Contents

Introduction   4

William Shakespeare: Life, Plays, Theater,
  Verse   6

The Tragedy of Othello, the Moor of Venice:
  Date, Source, Text   16

OTHELLO

Original Text Side-by-Side With Modern
  Version   19

Activities   294

Themes and Images   294

Characters   301

Examination Questions   315

Introduction

Shakespeare Made Easy is designed to help those who struggle with Shakespeare's language read his plays with greater ease and comprehension. William Shakespeare wrote his plays to appeal to a wide audience, but in the approximately four hundred years since the plays were written, the English language has undergone significant changes. Consequently, although Shakespeare is regarded by many as the greatest playwright in the English language, readers often find the language barrier insurmountable. Even though it is possible, with practice, to read the plays in the original language, many find the task too difficult and give up either in disgust or despair. Footnotes are helpful, but they can interrupt the flow of the language, and many readers become so discouraged with having to refer to footnotes that they simply give up.

Shakespeare Made Easy offers a helping hand not only to those who want to get better acquainted with Shakespeare's plays for their own sake but also to those who are required to study the plays but find the task of deciphering the language overwhelming. Of course, there is no substitute for reading and studying the plays themselves in Shakespeare's own words. The unmatched beauty of the language can never be duplicated, but the modern version will assist the reader in distinguishing between the characters and in understanding what is happening in the play.

There are a number of possible ways to use *Shakespeare Made Easy*. One option is to read the play in the original language, referring to the modern version only when necessary. Another possibility is to read the entire play in the modern version to know what is going on and then to read the original with this knowledge firmly in mind. The bracketed notations concerning the ways in which lines may be spoken by an actor—although giving only one of the possible interpretations—can be especially helpful. If the reader plans to view a filmed version of the play, reading the modern version in advance can help overcome the difficulty of trying to understand the spoken language, as well.

Whichever method you use, *Shakespeare Made Easy* will prove a valuable resource for your study of the play. It is not intended as a substitute for the original play, since even the most careful "translation" of the text will lose certain aspects such as poetic meter, alliteration, and verbal humor.

Whether you are studying the play for a class or reading it for enjoyment or to increase your acquaintance with Shakespeare's works, the Activities section at the end of the book will be helpful in pointing out themes or issues that may have escaped your notice as you read. If you need to write a paper about this play, this section will help you generate topic ideas. It will also help you as you write the paper to make sure that you have correctly interpreted a quote you are using in support of one of your points.

Using *Shakespeare Made Easy* will pave your way to a far better understanding of and appreciation for Shakespeare's plays and will remove the textual difficulties that may have caused you to stumble in past attempts. Not only will you gain confidence in discussing the plot and characters of the play, but you will also develop a greater awareness of the ways in which Shakespeare used language for poetic expression as well as for raising intriguing and challenging moral and philosophical issues.

Ever since the works of William Shakespeare entered the canon of English literature, they have excited the admiration of generations of scholars, readers, and theatergoers. Even if you've had negative experiences in the past with Shakespeare's plays—in fact, especially if you've had negative experiences—you will find yourself pleasantly surprised at just how entertaining his plays can be. We're glad you've chosen *Shakespeare Made Easy* as a companion on your journey to a better understanding of the plays of William Shakespeare.

William Shakespeare

His Life

Considering the impact that William Shakespeare has had on English literature, surprisingly little is known about his life. We do know that he was born to a prominent wool and leather merchant and his wife in 1564 (the actual day is in doubt but tradition sets it at April 23) in Stratford-upon-Avon, England. He is believed to have been educated at the local grammar school, although no lists of pupils survive from the sixteenth century. He did not attend university.

We also know from parish records that he married Anne Hathaway in 1582 when he was eighteen and she was twenty-six. They had three children; Susanna was their eldest, followed by twins, Judith and Hamnet. Their son, Hamnet, died at the age of about eleven, but the two daughters, Susanna and Judith, reached adulthood.

There are many stories about Shakespeare's life, such as the one alleging that he fled Stratford after having been caught poaching deer in the park belonging to Sir Thomas Lucy, a local justice of the peace. Like the rest of the tales about Shakespeare during this period of his life, this story cannot be verified and is probably untrue. Because his plays demonstrate extensive knowledge about a variety of subjects, articles have been written "proving" that Shakespeare must have temporarily pursued a career in either law, botany, or medicine or spent time as a soldier or sailor, to name a few of the occupations that he is speculated to have had.

The truth is, we simply don't know for sure what Shakespeare did for a living in the ten years following his marriage to Anne Hathaway. Ordinarily, as the eldest son he would have been expected to take over his father's business, but again there is no evidence to show that he did (or, for that matter, did not) serve an apprenticeship to his father. He may have spent some time with a traveling troupe of actors, but, aside from the baptismal records for his children, we have no actual records about him from the time of his marriage to Hathaway until 1592, by which time he had left Stratford and traveled to London. His wife and children remained in Stratford.

The next documented evidence pertaining to Shakespeare comes in 1592, when Shakespeare received his first critical recognition. It came in the form of a petulant outburst by fellow playwright Robert Greene who, apparently annoyed by the attention being received by this newcomer, complained bitterly in a pamphlet written from his deathbed about the "upstart crow . . . Shake-scene."

From about 1594 onward, Shakespeare was associated with a new theatrical company, The Lord Chamberlain's Men; by 1599 Shakespeare had become a shareholder in the company. The troupe gave command performances for Queen Elizabeth I as well as her successor, King James I. After King James' accession to the throne, the troupe took the name "The King's Men."

The King's Men performed at *The Globe* theater, which they owned. Of course, *The Globe* was not the only theater in London. *The Curtain* (built in 1577) and *The Rose* (1587), as well as a number of other theaters, also provided entertainment to the citizens. In addition to these open-air "public" theaters, there were many "private" or indoor theaters. Shakespeare and his friends purchased one of the private theaters, *The Blackfriars*, which was giving them especially stiff competition because of the popularity of the child actors who performed there.

With so many theaters in operation, the demand for plays was high. Shakespeare may have earned a living for a time by reworking older plays and by collaborating with others on new ones, and of course he also wrote his own plays. In addition to the uncertainty about many facts pertaining to his life, there even is debate about the exact number of plays Shakespeare wrote; some say he wrote thirty-seven, others say thirty-eight.

Shakespeare stopped writing for the stage in about 1611, and, having prospered not only from his writing but also from his shares in the theatrical company, he retired to Stratford, where he installed his family in New Place, one of the more expensive homes in Stratford. He died at the age of fifty-two on April 23, 1616.

His Plays

Many people are surprised to learn that none of the original handwritten manuscripts of Shakespeare's plays survives. At that time, plays were not considered to be "literature" in the same way that poetry was. In fact, when Shakespeare wrote his plays, they would have been the property of the producing company, which was concerned, not with publication of the plays, but with producing them on stage. The company would have bought them for about ten pounds apiece, and when a play finished its theatrical run and the copies were of no further use to the company, they often were discarded.

Roughly half of Shakespeare's plays were published during his lifetime in quarto (17 centimeters by 21 centimeters) volumes, although many of these were pirated copies. Booksellers often would hire someone to take shorthand notes during a performance, and then they would sell these unauthorized copies. This method for acquiring a copy of the play, needless to say, could result in numerous errors depending on the accuracy of the transcriber. In other instances of piracy, actors' scripts were purchased by a bookseller after the play had completed its run, but since each actor's copy would contain only his scenes, the actor would have to provide the rest of the text from memory, which often proved faulty. These pirated copies are referred to as "bad" Quartos. Even when a printer was working from a good manuscript (probably a prompt copy obtained from the theater), mistakes often contaminated the printed copy. In addition to all these problems, portions of the plays were sometimes censored for a variety of reasons, resulting in still further corruption of the text.

Fortunately, seven years after Shakespeare's death an authoritative version of his works, the First Folio (21 centimeters by 34 centimeters), edited by two of his theatrical partners and fellow actors, John Hemming and Henry Condell, was published. They claimed in the introduction to have used his original manuscripts, but that claim is unverified. The First Folio contained thirty-six of his plays and was titled *Comedies, Histories, and Tragedies*. Despite the Folio's apparent superiority to other printings of Shakespeare's plays, serious questions remain, and debate continues concerning discrepancies between the various early editions.

Because of the discrepancies between different editions of the plays, when one of Shakespeare's plays is published, editors must make decisions about which version to use. Often, the edition will contain lines from several of the oldest texts, but since in some cases there remains significant disagreement about which text is the "best" or most accurate, the reader may discover that there are differences between editions of the play. Many editions include notes at the end of the play to indicate the words or lines that have an alternate reading.

His Theater

In Elizabethan times, the London authorities viewed playgoing as both morally and politically questionable; they also believed that the large crowds that attended the plays created an increased risk for spreading the bubonic plague. In fact, the playhouses were closed twice during Shakespeare's lifetime as a result of outbreaks of the plague. Because of the hostile atmosphere created by the civil authorities, playhouses were typically built outside the city limits in order to place them beyond the jurisdiction of authorities.

When The Lord Chamberlain's Men (the troupe to which

Shakespeare belonged), first began performing, *The Theater*, owned by Richard and Cuthbert Burbage, was their theatrical home. Constructed in 1576 just outside the city limits of London, *The Theater* was the first of the public playhouses. Plays had previously been performed in England in the square- or rectangular-shaped yards of the inns where traveling bands of actors stayed, but this arrangement had a serious drawback—it was far too easy for customers to enter and leave the grounds without paying the price of admission. Playhouses like *The Theater* were therefore a significant improvement since the enclosed design made it possible to have a single opening where tickets could be taken from those entering.

The Chamberlain's Men were financially successful, but a problem arose in 1598 concerning the property on which *The Theater* stood. The owner of the property planned to have the playhouse torn down once the lease on the land expired, so in late 1598 the Chamberlain's Men dismantled the building and reassembled it a short distance from the south bank of the River Thames, renaming it *The Globe*.

In 1603, The Lord Chamberlain's Men regrouped under the patronage of King James I and took the name The King's Men; the shareholders were thenceforward considered to be members of the royal household. Unfortunately, the company's fortunes took a downturn in 1613 when, during a performance of *Henry VIII*, a cannon was fired, setting the thatched roof of *The Globe* ablaze. Within an hour, the building was destroyed.

The King's Men rebuilt the playhouse, and the new *The Globe* theater, completed in 1614, was circular in shape. The "wooden O" (as it is referred to in *Henry V*) of *The Globe* actually had twenty sides, with an outer diameter of about one hundred yards. Some historians have estimated that it could hold up to three thousand people, but others dispute that figure as being far too high.

Playbills would be posted around the city to advertise for new plays, but due to the fact that the roofs of "public" theaters such as *The Globe* were open to the elements, plays could be performed only in daylight and in good weather. The theatrical company would fly a flag from the roof of the building to notify people if a performance was to proceed. If, however, the flag was not flown, theatergoers would be spared an unnecessary trip.

Those attending a play paid the gatekeeper at the entrance. In addition to standing room around the stage, seats were available in the three tiers of the gallery which encircled the playhouse. For the price of one penny (about sixty cents today), the "groundlings," as they were called, gained admission to the pit. Those who could afford to do so paid for gallery seating; the lowest tier was the least expensive, with the price climbing to as high as one shilling (about seven dollars today) for seats in the uppermost tier. The roof shielded the patrons seated in the galleries either from the heat of the sun or, in case the weather turned bad, from a sudden downpour.

Plays typically had a theatrical run of ten performances, although, depending on the popularity of the piece, some were performed up to about sixteen times; less popular plays, however, might have only six performances. The performances proceeded without intermission and usually took about two hours, although a number of Shakespeare's plays run significantly longer. When the play was about to begin, a trumpet would sound three times.

Shakespeare's plays were performed on what is referred to as a "thrust" stage; it was about five feet high and measured $27\frac{1}{2}$ feet deep by 43 feet wide; it probably sloped downward at the front (downstage) and projected out into the pit. The stage was covered by a roof (referred to as "the heavens"), which was painted to resemble a starlit sky upon which the signs of the zodiac were depicted. The area beneath the stage was referred to as "hell"; a trapdoor in the floor of the stage allowed for the entrances and exits of ghosts, monsters, and devils.

There was no scenery, nor was there a curtain that could be closed at the end of scenes or acts, so playwrights used the lines spoken by the actors to set the scene and to indicate when a scene or act was ending. A rhyming couplet, for example, would often indicate the conclusion of a scene. The gallery directly behind the stage was used for scenes in which actors were required to be either in an upper story of a house, on the battlements of a castle, or in some other elevated position. Musicians and even spectators also occupied the gallery.

At the rear of the stage (upstage) was the "tiring house" where the actors dressed (attired themselves). The tiring house had two or three doors providing access to the stage. Even though many of the plays performed were set in earlier times, the actors did not wear period costumes; the period in which a play was set would merely be suggested by certain period touches in the costumes, such as spears or helmets. Consequently, a play such as *Julius Caesar* which was set around 44 B.C.E. would have been performed in the current fashions of Elizabethan England. However, despite being historically inaccurate, the costumes the actors wore were quite lavish and were therefore not a disappointment to the audience.

Since it was illegal for women to perform in public at that time, boys or young men played the women's roles in the plays. Often, in order for a boy actor to be tall enough to be convincing in the role of an adult woman, he had to wear chopines (wooden platforms strapped to the soles of the shoes); the long skirts, which were fashionable, hid the chopines from view. Because of the restriction on women performing, Shakespeare's plays had few female characters, and, in many of his plays, the heroine would spend much of the play disguised as a boy.

The plays of Shakespeare were of course crucial to the success of the company, but the troupe also had the most renowned actor of the time, Richard Burbage. Burbage was the first actor to portray Hamlet. Although Shakespeare was himself an actor, he is only known to have performed secondary roles.

Other noted actors in the troupe were William Kempe, a comedian, and Robert Asmin, a singer and dancer, both of whom were also shareholders in The King's Men. The average size for a theatrical company was twenty-five members, about half of whom would usually be shareholders. Other actors were employed part-time as needed.

Because actors in Shakespeare's time needed to project their voices for open-air performances, they tended to employ a more exaggerated, declamatory style of acting than would be acceptable to today's audiences. Some actors went to extremes, however. Shakespearean scholars generally agree that Hamlet's instruction to the Players not to "tear a passion . . . to very rags" reflects his views on the tendency to overact amongst his contemporaries. Shakespeare's presence during rehearsals of his plays would have given him the opportunity to personally instruct an actor in the way a line should be delivered.

His Verse

Although Shakespeare's dramatic output alone would have been sufficient to ensure his place among English writers, his reputation as an author does not rest solely upon his plays. He wrote poetry, as well, including the erotic narrative poems *Venus and Adonis* (1593) and *The Rape of Lucrece* (1594). He also composed 154 *Sonnets*, which were circulated in manuscript prior to their publication in 1609.

Shakespeare's poetic output was not confined to his poems, however. At the beginning of Shakespeare's career as a playwright, the prevailing style for dialog was rhyming couplets (that is, two succeeding lines of poetry that rhyme), so a high percentage of the lines in his earlier plays rhyme. In one of his early works, *Love's Labor's Lost*, for example, nearly half of the lines rhyme.

As time passed, however, Shakespeare used fewer rhymed couplets for dialog and began favoring blank verse for his plays. Blank verse consists of unrhymed lines of iambic pentameter; iambic pentameter is the technical term for lines ten syllables in length with alternating stresses (that is, an unstressed syllable followed by a stressed syllable). Although Shakespeare continued to use rhyming couplets in his plays when he wanted to indicate the end of a scene or when the situation might call for a more artificial style of speech, he favored a much more naturalistic form of expression in his later plays.

Even in his early plays, however, Shakespeare was outdoing his fellow playwrights. For example, because of the prevailing style of rhyming couplets, most of the characters in a play would sound the same; in other words, one character's "voice" could not be distinguished from that of another. In contrast, even early on Shakespeare's characters each spoke with a recognizable voice. Even without the speaker's identity being revealed, no one would have any difficulty distinguishing the innocent yet passionate utterances of Juliet from the prosaic vulgarity of her Nurse. Furthermore, if, during the course of a play, a character underwent a significant change, Shakespeare would indicate this change by altering the character's speech patterns. One example of this technique is Othello who begins to sound more and more like Iago as he becomes progressively more infected with the "pestilence" Iago pours into his ear.

Shakespeare also used speech patterns to indicate a character's social rank. In his plays, members of the nobility usually speak in blank verse, while those of lower station speak in prose, reflecting their limited education. Shakespeare also uses prose to indicate when the more highly ranked characters are speaking informally or are under stress.

Another one of the many noteworthy aspects of Shakespeare's technique is his use of setting to reinforce ideas in his plays. In *Antony and Cleopatra*, for example, the cold austerity of Rome reflects the emotional coldness and sterility of the Romans, whereas the sun-drenched setting of Egypt reflects the passionate love of the title characters.

Furthermore, Shakespeare used imagery not only to create atmosphere but also to convey themes. *Hamlet*, for example, contains numerous references to disease and decay, reinforcing the theme of the moral and political rot in Denmark. In addition to demonstrating his technical brilliance, Shakespeare's works reveal insights into human nature that none of his predecessors or contemporaries could begin to approach.

Shakespeare's technique and contributions to drama and literature place him at the pinnacle of his art. It's no surprise then that each succeeding generation sees new additions to the ranks of "Bardolators."

The Tragedy of Othello, the Moor of Venice

Date

The official date for *Othello* is 1604, since it was noted in official documents that it was performed at court before King James I on November 1 of that year. However, the "bad" quarto of *Hamlet* (dated 1603) contains what appear to be borrowings from *Othello*, giving rise to speculation that *Othello* may have been composed earlier than 1604. Furthermore, Act I Scene 3 is quoted in Knolles' *History of the Turks*, the preface to which indicates a publication date of September 1603, so the earlier date of composition seems likely.

Source

Othello is based on a novella by Giraldi Cinthio; it is part of his *Hecatommithi*, which was published in Venice in 1565. There was no English translation of the novella at that time, so it is believed that Shakespeare may have read a French translation of the novella. Shakespeare has made significant changes from his source. The Ensign (Iago is not given a name in Cinthio's version) is desperately in love with Disdemona, as she is called. She, however, is in love with Othello and has no interest in the Ensign. He decides that the reason for her lack of interest in him must be because she is in love with the Captain (Cassio). When the Captain is demoted for bad behavior, the Ensign uses Disdemona's attempts to have him reinstated to incite Othello to jealousy. The Ensign and Othello plot together to murder Disdemona and the Captain. However, after the Ensign beats Disdemona to death, Othello belatedly repents and cashiers the Ensign. Only then does the Ensign become the enemy of

Othello. The Ensign informs on Othello, whereupon Othello is arrested, tortured, and banished. At the conclusion of the story, Othello is assassinated by Disdemona's relatives. The moral, expressed by Disdemona before her death, is that it is a mistake to marry someone so different from oneself.

Text

Thomas Walkley published a quarto edition of *Othello* in 1622; the second printing of *Othello* was in the First Folio, which was published in 1623. The textual situation for *Othello* is especially problematic in that there are significant discrepancies between the First Quarto and the First Folio. The quarto contains roughly 13 lines or partial lines that are not found in the folio, and the folio contains 160 lines not found in the quarto. In addition, there are more than one thousand discrepancies in wording between the two editions. Consequently, editors are forced to decide whether they prefer to favor one version over the other— many choose the folio since it is the more "complete" version— or to pick and choose between the two depending on which version seems to have more authority in the individual instances.

★ Note: Because the First Folio is generally considered to be the superior text, for this edition the editors have chosen it as the primary text. However, due to editorial choice or from necessity, approximately 190 readings have been taken from the original First Folio.

Othello

Original Text and Modern Version

The characters:

Duke of Venice
Brabantio   a senator, Desdemona's father
Gratiano   an official of Venice, brother to Brabantio
Lodovico   an official of Venice, a relative of Brabantio and
   Desdemona
Othello   a noble Moor in the military service of Venice
Cassio   Othello's lieutenant
Iago   Othello's enemy and his ensign [*some texts refer to Iago
   as Othello's "ancient," an archaic form of the word "ensign"*]
Roderigo   a gentleman of Venice
Montano   Governor of Cyprus
Clown   servant to Othello
Desdemona   daughter to Brabantio and wife to Othello
Emilia   wife to Iago
Bianca   mistress to Cassio
First Senator
Second Senator
**Gentlemen of Cyprus, Sailors, Messenger, Herald,
   Officers, Musicians, Attendants, and Servants**

Synopsis:

Act I
  Scene I   A street in Venice.
                   The elopement is discovered.
  Scene II   Another street.
                   Othello is called upon to defend Cyprus from a
                   Turkish invasion.
  Scene III   A council chamber.
                   The senate discusses the Turkish attack.
                   Brabantio brings his grievance to the senate
                   concerning the elopement.

Act II
  Scene I   A seaport in Cyprus. An open place near the
                   quay.
                   A storm scatters the Turkish fleet.
  Scene II   A street in Cyprus.
                   Othello declares a celebration of his marriage and
                   of the defeat of the Turks.
  Scene III   A hall in the castle.
                   Iago causes Cassio's disgrace.

Act III
  Scene I   Before the castle.
                   Cassio requests a meeting with Desdemona.
  Scene II   A room in the castle.
                   Othello surveys the fortifications.
  Scene III   The garden of the castle.
                   Cassio asks Desdemona to speak to Othello about
                   him. Iago plants seeds of suspicion in Othello's
                   mind.
  Scene IV   Before the castle.
                   Othello tests Desdemona's virtue.

Act IV

Scene I — Before the castle.
Iago continues to poison Othello's mind.

Scene II — A room in the castle.
Othello accuses Desdemona of infidelity. She denies it.

Scene III — Another room in the castle.
Desdemona prepares for bed.

Act V

Scene I — A street in Cyprus.
Cassio is wounded by Roderigo. Roderigo is killed.

Scene II — A bedchamber in the castle where Desdemona is in bed asleep and a light is burning.
Othello kills Desdemona and then learns the truth.

Act one

Scene 1

Enter **Roderigo** *and* **Iago**.

Roderigo [Tush,] never tell me! I take it much unkindly
That thou, Iago, who hast had my purse
As if the strings were thine, shouldst know of this.

Iago ['Sblood,] but you'll not hear me.
5 If ever I did dream of such a matter,
Abhor me.

Roderigo Thou toldst me thou didst hold him in thy hate.

Iago Despise me if I do not. Three great ones of the city,
In personal suit to make me his lieutenant,
10 Off-capp'd to him; and, by the faith of man,
I know my price, I am worth no worse a place.
But he (as loving his own pride and purposes)
Evades them with a bumbast circumstance
Horribly stuff'd with epithites of war,
15 [And in conclusion,]
Nonsuits my mediators; for, "Certes," says he,
"I have already chose my officer."
And what was he?
Forsooth, a great airthmetician,
20 One Michael Cassio, a Florentine
(A fellow almost damn'd in a fair wife),
The never set a squadron in the field,
Nor the division of a battle knows
More than a spinster—unless the bookish theoric,
25 Wherein the [toged] consuls can propose
As masterly as he. Mere prattle, without practice,

24

Act one

Scene 1

A street in Venice late at night.

[**Roderigo** *and* **Iago** *enter.*]

Roderigo Bah! Don't even speak to me! I am very angry, that after I've let you, Iago, spend my money as if it were your own, you already knew about this.

Iago God's blood! You just aren't listening to me. If I had even imagined it, you'd have every right to despise me.

Roderigo You told me you hated him.

Iago Go ahead and despise me if I don't hate him. Three important citizens asked to speak to him personally about making me his lieutenant, greeting him with great courtesy, and, believe me, I know my own worth and that I deserve the promotion. But he's so conceited and stubborn about making his own decision that he avoids them, making all kinds of excuses, giving very important-sounding military matters as his reason, and, to be brief, refuses to see my supporters, because, he claims, "Actually, I have already chosen my officer." And what was he? Merely someone who's good with calculations, a man from Florence named Michael Cassio (he's cursed with having a beautiful wife) that has never even led a squadron of soldiers into battle and knows as little about military tactics as a housewife does—except what comes from a book, where any "armchair general" can sound like he's an expert. All fancy theory, with no experience; that's all that

Is all his soldiership. But he, sir, had th' election;
And I, of whom his eyes had seen the proof
At Rhodes, at Cyprus, and on [other] grounds
30   Christen'd and heathen, must be belee'd and calm'd
By debitor and creditor—this counter-caster,
He (in good time!) must his lieutenant be,
And I ([God] bless the mark!) his Moorship's ancient.

Roderigo   By heaven, I rather would have been his hangman.

35 **Iago**   Why, there's no remedy. 'Tis the curse of service;
Preferment goes by letter and affection,
And not by old gradation, where each second
Stood heir to th' first. Now, sir, be judge yourself
Whether I in any just term am affin'd
To love the Moor.

40 **Roderigo**   I would not follow him then.

Iago   O, sir, content you;
I follow him to serve my turn upon him.
We cannot all be masters, nor all masters
Cannot be truly follow'd. You shall mark
45   Many a duteous and knee-crooking knave
That (doting on his own obsequious bondage)
Wears out his time, much like his master's ass,
For nought but provender, and when he's old, cashier'd.
Whip me such honest knaves. Others there are
50   Who, trimm'd in forms and visages of duty,
Keep yet their hearts attending on themselves,
And throwing but shows of service on their lords,
Do well thrive by them; and when they have lin'd their coats,
Do themselves homage. These fellows have some soul,
55   And such a one do I profess myself. For, sir,
It is as sure as you are Roderigo,
Were I the Moor, I would not be Iago.
In following him, I follow but myself;

qualifies him. But he, sir, is the one chosen, and I, who have been in battle at Rhodes, at Cyprus, and on other battlefields both in Christian nations and heathen ones, am left without wind in my sails and unable to move forward concerning those who owe me money and to whom I am in debt—while this "accountant," is quickly promoted to be his lieutenant, and I, by God, am merely his Moorship's [*"his Moorship's," a combination of "Moor" and "his worship" (ordinarily a term of respect) is said here with deep sarcasm*] ensign.

Roderigo   By heaven, I would like to be his executioner!

Iago   Well, there's nothing to be done. It's the curse of being in the army. People are promoted because of personal recommendations and favoritism, and not as a result of seniority, as they once did, where the second person always followed the one ahead when it came time for promotions. Now, sir, decide for yourself whether I have any reason to feel affection for the Moor.

Roderigo   I would not be in his service then.

Iago   Oh, sir, don't worry, I only remain under his command in order to get even with him. We can't all be leaders, and not every leader will be loyally followed. You will see many an obedient and bowing rascal that (loving his own submissive bondage) puts in his time, much like his master's ass, for nothing but his meals, and when he's old, he's dismissed. I'd like to take a whip to that kind of honest servant! There are others who, giving every appearance in manner and even facial expression of being obedient still look out for themselves, and only giving an outward show of loyalty to their masters, watch out for their own prosperity, and when they have secretly lined their own pockets, become their own masters. These fellows have guts, and that's the kind of man I am. Because, sir, as surely as you are yourself, if I were the Moor, I wouldn't want to be Iago. In serving under him, I actually serve only myself. Heaven

Heaven is my judge, not I for love and duty,
60 But seeming so, for my peculiar end;
    For when my outward action doth demonstrate
    The native act and figure of my heart
    In complement extern, 'tis not long after
    But I will wear my heart upon my sleeve
65 For daws to peck at: I am not what I am.

Roderigo What a [full] fortune does the thick-lips owe
If he can carry't thus!

Iago   Call up her father.
Rouse him, make after him, poison his delight,
Proclaim him in the streets; incense her kinsmen,
70 And though he in a fertile climate dwell,
    Plague him with flies. Though that his joy be joy,
    Yet throw such [changes] of vexation on't,
    As it may lose some color.

Roderigo Here is her father's house, I'll call aloud.

Iago Do, with like timorous accent and dire yell
76 As when, by night and negligence, the fire
    Is spied in populous cities.

Roderigo What ho! Brabantio, Signior Brabantio, ho!

Iago Awake! what ho, Brabantio! thieves, thieves!
Look to your house, your daughter, and your bags!
81 Thieves, thieves!

    [*Enter* **Brabantio**] *above* [*at a window*]

Brabantio What is the reason of this terrible summons?
What is the matter there?

Roderigo Signior, is all your family within?

Iago Are your doors lock'd?

Brabantio   Why? Wherefore ask you this?

28

is my judge, I don't serve him out of love and duty, but only pretend to do so for my own purposes, because while my outward actions seem to show that the actions and feelings in my heart correspond with the way I behave, soon afterward I will reveal my true feelings so clearly that even the birds could peck at them: I am not what I am.

Roderigo [*sneeringly*] Thick-lips will be very lucky if he can succeed in his plans. [*Shakespeare has* **Roderigo** *refer to* **Othello** *as "Thick-lips" to demonstrate* **Roderigo***'s bigotry.*]

Iago Call out to her father. Wake him up, follow him, poison his happiness, tell the story in the streets, anger her relatives, and even though, in general, his life should be a pleasant one, annoy him on the slightest grounds. No matter what he is happy about, find some way to pester him about it so that it no longer gives him the same pleasure.

Roderigo Here is her father's house. I'll call out to him.

Iago Do it, in a voice sounding as if you are terrified and bring bad news as when, at night and because of negligence, a fire is suddenly seen in densely populated cities.

Roderigo [*shouting*] Hey! Brabantio, Signior Brabantio, hey!

Iago Wake up! Hey, Brabantio! Thieves, thieves! Look out for your house, your daughter, your belongings! Thieves, thieves!

[**Brabantio** *looks out a window above.*]

Brabantio Why are you making all this terrible noise? What's wrong down there?

Roderigo Sir, is everyone in your family in the house?

Iago Are your doors locked?

Brabantio Why? Why are you asking these things?

86 **Iago**   ['Zounds,] sir, y' are robb'd! For shame, put on your gown;
       Your heart is burst, you have lost half your soul;
       Even now, now, very now, an old black ram
       Is tupping your white ewe. Arise, arise!
90   Awake the snorting citizens with the bell,
       Or else the devil will make a grandsire of you.
       Arise, I say!

Brabantio   What, have you lost your wits?

Roderigo   Most reverend signior, do you know my voice?

Brabantio   Not I; what are you?

Roderigo   My name is Roderigo.

Brabantio   The worser welcome;
96   I have charg'd thee not to haunt about my doors.
       In honest plainness thou hast heard me say
       My daughter is not for thee; and now, in madness
       (Being full of supper and distemp'ring draughts),
100   Upon malicious [bravery] dost thou come
       To start my quiet.

Roderigo   Sir, sir, sir—

Brabantio   But thou must needs be sure
       My spirits and my place have in their power
       To make this bitter to thee.

Roderigo   Patience, good sir.

105 **Brabantio**   What tell'st thou me of robbing? This is Venice;
       My house is not a grange.

Roderigo   Most grave Brabantio,
       In simple and pure soul I come to you.

Iago   ['Zounds,] sir, you are one of those that will
       not serve God, if the devil bid you. Because we come
110   to do you service, and you think we are ruffians,

Iago   God's wounds, sir, you have been robbed! Shame on you, put on your robe! Your heart is broken, you have lost half your soul. Right now, now, at this very moment, an old black ram is having sex with your white ewe. Get up, get up! Wake up the other snoring citizens with the alarm bell, or else the devil will make a grandfather out of you.
Get up, I say!

Brabantio   Are you out of your minds?

Roderigo   Most honored signior, do you know my voice?

Brabantio   No, I don't. Who are you?

Roderigo   My name is Roderigo.

Brabantio   [*angrily*] You aren't welcome here. I have ordered you not to hang around my house. You have heard me plainly tell you that you cannot marry my daughter, and now, like some madman stuffed with your supper and drunk on alcohol, you defy me and come in anger to disturb my rest.

Roderigo   Sir, sir, sir—

Brabantio   You may be sure I not only desire but also have the power to cause you to deeply regret what you have done.

Roderigo   Calm down, good sir.

Brabantio   Why do you claim I have been robbed? This is Venice. My house is not some isolated farmhouse.

Roderigo   Most honored Brabantio, I have come to you in sincerity and with a pure heart.

Iago   God's wounds, sir, you would not even obey God, if the devil had told you to do so. Because we come to help you and yet you think we are roughnecks, you'll wind up with your

    you'll have your daughter cover'd with a Barbary
    horse, you'll have your nephews neigh to you; you'll
    have coursers for cousins, and gennets for germans.

114 **Brabantio**   What profane wretch art thou?

    Iago   I am one, sir, that comes to tell you your
    daughter and the Moor are [now] making the beast
    with two backs.

    Brabantio   Thou art a villain.

    Iago   You are a senator.

    Brabantio   This thou shalt answer; I know thee, Roderigo.

120 **Roderigo**   Sir, I will answer any thing. But I beseech you,
    If't be your pleasure and most wise consent
    (As partly I find it is) that your fair daughter,
    At this odd-even and dull watch o' th' night,
    Transported with no worse nor better guard
125   But with a knave of common hire, a gundolier,
    To the gross clasps of a lascivious Moor—
    If this be known to you, and your allowance,
    We then have done you bold and saucy wrongs;
    But if you know not this, my manners tell me
130   We have your wrong rebuke. Do not believe
    That, from the sense of all civility,
    I thus would play and trifle with your reverence.
    Your daughter (if you have not given her leave),
    I say again, hath made a gross revolt,
135   Tying her duty, beauty, wit, and fortunes
    In an extravagant and wheeling stranger
    Of here and every where. Straight satisfy yourself.
    If she be in her chamber or your house,
    Let loose on me the justice of the state
    For thus deluding you.

140 **Brabantio**   Strike on the tinder, ho!
    Give me a taper! Call up all my people!

daughter being bedded by a Barbary horse, your grandsons will neigh to you, you'll have horses for distant relatives and Spanish horses for close relatives.

Brabantio   Who are you, you foul-mouthed wretch?

Iago   I am someone, sir, who has come to tell you that your daughter and the Moor are at this very moment having sex.

Brabantio   You are a villain.

Iago   [*mockingly*] You are a senator.

Brabantio   You will pay for this! I know who you are, Roderigo.

Roderigo   Sir, I am willing to be held accountable for anything I say. But, please, if you don't mind and would agree to it, it seems that your beautiful daughter, at this midnight hour, has run away with no more trustworthy guard than a common hired gondolier, to the disgusting embraces of a lusty Moor. If you know about this and you have permitted it, then we have wronged you with our boldness and disrespectful words. But if you did not know of this, I am sure you have been wrong in rebuking us. Don't believe that, from a lack of manners, I would joke or try to fool you, honored sir. Your daughter—if you have not given her permission—I repeat, has rebelled against you, giving her duty, beauty, intelligence, and future well-being to a foreigner and a wandering stranger from who knows where. Go ahead and see for yourself. If she is in her room or your house, have me arrested for fooling you like this.

Brabantio   [*shouting in great agitation*]
Strike a tinder! Give me a candle! Call my servants!

This accident is not unlike my dream,
Belief of it oppresses me already.
Light, I say, light!

Exit [*above*].

Iago   Farewell; for I must leave you.
145   It seems not meet, nor wholesome to my place,
To be producted (as, if I stay, I shall)
Against the Moor; for I do know the state
(How ever this may gall him with some check)
Cannot with safety cast him, for he's embark'd
150   With such loud reason to the Cyprus wars
(Which even now stands in act) that, for their souls,
Another of his fadom they have none
To lead their business; in which regard,
Though I do hate him as I do hell-pains,
155   Yet, for necessity of present life,
I must show out a flag and sign of love,
Which is indeed but sign. That you shall surely find him,
Lead to the Sagittary the raised search;
And there will I be with him. So farewell.

Exit.

Enter [*below*] **Brabantio** [*in his night-gown*] *with* **Servants**
and torches.

160 **Brabantio**   It is too true an evil; gone she is;
And what's to come of my despised time
Is nought but bitterness. Now, Roderigo,
Where didst thou see her?—O unhappy girl!—
With the Moor, say'st thou?—Who would be a father!—
165   How didst thou know 'twas she?—O, she deceives me
Past thought!—What said she to you?—Get moe tapers;
Raise all my kindred.—Are they married, think you?

Roderigo   Truly, I think they are.

[*to himself*] This situation is like a dream I had, and my fear
that it's true frightens me already.
[*shouting to his* **Servants**] Light, I say, bring a light!

[**Brabantio** *hurriedly pulls his head back from the window.*]

Iago   Goodbye, for I must leave you. It seems like a bad idea,
and one which could jeopardize my position to have to give
evidence—as I must, if I don't leave—against the Moor. I know
how the government works; even if it must rebuke him, it
doesn't dare dismiss him from his position because he has
boarded a ship to go fight in the battles for Cyprus, which
are underway at this very time, because, truly, they have no
one else as capable as he is to carry out their battle plans.
Consequently, although I hate him as much as I hate hell's
torments, yet, because of the present circumstances, I must act
as if I am his close friend although I am actually only pretending.
If you want to be sure to find him, go to the Sagitarry Inn with a
search party, and I will be with him there. Good-bye.

[**Brabantio**, *wearing his nightclothes, comes out of the house
along with his servants.*]

Brabantio   [*to himself*] This horrible news is true; she is gone,
and the rest of my life will be filled with nothing but bitterness.
[*to* **Roderigo**] Now, Roderigo, where did you see her?
[*to the absent* **Desdemona**] Oh, unhappy girl!
[*to* **Roderigo**] She was with the Moor, did you say?
[*to himself*] Why would anyone want to be a father?
[*to* **Roderigo**] How did you know it was she?
[*to himself*] Oh, she has tricked me beyond anything I could
have believed possible!
[*to* **Roderigo**] What did she say to you?
[*to the* **Servants**] Get more candles. Wake up all my relatives.
[*to* **Roderigo**] Are they married, do you think?

Roderigo   Really, I think they are.

169 **Brabantio** O heaven! how got she out? O treason of the blood!
       Fathers, from hence trust not your daughters' minds
       By what you see them act. Is there not charms
       By which the property of youth and maidhood
       May be abus'd? Have you not read, Roderigo,
       Of some such thing?

       Roderigo   Yes, sir, I have indeed.

175 **Brabantio** Call up my brother.—O would you had had her!—
       Some one way, some another.—Do you know
       Where we may apprehend her and the Moor?

       Roderigo I think I can discover him, if you please
179   To get good guard and go along with me.

       Brabantio Pray you lead on. At every house I'll call
       (I may command at most).—Get weapons, ho!
       And raise some special officers of [night].—
       On, good Roderigo, I will deserve your pains.

                                                    Exeunt.

Scene 2

Enter **Othello**, **Iago**, **Attendants** *with torches.*

       Iago Though in the trade of war I have slain men,
       Yet do I hold it very stuff o' th' conscience
       To do no contriv'd murder. I lack iniquity
       Sometime to do me service. Nine or ten times
5   I had thought t' have yerk'd him here under the ribs.

Brabantio   Oh, heaven! How did she get out? Oh, the disloyalty of a blood relative! Fathers, from now on do not think you can believe your daughters are trustworthy just because they act as if they were.
[*to* **Roderigo**] Are there not magic spells by which a young maiden may be deceived? Haven't you read, Roderigo, about things like that?

Roderigo   Yes, sir, I certainly have.

Brabantio   [*to the* **Servants**] Call for my brother.
[*to* **Roderigo**] Oh, I wish you had had her!
[*to the* **Servants**] Some of you search one way, some go another.
[*to* **Roderigo**] Do you know where we may capture her and the Moor?

Roderigo   I think I can find him, if you will please assemble a good group of men and will come along with me.

Brabantio   Please lead on. At every house we pass I will request help; I could even demand it at most.
[*shouting to his* **Servants**] Get weapons, you there! And also bring some of the special night guards.
[*to* **Roderigo**] Lead on, Roderigo. I will reward you for your efforts.

[*They all leave.*]

Scene 2

Another street in Venice a short time later.

[**Othello** *and* **Iago** *enter along with* **Attendants** *carrying torches.*]

Iago   [*speaking to* **Othello**] Although in the act of war I have killed men, it is against my conscience to commit a premeditated murder. Sometimes I'm not wicked enough to accomplish my goals. Nine or ten times I thought about stabbing him here [*he points to a spot on his abdomen*] under his ribs.

Othello   'Tis better as it is.

Iago   Nay, but he prated,
And spoke such scurvy and provoking terms
Against your honor,
That with the little godliness I have
10   I did full hard forbear him. But I pray you, sir,
Are you fast married? Be assur'd of this,
That the magnifico is much belov'd,
And hath in his effect a voice potential
As double as the Duke's. He will divorce you,
15   Or put upon you what restraint or grievance
The law (with all his might to enforce it on)
Will give him cable.

Othello   Let him do his spite;
My services which I have done the signiory
Shall out-tongue his complaints. 'Tis yet to know—
20   Which, when I know that boasting is an honor,
I shall [provulgate]—I fetch my life and being
From men of royal siege, and my demerits
May speak, unbonneted, to as proud a fortune
As this that I have reach'd; for know, Iago,
25   But that I love the gentle Desdemona,
I would not my unhoused free condition
Put into circumscription and confine
For the sea's worth. But look, what lights come yond?

Enter **Cassio** *with* [**Officers** *and*] *torches.*

Iago   Those are the raised father and his friends.
You were best go in.

30 **Othello**   Not I; I must be found.
My parts, my title, and my perfect soul
Shall manifest me rightly. Is it they?

Othello   It's better this way.

Iago   No, but he talked idly and said such despicable and infuriating things against you, your honor, that it was only by my own paltry goodness that I kept my hands off him. But tell me, sir, are you actually married? I assure you that the noble Brabantio is very highly regarded and has so much influence that he's as powerful as the Duke himself. He [*Brabantio*] will either force you to get a divorce, or he will use every possible legal means to restrain you or to bring a complaint against you.

Othello   Let him do his worst. The services I have done for the Venetian government shall speak more loudly than his complaints. It is not yet public knowledge, but I shall be sure to boast of my own honors. I am myself descended from royalty and my merits may speak for me—I say this in all due modesty. I am descended from just as impressive a rank as that which I have now achieved. For you may be sure, Iago, that if I did not love the gentle Desdemona, I would not give up my unrestricted, free condition or submit to the limitations and confines of marriage for all the treasure in the sea. But look, who is coming this way carrying lights?

[**Cassio** *enters with* **Officers** *carrying torches.*]

Iago   [*mistaking the identity of those approaching*] Those are the father and his friends who have all been alerted. You had better go inside.

Othello   Not I. I must be found by them. My personal merits, my title, and my clear conscience shall testify for me. Is it they?

Iago   By Janus, I think no.

Othello   The servants of the [Duke]? and my lieutenant?
35   The goodness of the night upon you, friends!
What is the news?

Cassio   The Duke does greet you, general,
And he requires your haste-post-haste appearance,
Even on the instant.

Othello   What is the matter, think you?

Cassio   Something from Cyprus, as I may divine;
40   It is a business of some heat. The galleys
Have sent a dozen sequent messengers
This very night at one another's heels;
And many of the consuls, rais'd and met,
Are at the Duke's already. You have been hotly call'd for;
45   When, being not at your lodging to be found,
The Senate hath sent about three several quests
To search you out.

Othello   'Tis well I am found by you.
I will but spend a word here in the house,
And go with you.

                                        [*Exit.*]

Cassio   Ancient, what makes he here?

Iago   Faith, he to-night hath boarded a land carract.
51   If it prove lawful prize, he's made for ever.

Cassio   I do not understand.

Iago   He's married.

Cassio   To who?

[*Enter* **Othello**.]

Iago   By Janus [*in Roman mythology, a god with two faces*], I don't think it is.

Othello   Is it the servants of the Duke? And my lieutenant? [*to the approaching group*] Good evening, friends! What is the news?

Cassio   The Duke greets you, general, and orders that you report to him quickly. Immediately, in fact.

Othello   Do you know what is the matter?

Cassio   Something from Cyprus, as far as I can tell. It is an urgent situation. The galleys have sent a dozen messengers tonight, one after the other right on one another's heels, and many of the consuls have been sent for and are at the Duke's already. You have been urgently called for, and when you were not found at your home, three separate groups were sent to find you.

Othello   It's a good thing you have found me. I will just leave word here at the house, and then I'll go with you.

[**Othello** *exits.*]

Cassio   [*speaking to* **Iago**] Ensign, what is Othello doing here?

Iago   Faith, tonight he has boarded a merchant ship. If the treasure ends up being his legally, he's set for life.

Cassio   I don't understand.

Iago   He's married.

Cassio   To whom?

Iago   Marry, to—Come, captain, will you go?

Othello   Have with you.

Cassio   Here comes another troop to seek for you.

Enter **Brabantio**, **Roderigo**, *with* **Officers** [*with*] *torches* [*and weapons*].

55 **Iago**   It is Brabantio. General, be advis'd,
He comes to bad intent.

Othello   Holla, stand there!

Roderigo   Signior, it is the Moor.

Brabantio   Down with him, thief!

[*They draw on both sides.*]

Iago   You, Roderigo! come, sir, I am for you.

Othello   Keep up your bright swords, for the dew will rust them.
60   Good signior, you shall more command with years
Than with your weapons.

Brabantio   O thou foul thief, where hast thou stow'd my
daughter?
Damn'd as thou art, thou hast enchanted her,
For I'll refer me to all things of sense,
65   If she in chains of magic were not bound,
Whether a maid so tender, fair, and happy,
So opposite to marriage that she shunn'd
The wealthy curled [darlings] of our nation,
Would ever have, t' incur a general mock,
70   Run from her guardage to the sooty bosom
Of such a thing as thou—to fear, not to delight!
Judge me the world, if 'tis not gross in sense,
That thou hast practic'd on her with foul charms,

Iago   [*still speaking to* **Cassio**] Why, to . . .

[**Othello** *returns.*]
[*Iago interrupts himself to address* **Othello**.] Hello, captain. Will you go?

Othello   Yes, let's go.

Cassio   Here comes another troop to find you.

[**Brabantio** *and* **Roderigo** *enter, along with* **Officers** *carrying torches and weapons.*]

Iago   It's Brabantio. General, be warned; he comes with bad intentions toward you.

Othello   Greetings. Halt there.

Roderigo   [*to* **Brabantio**] Sir, it is the Moor.

Brabantio   [*to the* **Officers**] Attack that thief!

[*Both groups draw their swords.*]

Iago   You, Roderigo! Now, sir, I am going to attack you.
[**Iago** *plans to merely pretend to fight* **Roderigo** *so that neither of them will be injured.*]

Othello   Put away your bright swords, for the dew will make them rust.
[*to* **Brabantio**] Good sir, your seniority in years carries more authority than your weapons.

Brabantio   [*enraged*] You evil thief, where have you hidden my daughter? Cursed as you are, you must have cast a spell on her—common sense can plainly see that. If she were not bound by chains of magic, why would such a gentle, beautiful, and happy young girl—one so opposed to marriage that she rejected all the wealthy, attractive young men of our country—risk public ridicule by running away from her safe home to the sooty embrace of such a thing as you are—a frightening man, not a delightful one? May the world judge whether or not it is

43

Abus'd her delicate youth with drugs or minerals
75   That weakens motion. I'll have't disputed on,
'Tis probable, and palpable to thinking.
I therefore apprehend and do attach thee
For an abuser of the world, a practicer
Of arts inhibited and out of warrant.
80   Lay hold upon him, if he do resist
Subdue him at his peril.

Othello   Hold your hands,
Both you of my inclining, and the rest.
Were it my cue to fight, I should have known it
Without a prompter. Whither will you that I go
To answer this your charge?

Brabantio   To prison, till fit time
86   Of law and course of direct session
Call thee to answer.

Othello   What if [I] do obey?
How may the Duke be therewith satisfied,
Whose messengers are here about my side,
90   Upon some present business of the state,
To bring me to him?

Officer   'Tis true, most worthy signior;
The Duke's in council, and your noble self
I am sure is sent for.

Brabantio   How? the Duke in council?
In this time of the night? Bring him away;
95   Mine's not an idle cause. The Duke himself,
Or any of my brothers of the state,
Cannot but feel this wrong as 'twere their own;
For if such actions may have passage free,
Bond-slaves and pagans shall our statesmen be.

Exeunt.

perfectly obvious that you must have worked on her with evil spells or harmed her delicate innocence with drugs or other chemicals that weaken a person's mind. I'll have experts look into it, because it's very probable and obvious when one thinks about it. Therefore, I apprehend and arrest you for being a corrupter of the world, one who practices forbidden and illegal arts.

[*to his followers*] Lay hold of him and, if he resists, don't hesitate to use deadly force.

Othello [*to his followers as well as* **Brabantio's**] Hold back, both those who are my men as well as the rest of you. If it were my cue to fight, I would have known it without needing a prompter. Where do you want me to go to answer your accusations?

Brabantio To prison, until the proper time when the regular court sessions shall call upon you to answer.

Othello What if I do obey? How then will the Duke, whose messengers are right here at my side to bring me to him concerning some current business of the state, be satisfied?

Officer It's true, most worthy sir. The Duke is with his council, and I'm sure you yourself have been sent for.

Brabantio What? The Duke is with the council? At this time of night?

[*to his followers*] Bring Othello along.

[*to all those present*] My problem is not a trivial one. The Duke or any of my "brothers" in the government cannot help but feel as if this wrong had been done to them, because, if such actions as these may be freely allowed, even slaves and pagans shall be our statesmen.

[*They all exit.*]

Scene 3

Enter **Duke** [*and*] **Senators** [*set at a table, with lights*] *and*
Officers.

Duke   There's no composition in [these] news
That gives them credit.

1st Senator   Indeed, they are disproportioned;
My letters say a hundred and seven galleys.

Duke   And mine, a hundred forty.

2nd Senator   And mine, two hundred!
5   But though they jump not on a just accompt
(As in these cases where the aim reports,
'Tis oft with difference), yet do they all confirm
A Turkish fleet, and bearing up to Cyprus.

Duke   Nay, it is possible enough to judgment.
10   I do not so secure me in the error
But the main article I do approve
In fearful sense.

Sailor   (*Within.*)   What ho, what ho, what ho!

Enter **Sailor**.

Officer   A messenger from the galleys.

Duke   Now? what's the business?

Sailor   The Turkish preparation makes for Rhodes,
15   So was I bid report here to the state
By Signior Angelo.

[*Exit Sailor.*]

Scene 3

A council chamber.

[*The* **Duke, Senators,** *and* **Officers** *enter and sit at a lighted table.*]

Duke   These reports are too inconsistent to be credible.

First Senator   Indeed, they are contradictory. My letter says 107 galleys.

Duke   And mine, 140.

Second Senator   And mine, 200! But even though the reports don't agree about the numbers—as in these cases where the reports are only guesses, there are often differences—yet they all confirm that a Turkish fleet is headed for Cyprus.

Duke   No, it's probable enough to believe it. I do believe that the main item is true even though there are discrepancies.

Sailor   [*shouting from offstage*] What ho, what ho, what ho!

[*A* **Sailor** *enters.*]

Officer   [*to the assembled group*] A messenger from the galleys.

Duke   What is happening?

Sailor   I was instructed by Signior Angelo to report here to the government that the Turkish fleet is headed for Rhodes.

Duke   How say you by this change?

1ˢᵗ Senator   This cannot be
By no assay of reason; 'tis a pageant
To keep us in false gaze. When we consider
20   Th' importancy of Cyprus to the Turk,
And let ourselves again but understand
That, as it more concerns the Turk than Rhodes,
So may he with more facile question bear it,
For that it stands not in such warlike brace,
25   But altogether lacks th' abilities
That Rhodes is dress'd in—if we make thought of this,
We must not think the Turk is so unskillful
To leave that latest which concerns him first,
Neglecting an attempt of ease and gain
30   To wake and wage a danger profitless.

Duke   Nay, in all confidence, he's not for Rhodes.

Officer   Here is more news.

Enter a **Messenger**.

Messenger   The Ottomites, reverend and gracious,
Steering with due course toward the isle of Rhodes,
35   Have there injointed them with an after fleet.

1ˢᵗ Senator   Ay, so I thought. How many, as you guess?

Messenger   Of thirty sail; and now they do restem
Their backward course, bearing with frank appearance
Their purposes toward Cyprus. Signior Montano,
40   Your trusty and most valiant servitor,
With his free duty recommends you thus,
And prays you to believe him.

[*Exit Messenger.*]

Duke   [*to the assembled group*] What do you make of this altered report?

First Senator   Common sense indicates that it cannot be true. It is merely a false maneuver to divert our attention so that the Turks may capture Cyprus more easily. We must bear in mind the importance of Cyprus to them and remember that Cyprus is of greater concern to them than Rhodes is. Cyprus is not so prepared for war and lacks the military readiness of Rhodes. If we consider this fact, then we must not think that the Turks are so lacking in military skill to leave the thing which concerns them most [*that is, the conquest of Cyprus*] to be dealt with last. Also, they would not fail to do that which is easily accomplished [*the conquest of Cyprus*] to attempt a risky venture that would be more dangerous and less likely to succeed.

Duke   No, we may be sure the Turks aren't headed for Rhodes.

Officer   Here comes more news.

[*A* **Messenger** *enters.*]

Messenger   The Ottomites [*Turks*], honored sirs, steering toward the island of Rhodes, have met up with a following fleet.

First Senator   Yes, I thought so. How many ships, would you suppose?

Messenger   Thirty sail, and now they are retracing their course, openly heading toward Cyprus. Signior Montano, I, your faithful and most brave servant, inform you of this with his assurances of his unswerving loyalty and beg you to believe him.

[*The* **Messenger** *exits.*]

Duke   'Tis certain then for Cyprus.
Marcus Luccicos, is not he in town?

45 **1ˢᵗ Senator**   He's now in Florence.

Duke   Write from us to him, post-post-haste. Dispatch!

1ˢᵗ Senator   Here comes Brabantio and the valiant Moor.

Enter **Brabantio**, **Othello**, **Cassio**, **Iago**, **Roderigo**,
and **Officers**.

Duke   Valiant Othello, we must straight employ you
Against the general enemy Ottoman.
50 [*To Brabantio.*] I did not see you; welcome, gentle signior,
We lack'd your counsel and your help to-night.

Brabantio   So did I yours. Good your Grace, pardon me:
Neither my place, nor aught I heard of business,
Hath rais'd me from my bed, nor doth the general care
55 Take hold on me; for my particular grief
Is of so flood-gate and o'erbearing nature
That it engluts and swallows other sorrows,
And it is still itself.

Duke   Why? what's the matter?

Brabantio   My daughter! O, my daughter!

[*All.*]   Dead?

Brabantio   Ay, to me:
60 She is abus'd, stol'n from me, and corrupted
By spells and medicines bought of mountebanks;
For nature so prepost'rously to err
(Being not deficient, blind, or lame of sense)
Sans witchcraft could not.

Duke   Who e'er he be that in this foul proceeding
66 Hath thus beguil'd your daughter of herself,

Duke   It's certain then that it's Cyprus. Is Marcus Luccicos not in town?

First Senator   He's in Florence just now.

Duke   Write him for us most urgently. Go!

First Senator   Here comes Brabantio with the courageous Moor.

[**Brabantio, Othello, Cassio, Iago, Roderigo,** *and* **Officers** *enter.*]

Duke   Valiant Othello, we must immediately engage your services against the universal enemy, the Ottomans [*Turks*]. [*to* **Brabantio**] I didn't see you. Welcome, noble signior. We were lacking your advice and your help tonight.

Brabantio   As I did yours. Honored sir, forgive me; neither my political position nor anything I have heard of the affairs of state have roused me from my bed, nor do ordinary affairs of state concern me, because my private grief is so overwhelming and pressing in nature that it engulfs and swallows all other sorrows and yet remains unaltered.

Duke   Why? What is the matter?

Brabantio   [*in great distress*] My daughter! Oh, my daughter!

All   [*anxiously*] Dead?

Brabantio   Yes, to me she is. She has been deceived, stolen from me and corrupted by spells and potions bought from mountebanks, for nature—if it isn't defective, blind, or lacking sanity—will not go so shockingly astray unless it had been bewitched.

Duke   [*sternly*] You yourself shall decide the enforcement of the bitter letter of the law in all its fury upon whoever has thus

And you of her, the bloody book of law
You shall yourself read in the bitter letter
After your own sense; yea, though our proper son
Stood in your action.

70 **Brabantio**   Humbly I thank your Grace.
Here is the man—this Moor, whom now, it seems,
Your special mandate for the state affairs
Hath hither brought.

All.   We are very sorry for't.

Duke   [*To Othello*.] What, in your own part, can you say to this?

75 **Brabantio**   Nothing, but this is so.

Othello   Most potent, grave, and reverend signiors,
My very noble and approv'd good masters:
That I have ta'en away this old man's daughter,
It is most true; true I have married her;
80 The very head and front of my offending
Hath this extent, no more. Rude am I in my speech,
And little bless'd with the soft phrase of peace;
For since these arms of mine had seven years' pith,
Till now some nine moons wasted, they have us'd
85 Their dearest action in the tented field;
And little of this great world can I speak
More than pertains to feats of broils and battle,
And therefore little shall I grace my cause
In speaking for myself. Yet (by your gracious patience)
90 I will a round unvarnish'd tale deliver
Of my whole course of love—what drugs, what charms,
What conjuration, and what mighty magic
(For such proceeding I am charg'd withal)
I won his daughter.

Brabantio   A maiden, never bold;
95 Of spirit so still and quiet that her motion

52

bewitched your daughter by this evil plot from both her true self and from you; yes, even if our own son is the one you charge with this crime.

Brabantio I humbly thank you, your Grace.
[*pointing accusingly at* **Othello**] Here is the man—this Moor whom it now seems your special orders concerning state affairs has brought here.

All We're very sorry to hear of this.

Duke [*sternly, to* **Othello**] What do you have to say for yourself?

Brabantio [*bitterly*] Nothing but that this is so.

Othello [*to the assembled group*] Most honored, grave, and reverend signiors, my very noble and trustworthy good masters, it is very true that I have taken away this old man's daughter, and it is also true that I have married her. This and nothing more is the full extent of my offense. I am unskilled in speaking and not especially gifted in forming the gentle phrases of peace. From the time when I was a robust seven-year-old until just the last nine months, my strength has been devoted to battle, and I have little knowledge of the great world aside from matters concerning uprisings and battles. I, therefore, shall not greatly advance my cause in speaking for myself. Yet, by your gracious patience, I will tell you the plain story of my whole course of love . . . [*He speaks ironically here.*] by what drugs, charms, spells, and powerful magic (for such are the things I am charged with) I won Brabantio's daughter.

Brabantio [*to the assembled group*] She is a girl who is never brazen, so still and quiet in spirit that any stirring of her

Blush'd at herself; and she, in spite of nature,
Of years, of country, credit, every thing,
To fall in love with what she fear'd to look on!
It is a judgment main'd, and most imperfect,
100 That will confess perfection so could err
Against all rules of nature, and must be driven
To find out practices of cunning hell
Why this should be. I therefore vouch again
That with some mixtures pow'rful o'er the blood,
105 Or with some dram (conjur'd to this effect)
He wrought upon her.

Duke   To vouch this is no proof,
Without more wider and more [overt] test
Than these thin habits and poor likelihoods
Of modern seeming do prefer against him.

110 **1st Senator**   But, Othello, speak.
Did you by indirect and forced courses
Subdue and poison this young maid's affections?
Or came it by request, and such fair question
As soul to soul affordeth?

Othello   I do beseech you,
115 Send for the lady to the Sagittary,
And let her speak of me before her father.
If you do find me foul in her report,
The trust, the office I do hold of you,
Not only take away, but let your sentence
Even fall upon my life.

120 **Duke**   Fetch Desdemona hither.

[*Exeunt two or three.*]

Othello   Ancient, conduct them; you best know the place.

[*Exit Iago.*]

54

emotions made her blush. And yet, in spite of her nature, her youth, her country, her reputation, everything, she falls in love with something she was frightened even to look at! Only a person of damaged and very poor judgment would say that such perfection could so violate all the rules of nature, and, consequently, those having sound judgment must discover by what devilish practices this occurred. I, therefore, declare again that Othello has used some drugs having power over the emotions or that he bewitched her with some magic potion.

Duke   Simply declaring this is so is not proof, not without stronger or more clear evidence than these slight circumstances and flimsy suspicions amount to.

First Senator   But, Othello, tell us this. Did you by devious and coercive means capture and poison this young maiden's love? Or did it come about voluntarily, through the communion of one soul reaching out to another?

Othello   I beg you to send to the Saggitary Inn for the lady herself and let her defend me in her father's presence. If, by her report, you find me wicked, not only should you remove your trust as well as the official rank I have from you, but you should also allow the sentence you have pronounced fall upon me.

Duke   [*to* **Officers**] Go bring Desdemona here.

[*Several leave to find her.*]

Othello   [*to* **Iago**] Ensign, lead them there. You know exactly where the inn is.

And, [till] she come, as truly as to heaven
I do confess the vices of my blood,
So justly to your grave ears I'll present
125   How I did thrive in this fair lady's love,
And she in mine.

Duke   Say it, Othello.

Othello   Her father lov'd me, oft invited me;
Still question'd me the story of my life
From year to year—the [battles], sieges, [fortunes],
131   That I have pass'd.
I ran it through, even from my boyish days
To th' very moment that he bade me tell it;
Wherein I spoke of most disastrous chances:
135   Of moving accidents by flood and field,
Of hair-breadth scapes i' th' imminent deadly breach,
Of being taken by the insolent foe
And sold to slavery, of my redemption thence
And portance in my [travel's] history;
140   Wherein of antres vast and deserts idle,
Rough quarries, rocks, [and] hills whose [heads] touch heaven,
It was my hint to speak—such was my process—
And of the Cannibals that each [other] eat,
The Anthropophagi, and men whose heads
145   [Do grow] beneath their shoulders. These things to hear
Would Desdemona seriously incline;
But still the house affairs would draw her [thence],
Which ever as she could with haste dispatch,
She'ld come again, and with a greedy ear
150   Devour up my discourse. Which I observing,
Took once a pliant hour, and found good means
To draw from her a prayer of earnest heart
That I would all my pilgrimage dilate,
Whereof by parcels she had something heard,
155   But not [intentively]. I did consent,

[*to the remaining group*] And until she comes, as truthfully as I confess my sins to heaven will I honestly tell your ears, worthy sirs, how I came to be loved by this fair lady and how she came to love me.

Duke   Tell us, Othello.

Othello   Her father was fond of me and often invited me to spend time with him. He continually asked me to tell him the story of my life. I went through the account from the time I was boy up to the very moment of his asking me to tell him the story. In it I spoke of the most calamitous occurrences, of terrifying events concerning flood and battlefield, of hairsbreadth escapes from imminent death, of being captured by the insolent foe and sold into slavery, of my redemption from enslavement, and of my actions in the history of my travels. I spoke of vast caves and barren deserts, of rugged boulders and rocks, and of hills whose tops reach to heaven. I was also urged to speak, as I went along, of the Anthropophagi [*that is, cannibals*] who eat one another, and also of men whose heads grow beneath their shoulders. Desdemona would listen most closely to all these things, and when household matters would call her away she would, if possible, deal with them quickly and then come again and devour my tales with a hungry ear. When I observed this, I took a favorable time and gave her the chance to ask me to tell her the full story of my adventures. She had heard portions but had not been able to hear in full. I consented and often moved

And often did beguile her of her tears,
When I did speak of some distressful stroke
That my youth suffer'd. My story being done,
She gave me for my pains a world of [sighs];
She swore, in faith 'twas strange, 'twas passing strange;
161   'Twas pitiful, 'twas wondrous pitiful.
She wish'd she had not heard it, yet she wish'd
That heaven had made her such a man. She thank'd me,
And bade me, if I had a friend that lov'd her,
165   I should but teach him how to tell my story,
And that would woo her. Upon this hint I spake:
She lov'd me for the dangers I had pass'd,
And I lov'd her that she did pity them.
This only is the witchcraft I have us'd.
170   Here comes the lady; let her witness it.

Enter **Desdemona**, **Iago**, **Attendants**.

Duke   I think this tale would win my daughter too.
Good Brabantio,
Take up this mangled matter at the best;
Men do their broken weapons rather use
Than their bare hands.

Brabantio   I pray you hear her speak.
176   If she confess that she was half the wooer,
Destruction on my head if my bad blame
Light on the man! Come hither, gentle mistress.
Do you perceive in all this noble company
Where most you owe obedience?

Desdemona   My noble father,
181   I do perceive here a divided duty:
To you I am bound for life and education;
My life and education both do learn me
How to respect you; you are the lord of duty;
I am hitherto your daughter. But here's my husband;

her to tears when I spoke of some grievous blow I had suffered in my youth. When my story was done, she sighed and swore that truly it was strange, very strange, that it was pitiful, very pitiful. She wished she hadn't heard it, yet she wished that heaven had made her such a man. She thanked me and urged me, if I should have a friend that cared for her, to teach him how to tell my story and so to woo her. Upon hearing this hint, I spoke up. She loved me for the dangers I had experienced, and I loved her because she pitied me. This is the only "witchcraft" I have used.

[*He sees* **Desdemona,** **Iago,** *and* **Attendants** *approaching.*] Here comes the lady. Let her testify to it.

Duke   I think this story would win my daughter, too. [*to* **Brabantio**] Good Brabantio, make the best of this messy situation. [*The* **Duke** *quotes a proverb.*] "Men will use their broken weapons rather than their bare hands."

Brabantio   I ask you to hear her speak first. If she confesses that she did half the wooing, may destruction fall upon my head if I blame the man! [*to* **Desdemona**] Come here, gentle lady. Do you see in this noble company the one to whom you owe your greatest obedience?

Desdemona   My noble father, I am torn between my loyalties to my husband and to you. I am indebted to you for life and for my rearing; they teach me to honor you and to be loyal to you as your daughter. But here is my husband [*She points toward*

186   And so much duty as my mother show'd
       To you, preferring you before her father,
       So much I challenge that I may profess
       Due to the Moor, my lord.

       Brabantio   God be with you! I have done.
190   Please it your Grace, on to the state affairs.
       I had rather to adopt a child than get it.
       Come hither, Moor:
       I here do give thee that with all my heart
       Which but thou hast already, with all my heart
195   I would keep from thee. For your sake, jewel,
       I am glad at soul I have no other child,
       For thy escape would teach me tyranny,
       To hang clogs on them. I have done, my lord.

       Duke   Let me speak like yourself, and lay a sentence,
200   Which as a grise or step, may help these lovers
       [Into your favor].
       When remedies are past, the griefs are ended
       By seeing the worst, which late on hopes depended.
       To mourn a mischief that is past and gone
205   Is the next way to draw new mischief on.
       What cannot be preserv'd when Fortune takes,
       Patience her injury a mock'ry makes.
       The robb'd that smiles steals something from the thief;
       He robs himself that spends a bootless grief.

210 **Brabantio**   So let the Turk of Cyprus us beguile,
       We lose it not, so long as we can smile.
       He bears the sentence well that nothing bears
       But the free comfort which from thence he hears;
       But he bears both the sentence and the sorrow
215   That, to pay grief, must of poor patience borrow.
       These sentences, to sugar or to gall,
       Being strong on both sides, are equivocal.
       But words are words; I never yet did hear

Othello.], and even as my mother gave her loyalty to you, putting you before her father, so also do I declare that I owe my loyalty to the Moor, my husband.

Brabantio   [*with disappointed resignation*] God be with you. I am finished.

[*to the* **Duke**] With your permission, your Grace, let us discuss state affairs.

[*to himself, bitterly*] I would rather adopt a child than father it.

[*to* **Othello**, *resignedly*] Come here, Moor. I now give you that which I would keep from you if I were able to.

[*to* **Desdemona**, *bitterly*] Because of what you have done, my jewel, I am glad I have no other children, for your escape would make me a tyrant who would hang heavy weights on them [*that is, to keep them from doing something similar to what Desdemona had done*].

[*to the* **Duke**] I am finished, my lord.

Duke   Let me speak as you ought to and recite a proverb which to some degree may help these lovers win your favor:

"When there is no remedy, sorrows are ended
by seeing the worst, on which one once depended.
To mourn an injury that is over and done
is the way to bring new sorrows on.
What can't be kept when bad luck steals,
patience therein a deep wound heals.
The one who's robbed and smiles steals back from the thief,
but he steals from himself when yielding to pointless grief."

Brabantio   [*dutifully but despondently*]
So let's trick the Turks of Cyprus a while;
We can't lose as long as we can smile.
He endures his sentence well who doesn't bear
anything but the full comfort which there he hears.
But he gets both the sentence and the sorrow
who from endurance, to pay off grief, must borrow.
These proverbs, whether sweet or like gall

That the bruis'd heart was pierced through the [ear].
220   I humbly beseech you proceed to th' affairs of state.

Duke   The Turk with a most mighty preparation
makes for Cyprus. Othello, the fortitude of the place is
best known to you; and though we have there a
substitute of most allow'd sufficiency, yet opinion, a
225   sovereign mistress of effects, throws a more
safer voice on you. You must therefore be content to
slubber the gloss of your new fortunes with this more
stubborn and boist'rous expedition.

Othello   The tyrant custom, most grave senators,
230   Hath made the flinty and steel [couch] of war
My thrice-driven bed of down. I do agnize
A natural and prompt alacrity
I find in hardness; and do undertake
This present wars against the Ottomites.
235   Most humbly therefore bending to your state,
I crave fit disposition for my wife,
Due reference of place and exhibition,
With such accommodation and besort
As levels with her breeding.

Duke   [If you please,
Be't] at her father's.

240 **Brabantio**   I will not have it so.

Othello   Nor I.

Desdemona   Nor [I; I would not] there reside,
To put my father in impatient thoughts
By being in his eye. Most gracious Duke,
To my unfolding lend your prosperous ear,
245   And let me find a charter in your voice
T' assist my simpleness.

Duke   What would you, Desdemona?

Desdemona   That I [did] love the Moor to live with him,
My downright violence, and storm of fortunes,

are strong either way and puzzle all.

[*softly, to himself*] But words are just words. I never did hear
that the wounded heart could be healed through the ear.

[*to the* **Duke**] I humbly beg you to take up the affairs of state.

Duke   [*to the assembled group*] The Turk is headed toward
Cyprus with a mighty fleet.

[*to* **Othello**] Othello, you are the best acquainted with the
fortifications of the place, and although we have here a
representative whose reputation is well known, yet public
opinion has the final word on what should be done and
declares that you are the safer choice. You, therefore, must be
satisfied to allow this harsh and hazardous expedition to dull
the glow of your new happiness. [*The* **Duke** *bows to*
Desdemona.]

Othello   The tyrant of duty, most honored senators, has caused
my bed of softest down to be the hard and steely bed of war. I
admit that I am fully accustomed to hardship, and I will take up
this war with the Ottomites. I ask for suitable provision to be
made for my wife, for a suitable residence, and for a monetary
allowance, with such arrangements and companionship as are
appropriate to one of her birth.

Duke   If you will agree, let it be at her father's.

Brabantio   [*angrily*] I won't permit it.

Othello   Nor will I.

Desdemona   Nor I. I will not stay there and cause my father to
be upset by having to see me. Most gracious Duke, give me
your willing ear, and give my simple request your support.

Duke   What do you want to do, Desdemona?

Desdemona   I loved the Moor in order to live with him;
my bold actions and my having taken my fortunes into

250   May trumpet to the world. My heart's subdu'd
       Even to the very quality of my lord.
       I saw Othello's visage in his mind,
       And to his honors and his valiant parts
       Did I my soul and fortunes consecrate.
255   So that, dear lords, if I be left behind,
       A moth of peace, and he go to the war,
       The rites for why I love him are bereft me,
       And I a heavy interim shall support
       By his dear absence. Let me go with him.

260 **Othello**   Let her have your voice.
       Vouch with me, heaven, I therefore beg it not
       To please the palate of my appetite,
       Nor to comply with heat (the young affects
       In [me] defunct) and proper satisfaction;
265   But to be free and bounteous to her mind.
       And heaven defend your good souls, that you think
       I will your serious and great business scant
       [For] she is with me. No, when light-wing'd toys
       Of feather'd Cupid seel with wanton dullness
270   My speculative and offic'd [instruments],
       That my disports corrupt and taint my business,
       Let housewives make a skillet of my helm,
       And all indign and base adversities
       Make head against my estimation!

275 **Duke**   Be it as you shall privately determine,
       Either for her stay or going; th' affair cries haste,
       And speed must answer it.

     1ˢᵗ Senator   You must away to-night.

     [**Desdemona**   To-night, my lord?

     Duke   This night.]

     Othello   With all my heart.

my own hands declare this fact to the world. My heart has
been captured by my husband's noble character. I saw
Othello's true appearance in his inner being, and I consecrated
my soul and fortunes to his honor and his excellent qualities.
So if I am left behind to live parasitically in peace while he
goes to war, the benefits of being his wife are lost to me,
and I will be terribly sad during his absence. Let me go with
him.

Othello   [*with great joy*] Let her have your permission. Testify
for me, heavens, that I do not ask in order to satisfy the
hungers of my body nor to serve the lust—since the youthful
passions are past with me—of my private appetites, but to
fully and generously enjoy her mind. And may heaven keep
you from thinking that, because she is with me, I shall give
little attention to your serious and grave business [*that is,
concerning the war in Cyprus*]. No, when Cupid's frivolous toys
dull my faculties and perceptions so that my pleasures corrupt
and soil my sense of duty, may housewives turn my helmet
into a skillet and may all shameful and worthless troubles raise
an army against my reputation.

Duke   It shall be as you decide as to whether Desdemona stays
or goes. The crisis calls for haste, and it must be quickly
attended to.

First Senator   You must leave tonight.

Desdemona   [*She is very upset.*] Tonight, my lord?

Duke   This very night.

Othello   I am entirely ready to go.

Duke   At nine i' th' morning here we'll meet again.
280   Othello, leave some officer behind,
And he shall our commission bring to you;
And such things else of quality and respect
As doth import you.

Othello   So please your Grace, my ancient;
A man he is of honesty and trust.
285   To his conveyance I assign my wife,
With what else needful your good Grace shall think
To be sent after me.

Duke   Let it be so.
Good night to every one. [*To Brabantio.*] And, noble signior,
If virtue no delighted beauty lack,
290   Your son-in-law is far more fair than black.

1ˢᵗ Senator   Adieu, brave Moor, use Desdemona well.

Brabantio   Look to her, Moor, if thou hast eyes to see;
She has deceiv'd her father, and may thee.

Exeunt [Duke, Senators, Officers, etc.].

Othello   My life upon her faith! Honest Iago,
295   My Desdemona must I leave to thee.
I prithee let thy wife attend on her,
And bring them after in the best advantage.
Come, Desdemona, I have but an hour
Of love, of wordly matter and direction,
300   To spend with thee. We must obey the time.

Exit [with Desdemona].

Roderigo   Iago—

Iago   What say'st thou, noble heart?

Roderigo   What will I do, think'st thou?

Duke   [*to the assembled group*] We'll meet here again at nine in the morning.
[*to* **Othello**] Othello, leave some officer behind and he'll bring our orders to you, as well as whatever things you require in accordance with your rank and privilege.

Othello   With your permission, your Grace, let it be my ensign; he is an honorable and trustworthy man. I place my wife in his care, along with whatever else your Grace decides to send after me.

Duke   Let it be so.
[*to all*] Good night, everyone.
[*to* **Brabantio**] And, noble signior, [*The* **Duke** *again recites a proverb.*] "If honor compensates for beauty's lack, your son-in-law is far more light than black."

First Senator   Good-bye, brave Moor. Be good to Desdemona.

Brabantio   [*bitterly, to* **Othello**] Watch out, Moor, to see what is true; she deceived me; she may deceive you.

[**Duke, Senators, Officers,** *and* **Attendants** *all leave.*]

Othello   [*calls to the departing* **Brabantio**] I would wager my life upon her loyalty!
[*to* **Iago**] Honest Iago, I must leave my Desdemona in your care. I ask you to allow your wife to be her attendant, and also bring them with you at the earliest opportunity. Come, Desdemona, I have only one hour for love, for normal pursuits, to spend with you. We must watch the clock.

[**Othello** *and* **Desdemona** *leave.*]

Roderigo   Iago . . .

Iago   What is it, good friend?

Roderigo   What do you think I should do?

Iago   Why, go to bed and sleep.

305 **Roderigo**   I will incontinently drown myself.

Iago   If thou dost, I shall never love thee after.
Why, thou silly gentleman?

Roderigo   It is silliness to live, when to live is torment;
and then have we a prescription to die, when death is
310   our physician.

Iago   O villainous! I have look'd upon the world
for four times seven years, and since I could
distinguish betwixt a benefit and an injury, I never found
man that knew how to love himself. Ere I would say I
would drown myself for the love of a guinea hen,
316   I would change my humanity with a baboon.

Roderigo   What should I do? I confess it is my shame to
be so fond, but it is not in my virtue to amend it.

Iago   Virtue? a fig! 'tis in ourselves that we are
320   thus or thus. Our bodies are our gardens, to the
which our wills are gardeners; so that if we will plant
nettles or sow lettuce, set hyssop and weed up [tine],
supply it with one gender of herbs or distract it with
many, either to have it sterile with idleness or manur'd
325   with industry—why, the power and corrigible
authority of this lies in our wills. If the [beam] of our
lives had not one scale of reason to poise another of
sensuality, the blood and baseness of our natures would
conduct us to most prepost'rous conclusions. But we
330   have reason to cool our raging motions, our carnal
stings, [our] unbitted lusts; whereof I take this that
you call love to be a sect or scion.

Roderigo   It cannot be.

Iago   It is merely a lust of the blood and a
335   permission of the will. Come, be a man! Drown

Iago   Why, go to bed and get some sleep.

Roderigo   [*gloomily*] I'm going right out to drown myself.

Iago   [*trying to cheer* **Roderigo** *with a mild joke*] If you do, I won't be your friend anymore. [*more seriously*] Why, you foolish man?

Roderigo   [*refusing to be cheered up*] It's foolish to live when living is torment. Besides, when death is our doctor, we have a "prescription" [*a play on words meaning "a perfect right"*] to die.

Iago   Oh, what horrible nonsense! I have observed the world now for twenty-eight years, and ever since I could tell the difference between what can help or harm a person, I've never yet found a man that knew how to love himself as he should. Before I would talk about drowning myself for the love of a guinea hen [*a derogatory term for "woman"*], I'd turn myself into a baboon.

Roderigo   [*wails despairingly*] What should I do? I admit I'm embarrassed about loving Desdemona so much, but I can't change my nature.

Iago   [*laughs mockingly*] Nature? Ha! We have the power to choose what we are. [*persuasively*] Our bodies are like gardens, and our wills are the gardeners. If we sow weeds or lettuce, plant hyssop and weed out wild grasses, fill our "garden" with one kind of herb or vary it with many kinds, leave it barren with idleness or fertilized with hard work, why, the power for all of these changes is controlled by our wills. If our lives weren't held in balance between our minds and our lusts, the lower passions of our natures would lead us to do outrageous things. But we do have reason to cool down our heated passions, our fleshly impulses, our uncontrolled lusts. So I think what you call "love" is nothing more than a young "plant" [*which can be easily plucked out*].

Roderigo   [*He remains gloomy*] It can't be.

Iago   It's only a lust of your body which your will has permitted. [*heartily*] Come, be a man. Drown yourself? You'd be better off

thyself? drown cats and blind puppies! I have
profess'd me thy friend, and I confess me knit to thy
deserving with cables of perdurable toughness. I could
never better stead thee than now. Put money in thy
340   purse; follow thou the wars; defeat thy favor with
an usurp'd beard. I say put money in thy purse. It
cannot be long that Desdemona should continue her
love to the Moor—put money in thy purse—nor he his
to her. It was a violent commencement in her, and
345   thou shalt see an answerable sequestration—put
but money in thy purse. These Moors are changeable
in their wills—fill thy purse with money. The food
that to him now is as luscious as locusts, shall be to him
shortly as [acerb] as [the] coloquintida. She must change
350   for youth; when she is sated with his body, she
will find the [error] of her choice. [She must have
change, she must;] therefore put money in thy purse.
If thou wilt needs damn thyself, do it a more delicate
way than drowning. Make all the money thou canst.
355   If sanctimony and a frail vow betwixt an erring
barbarian and [a] super-subtle Venetian be not too hard
for my wits and all the tribe of hell, thou shalt enjoy
her; therefore make money. A pox of drowning thyself, it is clean out of the way. Seek thou rather to be
hang'd in compassing thy joy than to be drown'd and
361   go without her.

Roderigo   Wilt thou be fast to my hopes, if I depend on
the issue?

Iago   Thou art sure of me—go make money. I
365   have told thee often, and I retell thee again and
again, I hate the Moor. My cause is hearted; thine
hath no less reason. Let us be conjunctive in our
revenge against him. If thou canst cuckold him, thou
dost thyself a pleasure, me a sport. There are many

drowning cats and blind puppies! I have said I am your friend, and I assure you that I am bound to you with ropes of enduring strength. Put money in your pocket! [**Iago** *means that* **Roderigo** *should do so in order to buy jewels and other expensive gifts for* **Desdemona**. **Iago** *intends, however, to keep the jewels, etc., for himself.*] Go to war with the soldiers. Change your appearance with a false beard. I tell you, put money in your pocket. Desdemona won't continue to be in love with the Moor for very long—put money in your pocket—nor will his love for her last. It had an abrupt beginning and you shall see an equally sudden ending—just put money in your pocket. These Moors are always changing their minds—fill your pockets with money. The "food" which tastes as delicious as carob [*a substance with a flavor similar to chocolate*] will soon be as sour as a crab apple. She is young and fickle. When she has glutted herself on his body, she will see how wrong she was. She'll want something different. [**Roderigo** *looks doubtful so* **Iago** *reiterates.*] Yes, she will. So fill your pockets with money. If you have to send yourself to hell, find a better way to do it than by drowning. Make all the money you can. If a mere marriage ceremony and a weak vow between a wandering barbarian [*Othello*] and a highly refined Venetian [*Desdemona*] is not too difficult for my brains and all the demons in hell, you will enjoy her body. Therefore, make money. To hell with drowning yourself! It's ridiculous. You'd be better off being hanged for having sex with her than being drowned and not having had her.

Roderigo   [*doubtfully*] Will you faithfully support my goals if I do as you say?

Iago   You can count on me. Go make money! I've told you many times, and I'll say it again and again: I hate the Moor. My cause comes from the depths of my heart; yours is just as deeply felt. Let's work together to take revenge on him. If you can have sex with his wife, you will have your physical pleasure, and I will have a good laugh. Time is pregnant with many things to

events in the womb of time which will be deliver'd.
Traverse, go, provide thy money. We will have more
372   of this to-morrow. Adieu.

Roderigo   Where shall we meet i' th' morning?

Iago   At my lodging.

375 **Roderigo**   I'll be with thee betimes.

Iago   Go to, farewell. Do you hear, Roderigo?

[**Roderigo**   What say you?

Iago   No more of drowning, do you hear?

Roderigo   I am chang'd.

Iago   Go to, farewell. Put money enough in your
381   purse.]

Roderigo   I'll sell all my land.

Exit.

Iago   Thus do I ever make my fool my purse;
For I mine own gain'd knowledge should profane
385   If I would time expend with such [a] snipe
But for my sport and profit. I hate the Moor,
And it is thought abroad that 'twixt my sheets
[H'as] done my office. I know not if't be true,
But I, for mere suspicion in that kind,
390   Will do as if for surety. He holds me well,
The better shall my purpose work on him.
Cassio's a proper man. Let me see now:
To get his place and to plume up my will
In double knavery—How? how?—Let's see—
395   After some time, to abuse Othello's [ear]
That he is too familiar with his wife.
He hath a person and a smooth dispose
To be suspected—fram'd to make women false.

which it will give birth. Onward, go, get your money. We'll talk more about this tomorrow.

Roderigo   Where shall we meet in the morning?

Iago   At my place.

Roderigo   I'll get there early.

Iago   Go on, good-bye. [**Roderigo** *seems distracted, so* **Iago** *speaks more loudly.*] Do you hear me, Roderigo?

Roderigo   What did you say?

Iago   No more talk about drowning, by the way.

Roderigo   I've changed my mind.

Iago   Go on, good-bye. [*As* **Roderigo** *walks away,* **Iago** *calls after him.*] Put plenty of money in your pocket.

Roderigo   I'll sell all my property. [**Roderigo** *leaves.*]

Iago   [*to himself, contemptuously*] And so I use this fool as my wallet. As if I would be stupid enough to waste my time with such an idiot unless I hoped to have some laughs or make some money out of it. I hate the Moor. Also, there is a rumor circulating that he has had sex with my wife. I don't know if the rumor is true, but based only on that suspicion I will act as if it is a proven fact. Othello respects me, which makes my plot easier to carry out.
Cassio is a good-looking man. Let me see now. How can I take over Cassio's military rank and feed my ego at the same time? How? How? [*He stops to think.*] Let's see . . . in a little while I could give Othello the painful "news" that Cassio is too intimate with Desdemona. Cassio has such good looks and polished manners that it would be believable—he's the kind

The Moor is of a free and open nature,
400   That thinks men honest that but seem to be so,
And will as tenderly be led by th' nose
As asses are.
I have't. It is engend'red. Hell and night
Must bring this monstrous birth to the world's light.

[*Exit.*]

just made to tempt women to be unfaithful. The Moor has an open and trusting nature; he believes men to be honest simply because they seem to be, so he can be as easily led about by the nose as jackasses are.

[*triumphantly*] I know! It's germinating in my mind. Hell and the night will bring this monstrous plan into the light of day.

[*He leaves.*]

Act two

Scene 1

Enter **Montano** *and two* **Gentlemen**.

Montano   What from the cape can you discern at sea?

1ˢᵗ Gentleman   Nothing at all, it is a high-wrought flood.
I cannot, 'twixt the heaven and the main,
Descry a sail.

Montano   Methinks the wind hath spoke aloud at land,
6   A fuller blast ne'er shook our battlements.
If it hath ruffian'd so upon the sea,
What ribs of oak, when mountains melt on them,
Can hold the mortise? What shall we hear of this?

10 **2ⁿᵈ Gentleman**   A segregation of the Turkish fleet:
For do but stand upon the foaming shore,
The chidden billow seems to pelt the clouds,
The wind-shak'd surge, with high and monstrous mane,
Seems to cast water on the burning Bear,
15   And quench the guards of th' ever-fixed Pole;
I never did like molestation view
On the enchafed flood.

Montano   If that the Turkish fleet
Be not enshelter'd and embay'd, they are drown'd;
It is impossible to bear it out.

Enter a [third] **Gentleman**.

20 **3ʳᵈ Gentleman**   News, lads! our wars are done.
The desperate tempest hath so bang'd the Turks,

Act two

Scene 1

The following day, a seaport in Cyprus. An open place near the quay.

[**Montano** *and two* **Gentlemen** *enter. They anxiously gaze toward the sea.*]

Montano   Can you see anything out at sea from the cape?

First Gentleman   [*He scans the horizon.*] Nothing at all. The waves are too high. I can't see so much as a sail on the horizon.

Montano   The wind is howling over the land; our fortifications have never had to withstand such shaking. If this wind so churns up the sea, what ships' timbers could possibly hold together with waves as high as mountains crashing against them? What news are we likely to hear about all this?

Second Gentleman   That the Turkish fleet has been dispersed. Just stand on the foaming shore and see—the scudding waves seem to fling themselves up to the clouds; the rushing tide seems to furiously hurl water at Ursa Major [*the Great Bear, a constellation*] and even to quench the two stars that guard the pole star [*the North star*]. I've never seen such turbulence of the sea.

Montano   If the Turkish fleet hasn't sailed into some sheltered bay, the sailors must have drowned. They couldn't possibly survive this storm.

[*A* **Third Gentleman** *enters.*]

Third Gentleman   Here's news, men! The war is over. The violent tempest has so bombarded the Turks that their

That their designment halts. A noble ship of Venice
Hath seen a grievous wrack and sufferance
On most part of their fleet.

Montano   How? is this true?

3ʳᵈ Gentleman   The ship is here put in,
26   A Veronesa; Michael Cassio,
Lieutenant to the warlike Moor Othello,
Is come on shore; the Moor himself at sea,
And is in full commission here for Cyprus.

30 **Montano**   I am glad on't; 'tis a worthy governor.

3ʳᵈ Gentleman   But this same Cassio, though he speak of
comfort
Touching the Turkish loss, yet he looks sadly,
And [prays] the Moor be safe; for they were parted
With foul and violent tempest.

Montano   Pray [heaven] he be;
35   For I have serv'd him, and the man commands
Like a full soldier. Let's to the sea-side, ho!
As well to see the vessel that's come in
As to throw out our eyes for brave Othello,
Even till we make the main and th' aerial blue
An indistinct regard.

40 **3ʳᵈ Gentleman**   Come, let's do so;
For every minute is expectancy
Of more [arrivance].

Enter **Cassio**.

Cassio   Thanks you, the valiant of [this] warlike isle,
That so approve the Moor! O, let the heavens
45   Give him defense against the elements,
For I have lost him on a dangerous sea.

advance is halted. One of Venice's noble ships has seen the terrible damage most of their ships have sustained.

Montano   Really? Is this true?

Third Gentleman   The ship, a Veronesa has docked here. [*The meaning of "Veronesa" is unclear. It may refer to a ship from Verona which is assisting Venice, or it may refer to a particular design of ship.*] Michael Cassio, lieutenant to the warlike Moor, Othello, has come on shore. The Moor is coming by sea to Cyprus to take charge.

Montano   I'm glad to hear it; he's a capable administrator.

Third Gentleman   But this same Cassio, although he brings encouraging news concerning the Turks' losses, looks worried and says he hopes the Moor is safe, because they were separated by the terrible and violent storm.

Montano   I pray that he is, for I have served under him, and the man leads like a true soldier. Let's go down to the shore. We'll be able to see the ship that has arrived, and we can also scan the distant horizon for the brave Othello.

Third Gentleman   Come, let's do so, for we can expect new arrivals at any moment.

[**Cassio** *enters.*]

Cassio   Thanks to you, you brave soldiers of this warlike isle, who so admire the Moor! May the heavens protect him from the elements, for I have become separated from him on the dangerous sea.

Montano   Is he well shipp'd?

Cassio   His bark is stoutly timber'd, and his pilot
Of very expert and approv'd allowance;
50   Therefore my hopes (not surfeited to death)
Stand in bold cure.   *Within,* "A sail, a sail, a sail!"

[*Enter a* **Messenger**.]

Cassio   What noise?

[**Messenger**]   The town is empty; on the brow o' th' sea
Stand ranks of people, and they cry, "A sail!"

55 **Cassio**   My hopes do shape him for the governor.

[*A shot.*]

2ⁿᵈ Gentleman   They do discharge their shot of
courtesy;
Our friends at least.

Cassio   I pray you, sir, go forth,
And give us truth who 'tis that is arriv'd.

2ⁿᵈ Gentleman   I shall.

Exit.

Montano   But, good lieutenant, is your general wiv'd?

Cassio   Most fortunately: he hath achiev'd a maid
62   That paragons description and wild fame;
One that excels the quirks of blazoning pens,
And in th' essential vesture of creation
Does tire the [ingener].

Enter [**Second**] **Gentleman**.

How now? who has put in?

66 **2ⁿᵈ Gentleman**   'Tis one Iago, ancient to the general.

Montano   Is his ship a strong one?

Cassio   His ship is well constructed, and his pilot has a reputation as being very skilled. My hopes, therefore, have not died, and I think they will be borne out.

[*A voice in the distance cries, "A sail, a sail, a sail!"*]
[*A* **Messenger** *enters.*]

Cassio   What's all the noise about?

Messenger   The town is empty; rows of people stand on the cliffs overlooking the sea and cry out, "A sail!"

Cassio   I hope it is Othello.

[*In the distance, a volley is fired.*]

Second Gentleman   They're firing the guns as a salute, so it must be our allies, at the least.

Cassio   [*to* **Second Gentleman**] Please, sir, go and find out the truth about who has actually arrived.

Second Gentleman   I shall.

[*He leaves.*]

Montano   [*to* **Cassio**] But, good lieutenant, has your general truly gotten married?

Cassio   Yes, and very well indeed. He has acquired a young lady who defies both description and extravagant praise, one who defeats the attempts of pens to describe her qualities and whose natural beauty would exhaust the poet who tries to portray her.

[**Second Gentleman** *enters.*]

Cassio   [*to* **Second Gentleman**] What news? Who has arrived?

Second Gentleman   It's Iago, the general's ensign.

Cassio H'as had most favorable and happy speed:
Tempests themselves, high seas, and howling winds,
The gutter'd rocks and congregated sands,
70 Traitors ensteep'd to enclog the guiltless keel,
As having sense of beauty, do omit
Their mortal natures, letting go safely by
The divine Desdemona.

Montano   What is she?

Cassio She that I spake of, our great captain's captain,
75 Left in the conduct of the bold Iago,
Whose footing here anticipates our thoughts
A se'nnight's speed. Great Jove, Othello guard,
And swell his sail with thine own pow'rful breath,
That he may bless this bay with his tall ship,
80 Make love's quick pants in Desdemona's arms,
Give renew'd fire to our extinced spirits,
[And bring all Cyprus comfort!]

Enter **Desdemona**, **Iago**, **Roderigo**, *and* **Emilia**, [*with*
Attendants].

                              O, behold,
The riches of the ship is come on shore!
You men of Cyprus, let her have your knees.
85 Hail to thee, lady! and the grace of heaven,
Before, behind thee, and on every hand,
Enwheel thee round!

Desdemona   I thank you, valiant Cassio.
What tidings can you tell [me] of my lord?

Cassio He is not yet arriv'd, nor know I aught
90 But that he's well and will be shortly here.

Desdemona O, but I fear—How lost you company?

Cassio   He's had favorable winds and made good speed. Even tempests, high seas, and howling winds, jagged rocks and sand bars like submerged traitors attempting to snag the ship's unsuspecting keel, all behave contrary to their natures and, recognizing the divine Desdemona's beauty, allow her to pass safely by.

Montano   Who is she?

Cassio   She is the one I spoke of, [*making a mildly joking play on words*] the "captain" of our great captain. She was left in the care of Iago who has arrived here a week earlier than what we expected. Great Jove [*Jupiter, the supreme god of Roman mythology*], guard Othello and fill his sails with your own powerful breath so that he may bring blessings to this bay by arriving in his tall ship, so that he may experience the breathlessness of love in Desdemona's arms, and so that he may rekindle our drooping spirits and bring encouragement to all Cyprus!

[**Desdemona, Iago, Roderigo, Emilia** *and* **Attendants** *enter.*]

Oh, look, the treasures of the ship [**Cassio** *refers to* **Desdemona and Emilia.**] have come ashore!
[*to those already present*] You men of Cyprus, kneel before Desdemona.
[*to* **Desdemona**] Welcome and praise to you, lady! May the blessings of heaven go before you, follow behind you, and completely surround you!

Desdemona   Thank you, brave Cassio. What news can you tell me of my husband?

Cassio   He hasn't yet arrived, but, as far as I know, he is well and will soon be here.

Desdemona   [*anxiously*] Oh, but I'm afraid . . . [*She hesitates, not wanting to speak her fears aloud.*] How did you become separated?

Cassio   The great contention of [the] sea and skies
Parted our fellowship.

Within, "A sail, a sail!"   [*A shot.*]

But hark! a sail.

2nd Gentleman   They give [their] greeting to the citadel.
This likewise is a friend.

95 **Cassio**   See for the news.

[*Exit Second Gentleman.*]

Good ancient, you are welcome. [*To Emilia.*] Welcome,
    mistress.
Let it not gall your patience, good Iago,
That I extend my manners; 'tis my breeding
99 That gives me this bold show of courtesy.

[*Kissing her.*]

Iago   Sir, would she give you so much of her lips
As of her tongue she oft bestows on me,
You would have enough.

Desdemona   Alas! she has no speech.

Iago   In faith, too much;
I find it still, when I have [list] to sleep.
105 Marry, before your ladyship, I grant,
She puts her tongue a little in her heart,
And chides with thinking.

Emilia   You have little cause to say so.

Iago   Come on, come on; you are pictures out [a' doors],
110 Bells in your parlors, wild-cats in your kitchens,
Saints in your injuries, devils being offended,
Players in your huswifery, and huswives in your beds.

Cassio   The violence of the sea and the winds drove us apart.

[*In the distance, a voice cries, "A sail, a sail!"*]

[*A volley is fired.*]

Cassio   Look! A sail!

Second Gentleman   The ship is firing a salute to the citadel. This must also be a friendly ship.

Cassio   [*to the* **Second Gentleman**] Go learn the news.

[*The* **Second Gentleman** *leaves.*]

[*to Iago*] Don't be too upset, good Iago, about my showing courtesy to your wife. My upbringing causes me to make these gallantries. [*He kisses* **Emilia**.]

Iago   [*snidely*] Sir, if she were to give you as many kisses as she gives me words, you would have your fill of them.

Desdemona   [*laughing*] Alas, she says nothing.

Iago   Actually, she says too much; I find that out whenever I try to sleep. [**Emilia** *looks indignant.*] Truly, my lady Desdemona, I admit, she doesn't care what she says, and she scolds about everything she can think of.

Emilia   [*sullenly*] You have little excuse for saying so.

Iago   Come, come! You women are as silent as a picture when you're with other people, but you're never quiet at home— you're like wildcats in your own kitchen. [*As he speaks,* **Emilia** *becomes more and more angry.*] You act as if you were saints even when you offend someone else, yet you rage like the devil himself if you are offended. You put on a big show about your abilities as housewives, and you're housewives [*an insulting use of the word meaning "whores"*] in your beds.

85

Desdemona   O, fie upon thee, slanderer!

Iago   Nay, it is true, or else I am a Turk:
115   You rise to play, and go to bed to work.

Emilia   You shall not write my praise.

Iago   No, let me not.

Desdemona   What wouldst write of me, if thou shouldst
        praise me?

Iago   O gentle lady, do not put me to't,
        For I am nothing if not critical.

Desdemona   Come on, assay.—There's one gone to the
120   harbor?

Iago   Ay, madam.

Desdemona   I am not merry; but I do beguile
        The thing I am by seeming otherwise.—
        Come, how wouldst thou praise me?

125 **Iago**   I am about it, but indeed my invention
        Comes from my pate as birdlime does from frieze,
        It plucks out brains and all. But my Muse labors,
        And thus she is deliver'd:
        If she be fair and wise, fairness and wit,
130   The one's for use, the other useth it.

Desdemona   Well prais'd! How if she be black and witty?

Iago   If she be black, and thereto have a wit,
        She'll find a white that shall her blackness [hit].

Desdemona   Worse and worse.

135 **Emilia**   How if fair and foolish?

Iago   She never yet was foolish that was fair,
        For even her folly help'd her to an heir.

Desdemona [*dismissing his remarks as a joke*] Shame on you, you slanderer!

Iago If it's not true, I'm a Turk. You women get out of bed to play, and do your "work" when you do go to bed.

Emilia You'd never write a poem praising me [*as lovers often did at the time*].

Iago No, I wouldn't.

Desdemona What would you write about me if you decided to write a poem in praise of me?

Iago Don't ask me to, for I only know how to criticize.

Desdemona Come, try it. [*She abruptly changes the subject and asks anxiously.*] Has someone gone to the harbor?

Iago Yes, madam.

Desdemona [*to herself*] I'm not really cheerful just now, but I'm trying to distract myself by acting as if I were.
[*to* **Iago**] Come now, how would you praise me?

Iago I'm trying, but it's as difficult to get my creative juices flowing as it is to get birdlime [*a sticky substance used to trap birds*] out of wool; my efforts yank out my brains along with them. But my Muse [*in Greek mythology, one of the nine goddesses who inspired the creative arts*] is in labor and now she gives birth:
[*reciting an old saying*] "If she is a beautiful blonde and clever, she puts her cleverness to use by using her beauty."

Desdemona Well done! What if she's a brunette and is clever?

Iago [*reciting again*] "If she's a brunette and knows how to use her brains, she'll catch a man with her good looks."

Desdemona [*laughingly protesting*] Worse and worse!

Emilia [*sourly*] What if she's blonde and stupid?

Iago [*recites once more*] "There is no such thing as a stupid blonde, for even her stupidity helps her attract a husband."

Desdemona   These are old fond paradoxes to make fools
laugh i' th' alehouse. What miserable praise hast thou
140   for her that's foul and foolish?

Iago   There's none so foul and foolish thereunto,
But does foul pranks which fair and wise ones do.

Desdemona   O heavy ignorance! thou praisest the worst
144   best. But what praise couldst thou bestow on a
deserving woman indeed—one that in the authority of
her merit, did justly put on the vouch of very malice
itself?

Iago   She that was ever fair, and never proud,
Had tongue at will, and yet was never loud,
150   Never lack'd gold, and yet went never gay,
Fled from her wish, and yet said, "Now I may";
She that being ang'red, her revenge being nigh,
Bade her wrong stay, and her displeasure fly;
She that in wisdom never was so frail
155   To change the cod's head for the salmon's tail;
She that could think, and nev'r disclose her mind,
See suitors following, and not look behind:
She was a wight (if ever such [wight] were)—

159   **Desdemona**   To do what?

Iago   To suckle fools and chronicle small beer.

Desdemona   O most lame and impotent conclusion! Do
not learn of him, Emilia, though he be thy husband.
How say you, Cassio? is he not a most profane and
liberal counsellor?

Cassio   He speaks home, madam. You may relish him
166   more in the soldier than in the scholar.

Iago   [*Aside.*] He takes her by the palm; ay, well
said, whisper. With as little a web as this will I en-

Desdemona   These are just stupid old paradoxes that fools in taverns laugh over. So what horrid "praise" do you have for the woman who is ugly and stupid?

Iago   [*still reciting*] "No woman is so ugly and stupid that she can't use the same tricks used by the beautiful and clever."

Desdemona   [*in exasperation*] Oh, what deliberate ignorance! You give the best praise to the worst woman! But what can you say in praise of a truly deserving woman—one whose merits compel even critics to speak favorably?

Iago   [*reciting once again*] "The woman who was always beautiful and never vain,
Knew how to speak at the right time, and yet was never loud,
Never was poor, and yet didn't wear extravagant clothing,
Didn't indulge herself, and yet she was free to do so,
Told her hurt feelings to be quiet and her anger to fly away,
Was never so foolish as to trade something valuable for something worthless,
Who could think, yet not reveal her thoughts,
She was a woman indeed—if there ever was such a woman
. . ." [*He pauses provocatively.*]

Desdemona   To do what?

Iago   To tend babies and keep house.

Desdemona   [*Protesting laughingly*] Oh, what a feeble and stupid conclusion!
[*to* **Emilia**] Don't listen to him, Emilia, even if he is your husband.
[*to* **Cassio**] What do you think, Cassio? Isn't he a vulgar and loose talker?

Cassio   [*ruefully*] He's very blunt, madam. You would probably like him better as a soldier than as a philosopher.

Iago   [*to himself*] Cassio is taking her hand . . . Yes, go on, whisper to her. With as small a web as this I will catch as big a

snare as great a fly as Cassio. Ay, smile upon her, do;
170   I will gyve thee in thine own courtship. You
say true, 'tis so indeed. If such tricks as these strip
you out of your lieutenantry, it had been better you
had not kiss'd your three fingers so oft, which now
again you are most apt to play the sir in. Very good;
175   well kiss'd! [an] excellent [courtesy]! 'Tis so
indeed. Yet again, your fingers to your lips? Would
they were clyster-pipes for your sake! [*Trumpets
within.*]—The Moor! I know his trumpet.

Cassio   'Tis truly so.

180 **Desdemona**   Let's meet him and receive him.

Cassio   Lo, where he comes!

Enter **Othello** *and* **Attendants**.

Othello   O my fair warrior!

Desdemona   My dear Othello!

Othello   It gives me wonder great as my content
To see you here before me. O my soul's joy!
185   If after every tempest come such calms,
May the winds blow till they have waken'd death!
And let the laboring bark climb hills of seas
Olympus-high, and duck again as low
As hell's from heaven! If it were now to die,
190   'Twere now to be most happy; for I fear
My soul hath her content so absolute
That not another comfort like to this
Succeeds in unknown fate.

Desdemona   The heavens forbid
But that our loves and comforts should increase
Even as our days do grow!

195 **Othello**   Amen to that, sweet powers!
I cannot speak enough of this content,

fly as Cassio. I will ensnare you in your own courtly manners. Yes, you're so right; it's true indeed. [**Iago** *is encouraging* **Cassio** *to continue his gallantries to* **Desdemona**, *although not with the intention of being heard.*] If courtesies such as these cause you to be stripped of your lieutenancy, you'd have been better off not to have kissed your three fingers so often as you now do in order to look like a fancy gentleman. [*sarcastically*] Very good! Fine hand kissing! An excellent bow! Indeed, it is. You kiss the hand again? I wish you were kissing enema tubes! [*Trumpets sound in the distance.*]

[*to* **Desdemona, Cassio,** *and* **Emilia**] It's the Moor! I know his trumpet signal.

Cassio   It is indeed.

Desdemona   [*eagerly*] Let's go meet and welcome him.

Cassio   Look, here he comes!

[**Othello** *and* **Attendants** *approach.*]

Othello   [*to* **Desdemona**] My beautiful warrior!

Desdemona   My dear Othello!

Othello   I am awed and happy to find you here. Oh, my soul's joy! If every storm is to be followed by such peace, may the winds blow till they awake the dead, and let the struggling ship climb waves as high as Mount Olympus and plunge down again as far below heaven as hell is! If I were to die now, this would be my happiest moment, for I am afraid my soul is so completely contented that no delight as great as this could follow in the uncertain future.

Desdemona   May the heavens forbid anything except that our love and contentment should keep growing as long as we live!

Othello   Amen to that, kindly powers of heaven! I can barely express my contentment. I am unable to speak; my joy is so

It stops me here; it is too much of joy.
And this, and this, the greatest discords be

[They kiss.]

That e'er our hearts shall make!

Iago   *[Aside.]* O, you are well tun'd now!
200   But I'll set down the pegs that make this music,
As honest as I am.

Othello   Come; let us to the castle.
News, friends: our wars are done; the Turks are drown'd.
How does my old acquaintance of this isle?
Honey, you shall be well desir'd in Cyprus,
I have found great love amongst them. O my sweet,
206   I prattle out of fashion, and I dote
In mine own comforts. I prithee, good Iago,
Go to the bay and disembark my coffers.
Bring thou the master to the citadel;
210   He is a good one, and his worthiness
Does challenge much respect. Come, Desdemona,
Once more, well met at Cyprus.

*Exeunt Othello and Desdemona [with all but
Iago and Roderigo].*

Iago   *[To an Attendant, as he is going out.]* Do thou
meet me presently at the harbor.—Come [hither]. If
215   thou be'st valiant (as they say base men being in
love have then a nobility in their natures more than is
native to them), list me. The lieutenant to-night
watches on the court of guard. First, I must tell thee
this: Desdemona is directly in love with him.

220 **Roderigo**   With him? why, 'tis not possible.

Iago   Lay thy finger thus; and let thy soul be instructed. Mark me with what violence she first lov'd

overwhelming. May this [*He kisses her.*] and this [*He kisses her again.*] be the greatest problems our hearts shall have!

Iago   [*to himself*] Oh, you're in harmony now! But I'll loosen the pegs that tune your instruments [*to cause them to be "out of tune" with one another*], I promise you.

Othello   [*to **Desdemona***] Come, let us go to the castle.
[*to all*] Good news, friends; our wars are over. The Turks have been drowned. How are you, my old friends of this island?
[*to **Desdemona***] Honey, you will be greatly loved in Cyprus; I have found the people to be very kind. Oh, my sweet, I'm babbling on and on and sounding like a fool, I'm so happy.
[*to **Iago***] Iago, please go to the bay and unload my baggage. Bring the captain of the ship to the citadel; he's a good captain, and he's worthy of great respect.
[*to **Desdemona***] Come, Desdemona.
[*to all*] Once again, I greet you citizens of Cyprus. [*The Cypriots cheer loudly.*]

[**Othello** *and* **Desdemona** *leave. The citizens and others depart separately.* **Iago** *and* **Roderigo** *remain.*]

Iago   [*to an **Attendant** as he is departing*] Meet me at the harbor in a little while.
[*to **Roderigo***] Come here. People say that even ordinary men, when in love, become better people than they ordinarily are, so, if you are brave [*because of his love for Desdemona*], listen to me. Lieutenant Cassio stands watch in the court of the guard tonight. But first I need to tell you this; Desdemona is clearly in love with him.

Roderigo   [*in dismay and disbelief*] With him? Why, it isn't possible.

Iago   Be silent a moment and let me give you some advice. Think about how intensely she began loving the Moor, and for

the Moor, but for bragging and telling her fantastical
lies. To love him still for prating—let not thy discreet
225   heart think it. Her eye must be fed; and what delight shall she have to look on the devil? When the
blood is made dull with the act of sport, there should
be, [again] to inflame it and to give satiety a fresh
appetite, loveliness in favor, sympathy in years,
230   manners, and beauties—all which the Moor is defective in. Now for want of these requir'd conven-
iences, her delicate tenderness will find itself abus'd,
begin to heave the gorge, disrelish and abhor the Moor;
very nature will instruct her in it and compel her to
235   some second choice. Now, sir, this granted (as it
is a most pregnant and unforc'd position), who stands
so eminent in the degree of this fortune as Cassio
does? a knave very voluble; no further conscionable
than in putting on the mere form of civil and humane
seeming, for the better compass of his salt and most
hidden loose affection? Why, none, why, none—a
242   slipper and subtle knave, a finder[-out] of occasion;
that [has] an eye can stamp and counterfeit advantages,
though true advantage never present itself; a devilish
245   knave. Besides, the knave is handsome, young,
and hath all those requisites in him that folly and
green minds look after; a pestilent complete knave,
and the woman hath found him already.

Roderigo   I cannot believe that in her, she's full of most
250   bless'd condition.

Iago   Bless'd fig's-end! The wine she drinks is
made of grapes. If she had been bless'd, she would
never have lov'd the Moor. Bless'd pudding! Didst
thou not see her paddle with the palm of his hand?
255   Didst not mark that?

Roderigo   Yes, that I did; but that was but courtesy.

nothing more than his bragging and telling her outlandish lies. But to continue loving him for his boasting? Don't think it for a minute! She needs something handsome to look at, and what pleasure can she have looking at that devil? When she's satisfied her physical desires with sex, she will need, in order to make her hungry again, a handsome face, similarity in age, manners, and attractiveness—all of which the Moor lacks. Then, because these traits are lacking in him, her refined senses will begin to grow disgusted, to become revolted, to loath and despise the Moor. Nature itself will teach her this and compel her to choose another. Now, sir, granted this very obvious and unarguable fact, who stands a better chance of being chosen than Cassio? A young fool who is full of compliments, never hesitates to put on a show of being extremely polite and courteous in order to hide his lust and his lewd desires? Why, none! Why, none! A slippery and subtle villain, a man who's always on the lookout for a chance to get ahead, who readily creates his own opportunities even where they aren't apparent; a devilish rogue. Besides, the rogue is handsome, young, and has everything that a lusty and inexperienced woman looks for. He's a totally disgusting fellow, and Desdemona has noticed him already.

Roderigo   I can't believe it of her! She has such a saintly character.

Iago   [*in disgust*] Blessed fig's end [*a vulgar expression, based on an obscene gesture*]! The wine she drinks is made from grapes. If she were really a saint, she'd never have fallen in love with the Moor. Blessed sausage [*another vulgarism*]! Didn't you see her caressing the palm of Cassio's hand? Didn't you notice that?

Roderigo   Yes, I did, but she was just being polite.

Iago   Lechery, by this hand; an index and obscure
258   prologue to the history of lust and foul thoughts.
They met so near with their lips that their breaths
embrac'd together. Villainous thoughts, Roderigo!
When these [mutualities] so marshal the way, hard at
262   hand comes the master and main exercise, th'
incorporate conclusion. Pish! But, sir, be you rul'd by
me. I have brought you from Venice. Watch you to-
night; for the command, I'll lay't upon you. Cassio
knows you not. I'll not be far from you. Do you find
267   some occasion to anger Cassio, either by speaking too loud, or tainting his discipline, or from what
other course you please, which the time shall more
270   favorably minister.

Roderigo   Well.

Iago   Sir, he's rash and very sudden in choler, and
happily may strike at you—provoke him that he may;
for even out of that will I cause these of Cyprus to
mutiny, whose qualification shall come into no true
taste again but by the displanting of Cassio. So shall
277   you have a shorter journey to your desires by the
means I shall then have to prefer them; and the impedi-
ment most profitably remov'd, without the which
280   there were no expectation of our prosperity.

Roderigo   I will do this, if you can bring it to any
opportunity.

Iago   I warrant thee. Meet me by and by at the
citadel. I must fetch his necessaries ashore. Farewell.

285 **Roderigo**   Adieu.

Exit.

Iago   That Cassio loves her, I do well believe't;
That she loves him, 'tis apt and of great credit.
The Moor (howbeit that I endure him not)

Iago   That was lust, I swear it. It's the introduction and the table
of contents to the story of their lust and evil desire. Their lips
were so close together, their breath was making love. They
have evil intentions, Roderigo. When these kinds of intimacies
pave the way, the principle deed—the act of sex—soon
follows. Pish! But, sir, let me tell you what to do. I have brought
you from Venice. Stand guard with the night watchman
tonight; I'll arrange for the official orders for it. Cassio doesn't
know you. I'll be nearby. Think up some way to anger Cassio;
either talk too loudly, or undermine his authority, or whatever
else you choose to do as the situation may suggest.

Roderigo   All right.

Iago   Sir, Cassio is very impulsive and quick to anger, and he'll
probably try to hit you—provoke him to do so. I'll use this
small incident to incite the people of Cyprus to riot, and they
won't be satisfied unless Cassio is removed from his post. You
will reach your goal more quickly by the steps I am taking to
advance your cause. And we will both benefit when this
roadblock is removed, for without its removal neither of us can
hope to get what we want.

Roderigo   [*reluctantly*] I'll do it if you can create an opportunity.

Iago   I assure you I can. Meet me in a little while near the citadel.
I must bring Othello's baggage ashore. Farewell.

Roderigo   Goodbye.

[*He leaves.*]

Iago   [*to himself*] I can easily believe that Cassio loves
Desdemona; that she loves him is both probable and
believable. I must admit that the Moor, even though I despise

Is of a constant, loving, noble nature,
290 And I dare think he'll prove to Desdemona
A most dear husband. Now I do love her too,
Not out of absolute lust (though peradventure
I stand accomptant for as great a sin),
But partly led to diet my revenge,
295 For that I do suspect the lusty Moor
Hath leap'd into my seat; the thought whereof
Doth (like a poisonous mineral) gnaw my inwards;
And nothing can or shall content my soul
Till I am even'd with him, wife for wife;
300 Or failing so, yet that I put the Moor
At least into a jealousy so strong
That judgment cannot cure. Which thing to do,
If this poor trash of Venice, whom I trace
For his quick hunting, stand the putting on,
305 I'll have our Michael Cassio on the hip,
Abuse him to the Moor in the [rank] garb
(For I fear Cassio with my night-cap too),
Make the Moor thank me, love me, and reward me,
For making him egregiously an ass,
310 And practicing upon his peace and quiet
Even to madness. 'Tis here; but yet confus'd,
Knavery's plain face is never seen till us'd.

Exit.

Scene 2

*Enter Othello's **Herald** with a proclamation; [people following].*

Herald   It is Othello's pleasure, our noble and valiant
general, that upon certain tidings now arriv'd, import-
ing the mere perdition of the Turkish fleet, every man

him, has a faithful, loving, and noble nature, but I think he's going to turn out to be a very "expensive" husband to Desdemona. In fact, I love her too, and not entirely because of lust—although I suppose I am also guilty of that great sin. But part of the reason I long for revenge is that I suspect that the lusty Moor has slept with my wife, and the mere thought of this eats at my guts like poison. Nothing, therefore, will satisfy me until I am even with him, wife for wife. Or, if I fail to do that, I at least can put the Moor into such a state of jealousy that no amount of sound judgment can overcome. If I can incite the rabble of Venice to do what I want them to do, I'll have our Michael Cassio right where I want him. I'll tell false tales to the Moor, speaking in a vulgar manner—for I too fear that Cassio could seduce my wife—and make the Moor thank me, love me, and reward me for making a complete jackass of him and for disturbing his peace and quiet to the point of driving him insane. The plan is right here [*He taps his forehead.*], but I haven't worked out all the details. My villainy doesn't seem to want to entirely show its face until the scheme has been set in motion.

[*He leaves.*]

Scene 2

A street in Cyprus.

[**Othello***'s* **Herald** *enters with a proclamation. The people of the city gather to listen.*]

Herald   [*loudly, making an announcement to all citizens*] It is the desire of our noble and brave general Othello, now that

put himself into triumph; some to dance, some to make
5   bonfires, each man to what sport and revels his
[addiction] leads him; for besides these beneficial
news, it is the celebration of his nuptial. So much was
his pleasure should be proclaim'd. All offices are open,
and there is full liberty of feasting from this present
hour of five till the bell have told eleven. [Heaven]
11   bless the isle of Cyprus and our noble general
Othello!

Exeunt.

[Scene 3]

Enter **Othello**, **Desdemona**, **Cassio**, *and* **Attendants**.

Othello   Good Michael, look you to the guard to-night.
Let's teach ourselves that honorable stop,
Not to outsport discretion.

Cassio   Iago hath direction what to do;
5   But notwithstanding with my personal eye
Will I look to't.

Othello   Iago is most honest.
Michael, good night. To-morrow with your earliest
Let me have speech with you. [*To Desdemona.*] Come,
    my dear love,
The purchase made, the fruits are to ensue;
10   That profit's yet to come 'tween me and you.—
Good night.

Exit [with Desdemona and Attendants].

Enter **Iago**.

verified reports have arrived concerning the complete destruction of the Turkish fleet, that everyone should celebrate. Dance, build bonfires, celebrate in whatever way you wish, for, in addition to the good news, he wants you to celebrate his marriage. It was his desire to have this proclaimed. All the storehouses are opened, and he proclaims a free feast from now, five o'clock, until eleven o'clock. May heaven bless the island of Cyprus and our noble general Othello!

[*All cheer and then leave, celebrating.*]

Scene 3

Several hours later. A hall in the citadel at Cyprus.

[**Othello, Desdemona, Cassio,** *and* **Attendants** *enter.*]

Othello   My good friend, Michael, you shall be the head of the guard tonight. We must exercise self-control and not celebrate uncontrollably.

Cassio   Iago has his orders, but I will personally keep an eye on things nonetheless.

Othello   Iago is very trustworthy. Michael, good night. First thing tomorrow I want to speak with you.
[*to* **Desdemona**] Come, my love, we have made our purchase, and the enjoyment of it awaits us. The profit of our purchase is still to come for you and me.
[*to the rest*] Good night.

[**Othello** *and* **Desdemona** *leave, followed by* **Attendants.**]

[**Iago** *enters.*]

Cassio   Welcome, Iago; we must to the watch.

Iago   Not this hour, lieutenant; 'tis not yet ten o'
th' clock. Our general cast us thus early for the love
15   of his Desdemona; who let us not therefore
blame. He hath not yet made wanton the night with
her; and she is sport for Jove.

Cassio   She's a most exquisite lady.

19 **Iago**   And I'll warrant her, full of game.

Cassio   Indeed she's a most fresh and delicate
creature.

Iago   What an eye she has! Methinks it sounds a
parley to provocation.

Cassio   An inviting eye; and yet methinks right
25   modest.

Iago   And when she speaks, is it not an alarum to
love?

Cassio   She is indeed perfection.

Iago   Well—happiness to their sheets! Come,
30   lieutenant, I have a stope of wine, and here without
are a brace of Cyprus gallants that would fain have a
measure to the health of black Othello.

Cassio   Not to-night, good Iago, I have very poor
and unhappy brains for drinking. I could well wish
courtesy would invent some other custom of entertain-
36   ment.

Iago   O, they are our friends—but one cup, I'll
drink for you.

Cassio   I have drunk but one cup to-night—and that
was craftily qualified too—and behold what innova-
tion it makes here. I am infortunate in the infirmity,
42   and dare not task my weakness with any more.

Cassio   Welcome, Iago. We must go stand watch.

Iago   Not for another hour, lieutenant. It's not yet ten o'clock. Our general has dismissed us early so he can enjoy the love of Desdemona, and we certainly can't blame him for that. He hasn't slept with her yet, and she's enough woman to satisfy a god. [*He laughs suggestively.*]

Cassio   She is a very beautiful lady.

Iago   And I'll bet she's lively in bed. [*He winks and nudges* **Cassio**.]

Cassio   [**Cassio** *tries to ignore* **Iago***'s suggestive remarks.*] She is certainly a young and lovely creature.

Iago   What an eye she has! I think it signals a desire to flirt.

Cassio   A friendly eye, yes, but I think it's completely modest.

Iago   And when she speaks, isn't it an invitation to make love?

Cassio   [**Cassio** *continues to try to ignore* **Iago***'s suggestive remarks.*] She is certainly perfection itself.

Iago   Well, may their marriage bed be happy. Come, lieutenant, I have a tankard of wine, and here are some fellows of Cyprus who will gladly drink to the health of the black Othello.

Cassio   Not tonight. I have a very weak head for drinking. I very much wish some other custom for showing good will could be invented.

Iago   [*persuasively*] Oh, but these are our friends. Just one cup; I'll do your drinking for you.

Cassio   I've had only one cup tonight—and, wisely, I even diluted it—and look at how much it affects me. I am unfortunate to have this problem, and I don't dare test my weakness with any more drinking.

Iago   What, man? 'Tis a night of revels, the
gallants desire it.

45 **Cassio**   Where are they?

Iago   Here, at the door; I pray you call them in.

Cassio   I'll do't, but it dislikes me.

Exit.

Iago   If I can fasten but one cup upon him,
With that which he hath drunk to-night already,
50 He'll be as full of quarrel and offense
As my young mistress' dog. Now, my sick fool Roderigo,
Whom love hath turn'd almost the wrong side out,
To Desdemona hath to-night carous'd
Potations pottle-deep; and he's to watch.
55 Three else of Cyprus, noble swelling spirits
That hold their honors in a wary distance,
The very elements of this warlike isle,
Have I to-night fluster'd with flowing cups,
And they watch too. Now 'mongst this flock of drunkards
60 Am I [to put] our Cassio in some action
That may offend the isle. But here they come.

Enter **Cassio**, **Montano**, *and* **Gentlemen**;
[**Servants** *follow with wine*].

If consequence do but approve my dream,
My boat sails freely, both with wind and stream.

Cassio   'Fore [God], they have given me a rouse
65 already.

Montano   Good faith, a little one; not past a pint, as I
am a soldier.

Iago   Some wine ho!
[*Sings.*]   "And let me the canakin clink, clink;
70   And let me the canakin clink.
                  A soldier's a man;

104

Iago   What, man? It's a night for parties; the young men want to celebrate.

Cassio   [*doubtfully*] Where are they?

Iago   [*pointing*] Here, at the door. Please invite them in.

Cassio   [*reluctantly*] I'll do it, but I don't like the idea.

[*He exits.*]

Iago   [*to himself*] If I can persuade him to have just one drink, added to what he's already drunk tonight, he'll be as ready to quarrel and take offense as a fine lady's spoiled lap dog. Now, my lovesick fool Roderigo, who has been nearly turned inside out by love, has drunk deeply to Desdemona tonight, and he's the night watchman. Tonight I have also gotten three other men of Cyprus drunk—they're noble, proud fellows, typical of this warlike island. They're very touchy about their honor, and they're standing watch, too. Now, amongst this flock of drunkards I will cause Cassio to do something which should offend everyone on this island.

[*He hears sounds of others approaching.*]
Here they come.

[**Cassio, Montano,** *and* **Gentlemen** *enter, followed by* **Servants** *carrying wine and cups.*]
[*still speaking to himself*] If my hopes are fulfilled, my boat will sail freely with both the wind and the tide.

Cassio   [*staggers in, laughing and clearly already drunk*] By God, they've given me a drink already.

Montano   [*also laughing and somewhat intoxicated*] Truly, my friend, not more than a pint. I swear on my honor as a soldier.

[**Cassio** *and his companions continue drinking and laughing as the conversation continues.* **Iago** *pretends to become drunk like the rest.*]

Iago   [*to a* **Servant**] Bring some wine, you!
[**Iago** *sings loudly*] "And let me the tankard clink, clink;
[*At the word "clink,"* **Iago** *and the others clink their cups together.*]
And let me the tankard clink, clink.

O, man's life's but a span;
Why then let a soldier drink."
Some wine, boys!

75 **Cassio** 'Fore [God], an excellent song.

Iago I learn'd it in England, where indeed they
are most potent in potting; your Dane, your German,
and your swag-bellied Hollander—Drink ho!—are
nothing to your English.

Cassio Is your [Englishman] so exquisite in his
81 drinking?

Iago Why, he drinks you, with facility, your Dane
dead drunk; he sweats not to overthrow your Almain;
he gives your Hollander a vomit ere the next pottle
85 can be fill'd.

Cassio To the health of our general!

Montano I am for it, lieutenant; and I'll do you justice.

Iago O sweet England!
[*Sings.*]
"King Stephen was and-a worthy peer,
90   His breeches cost him but a crown;
He held them sixpence all too dear,
With that he call'd the tailor lown;
He was a wight of high renown,
And thou art but of low degree.
95 'Tis pride that pulls the country down,
[Then] take thy auld cloak about thee."
Some wine ho!

Cassio ['Fore God,] this is a more exquisite song than
the other.

100 **Iago** Will you hear't again?

Cassio No; for I hold him to be unworthy of his place
that does those things. Well, [God's] above all; and

A soldier's a man, Oh, man's life's but a span [*that is, a short time*].
Why, then let a soldier drink."
[*to the* **Servants**] Some wine, boys!

Cassio   [*becoming more drunk by the minute*] By God, that's an excellent song!

Iago   I learned it in England, where you will surely find strong drinkers. Your Dane, your German, and your pot-bellied Hollander . . .
[*He pauses and calls to* **Servants**.] Bring me a drink!
[*resumes, to* **Cassio**] . . . are nothing to your Englishman.

Cassio   Are the English really such great drinkers?

Iago   Why, the Englishman can easily drink until the Dane is dead drunk, he doesn't even break into a sweat out-drinking the German, and the Hollander will be vomiting while the Englishman is filling his next glass.

Cassio   [*shouting*] To our general's health!

Montano   I'll drink to that, lieutenant, and I'll match your toast.

Iago   [*sings*] "King Stephen was a worthy peer,
His pants cost him just a crown [*a unit of money*].
He thought they were sixpence too dear [*that is, too costly*],
So he called the tailor lown [*that is, a scoundrel*].
He was a man of great renown,
And you're just of low degree.
It's pride that pulls the country down,
Then wrap your old cloak 'round thee."
[*to* **Servants**] More wine here!

Cassio   [*He's now extremely drunk.*] By God, that's an even better song than the other.

Iago   Would you like to hear it again?

Cassio   No, because only someone unworthy of his rank would want that.
[*rambling drunkenly*] Well, God is greater than anything, and

107

there be souls must be sav'd, and there be souls must
not be sav'd.

105 **Iago**   It's true, good lieutenant.

Cassio   For mine own part—no offense to the general,
nor any man of quality—I hope to be sav'd.

Iago   And so do I too, lieutenant.

Cassio   Ay; but by your leave, not before me; the
110   lieutenant is to be sav'd before the ancient. Let's
have no more of this; let's to our affairs.—[God] forgive
us our sins!—Gentlemen, let's look to our business. Do not think, gentlemen, I am drunk: this is my
ancient, this is my right hand, and this is my left
[hand]. I am not drunk now; I can stand well enough,
116   and I speak well enough.
[*All.*] Excellent well.

Cassio   Why, very well then; you must not think then
that I am drunk.

Exit.

Montano   To th' platform, masters, come, let's set the
watch.

[*The Gentlemen follow Cassio off.*]

121 **Iago**   You see this fellow that is gone before:
He's a soldier fit to stand by Caesar
And give direction; and do but see his vice,
'Tis to his virtue a just equinox,
125   The one as long as th' other. 'Tis pity of him.
I fear the trust Othello puts him in,
On some odd time of his infirmity,
Will shake this island.

108

there are souls who will be saved and souls who won't
be saved.

Iago   That's true, good lieutenant.

Cassio   As for me—no offense to the general or to any noble
man—I hope to be saved.

Iago   And so do I, lieutenant.

Cassio   Yes, but with your permission, not before I am; the lieutenant
should be saved before the ensign. [**Cassio** *refers to military
protocol.* **Iago** *looks furious but swiftly hides his feelings.*]
But let's change the subject; let's get back to our business.
[*to entire the group*] Do not think, gentlemen, that I am drunk.
[*He points to Iago.*] This is my ensign [**Iago** *bows and the others
cheer and applaud.* **Cassio** *then holds up one hand.*], this is my
right hand [*He realizes he is holding up the wrong hand and
quickly switches hands as the others laugh good-naturedly.*
Cassio *next holds up the other hand.*], and this is my left hand.
I am not drunk just now. I can stand well enough [*He nearly falls
over as he says this. The others laugh again.*], and I can speak
well enough [*He slurs his words badly.*].

All   [*agreeing drunkenly*] Yes, very well.

Cassio   [*Because he is so drunk, he takes their words literally,
thinking they are saying that he can speak very well.*] Why,
very well then. You mustn't think then that I am drunk.

Montano   [*calls out*] To the ramparts, men! Come, let's take up
the watch.

[*The* **Gentlemen** *follow* **Cassio** *offstage.* **Montano** *and* **Iago**
remain behind.]

Iago   [*No longer acting as if drunk,* **Iago** *speaks to* **Montano** *with
false concern and regret.*] Did you see that fellow who just left?
He's a soldier fit to serve with Julius Caesar and to lead others,
yet just look at this weakness of his. It's the exact opposite to
his good qualities; his fault is as extensive as his merits. It's
very sad. I'm worried that the trust Othello has placed in him,
at some time when Cassio's weakness afflicts him, will
threaten the security of this island.

Montano   But is he often thus?

Iago   'Tis evermore [the] prologue to his sleep.
130   He'll watch the horologe a double set
If drink rock not his cradle.

Montano   It were well
The general were put in mind of it.
Perhaps he sees it not, or his good nature
Prizes the virtue that appears in Cassio,
135   And looks not on his evils. Is not this true?

Enter **Roderigo**.

Iago   [*Aside to him.*] How now, Roderigo?
I pray you, after the lieutenant, go.

[*Exit Roderigo.*]

Montano   And 'tis great pity that the noble Moor
Should hazard such a place as his own second
140   With one of an ingraft infirmity;
It were an honest action to say
So to the Moor.

Iago   Not I, for this fair island.
I do love Cassio well; and would do much
To cure him of this evil.

[*Cry within:* "Help! Help!"]

But hark, what noise?

Enter **Cassio** *pursuing* **Roderigo**.

145 **Cassio**   ['Zounds,] you rogue! you rascal!

Montano   What's the matter, lieutenant?

Cassio   A knave teach me my duty? I'll beat the knave
into a twiggen bottle.

Montano   [*with great concern*] But is he often this way?

Iago   [*He lies intentionally.*] He does it every night. [**Montano** *is clearly shocked and dismayed.*] He'd be capable of standing a double watch if drink didn't put him to sleep.

Montano   It would be wise to tell the general of this. Perhaps he hasn't observed it, or perhaps his kind heart appreciates Cassio's good qualities and doesn't see his faults. Don't you think so?

[**Roderigo** *enters.*]

Iago   [*softly to* **Roderigo** *so* **Montano** *doesn't hear them*] How goes it, Roderigo? Go follow the lieutenant, please.

[**Roderigo** *leaves.*]

Montano   [*shaking his head sadly*] It's a great pity that the noble Moor should take such a chance by having as second in command someone with such an innate weakness. It would be best to tell this to the Moor.

Iago   Not I, even if you were to give me this entire beautiful island. I care very much for Cassio and would do much to cure him of this problem.

[*A cry from offstage: "Help! Help!"*]

But listen! What's this commotion?

[**Cassio** *enters, pursuing* **Roderigo**.]

Cassio   [*cursing and shouting drunkenly*] God's wounds, you rogue! You rascal!

Montano   [*alarmed*] What's the matter, lieutenant?

Cassio   Shall I let a scoundrel teach me my duty? I'll beat the scoundrel till he's small enough to fit into a bottle.

149 **Roderigo**   Beat me?

Cassio   Dost thou prate, rogue?

[*Striking Roderigo.*]

Montano   Nay, good lieutenant; I pray you, sir, hold
your hand.

[*Staying him.*]

Cassio   Let me go, sir, or I'll knock you o'er the
mazzard.

155 **Montano**   Come, come—you're drunk.

Cassio   Drunk?

[*They fight.*]

Iago   [*Aside to Roderigo.*] Away, I say; go out and
cry a mutiny.

[*Exit Roderigo.*]

Nay, good lieutenant—[God's will], gentlemen—
Help ho!—lieutenant—sir—Montano—[sir]—
160 Help, masters!—Here's a goodly watch indeed!

[*A bell rung.*]

Who's that which rings the bell? *Diablo*, ho!
The town will rise. [God's will], lieutenant, [hold]!
You'll be asham'd for ever.

Enter **Othello** *and* [**Gentlemen** *with weapons*].

Othello   What is the matter here?

Montano   ['Zounds,] I bleed still,
I am hurt to th' death. He dies.

[*Assailing Cassio again.*]

112

Roderigo   Beat me?

Cassio   Are you babbling, scoundrel?

[*He strikes* **Roderigo**.]

Montano   [**Montano** *tries to restrain* **Cassio**.] No, good
lieutenant. I beg you, sir, to restrain yourself.

Cassio   [*struggling*] Let me go, sir, or I'll hit you on the head!

Montano   Come, come, you're drunk.

Cassio   [*indignantly*] Drunk?

[**Cassio** *begins fighting with* **Montano**.]

Iago   [*quietly to* **Roderigo** *so that the others cannot hear him*]
Go on, I tell you. Go out and shout that there is an insurrection.

[**Roderigo** *runs offstage*.]
[*to* **Cassio**] No, good lieutenant . . . [**Iago** *again tries to restrain*
Cassio.]
[*to the others present*] For God's sake, gentlemen . . . [**Iago** *and*
Cassio *struggle*.] Help me here!
[*to* **Cassio**, *as they continue to struggle*] Lieutenant . . . sir . . .
[*to* **Montano**, *trying to stop him as well*] Montano . . . sir . . .
[*to others*] Help me, gentlemen!
[*disgustedly, as the rest join in the brawl*] A fine night watch this is!
[*In the distance, an alarm bell is rung*]
Who's ringing that bell? What the devil . . . ? The whole town
will awaken.
[*to* **Cassio**] For God's sake, lieutenant, stop! You'll be disgraced
forever!

[**Othello** *and* **Gentlemen** *with weapons enter*.]

Othello   [*roars*] What is the matter here?

Montano   Good God, I'm bleeding! I'm going to die!

[*to* **Cassio**] You will die for this! [**Montano** *attacks* **Cassio**.]

165 **Othello**   Hold, for your lives!

Iago   Hold ho! Lieutenant—sir—Montano—gentlemen—
Have you forgot all place of sense and duty?
Hold! the general speaks to you; hold, for shame!

Othello   Why, how now ho? from whence ariseth this?
170 Are we turn'd Turks, and to ourselves do that
Which heaven hath forbid the Ottomites?
For Christian shame, put by this barbarous brawl.
He that stirs next to carve for his own rage
Holds his soul light; he dies upon his motion.
175 Silence that dreadful bell, it frights the isle
From her propriety. What is the matter, masters?
Honest Iago, that looks dead with grieving,
Speak: who began this? On thy love, I charge thee!

Iago   I do not know. Friends all, but now, even now;
180 In quarter, and in terms like bride and groom
Devesting them for bed; and then, but now
(As if some planet had unwitted men),
Swords out, and tilting one at other's [breast],
In opposition bloody. I cannot speak
185 Any beginning to this peevish odds;
And would in action glorious I had lost
Those legs that brought me to a part of it.

Othello   How comes it, Michael, you are thus forgot?

Cassio   I pray you pardon me, I cannot speak.

Othello [*even more loudly*] Stop if you wish to live!

Iago [*again tries to separate* **Cassio** *and* **Montano**] Stop!
[*to* **Cassio**] Lieutenant . . . sir . . .
[*to* **Montano**] Montano . . .
[*to all the brawlers*] Gentlemen. . . . Have you forgotten your
rank and your duties? Stop! [**Iago** *tries once again to stop the
fighting.*] The general is speaking to you. Stop fighting. You
should be ashamed. [*Order is gradually restored. Some
combatants look embarrassed; others look sullen.*]

Othello [*sternly*] What is all this? What has caused this
commotion? Have we become Turks ourselves, inflicting the
damage on ourselves that heaven prevented the Ottomites
from doing? Christians should be ashamed to behave this way.
Now stop this barbaric fighting. The next one to indulge his
rage sets little value on his life; he'll die if he makes a move.
[*impatiently, to his* **Attendants**] Tell them to stop ringing that
dreadful alarm bell. The whole island will be in an uproar.
[The **Attendants** *leave to carry out* **Othello**'s *orders.*]
[*to the brawlers*] What is the matter, men? [*They hesitate,
reluctant to answer.*]
[*to* **Iago**] Honest Iago, you look terribly upset. Tell me, who
started this? I order you, in loyalty to me, to speak!

Iago [*hesitating as if reluctant to answer*] I don't know. All these
friends just a short time ago were getting along; they were as
friendly as a bride and groom getting ready to go to bed. Then,
as if some strange influence had taken hold of their minds,
they drew their swords and started fighting violently. I can't
even tell you what started this foolish quarrel, but I would
rather my legs had been lost in battle than that they had
brought me here.

Othello [*to* **Cassio**] How can it be, Michael, that you have
forgotten yourself to this extent?

Cassio I beg you to pardon me. I cannot speak.

Othello   Worthy Montano, you were wont to be civil;
191   The gravity and stillness of your youth
The world hath noted, and your name is great
In mouths of wisest censure. What's the matter
That you unlace your reputation thus,
195   And spend your rich opinion for the name
Of a night-brawler? Give me answer to it.

Montano   Worthy Othello, I am hurt to danger.
Your officer, Iago, can inform you—
While I spare speech, which something now offends me—
200   Of all that I do know, nor know I aught
By me that's said or done amiss this night,
Unless self-charity be sometimes a vice,
And to defend ourselves it be a sin
When violence assails us.

Othello   Now by heaven,
205   My blood begins my safer guides to rule,
And passion, having my best judgment collied,
Assays to lead the way. ['Zounds,] if I stir,
Or do but lift this arm, the best of you
Shall sink in my rebuke. Give me to know
210   How this foul rout began; who set it on;
And he that is approv'd in this offense,
Though he had twinn'd with me, both at a birth,
Shall lose me. What, in a town of war,
Yet wild, the people's hearts brimful of fear,
215   To manage private and domestic quarrel?
In night, and on the court and guard of safety?
'Tis monstrous. Iago, who began't?

Montano   If partially affin'd, or [leagu'd] in office,
Thou dost deliver more or less than truth,
Thou art no soldier.

220 **Iago**   Touch me not so near;
I had rather have this tongue cut from my mouth

Othello [*to* **Montano**] Worthy Montano, you usually are well-mannered; everyone has noticed that you are a serious and calm young man, and you are highly regarded by even the sternest critic. What has caused you to risk your reputation in this way, to squander the high esteem in which you are held and to act like a common night-brawler? What is your defense?

Montano Worthy Othello, I am gravely wounded. Your officer, Iago, can tell you what has happened. . . . [*He pauses, gasping for breath.*] I must limit my speaking because it is causing me pain. . . . This I do know, that I have done nothing wrong tonight, unless watching out for oneself is sometimes wrong and defending oneself from attack is a sin.

Othello [*losing patience*] Now by heaven, my self-control begins to be overcome by my anger, and my best judgment is darkened by my passions. By God, if I so much as move or raise my arm, the bravest men among you shall fall before my rebuke. Tell me how this horrible brawl began and who started it, and whoever is convicted of this offense—even if he were my own brother—shall lose my support. [*As he speaks,* **Othello** *grows more and more enraged.*] What do you think you are doing carrying on a personal and private quarrel in public in a town that is still stirred up from war, the people's hearts still full of fear? It's monstrous.
[*to* **Iago**] Iago, who started this fight?

Montano [*softly, to* **Iago**] If you give a biased account because Cassio is your fellow officer, or if you tell either more or less than the truth, you are no soldier.

Iago [*to* **Othello**] Don't press me for an answer. I would rather have my tongue cut out of my mouth than say anything to harm Michael Cassio.

Than it should do offense to Michael Cassio;
yet I persuade myself, to speak the truth
Shall nothing wrong him. [Thus] it is, general:

225   Montano and myself being in speech,
There comes a fellow crying out for help,
And Cassio following him with determin'd sword
To execute upon him. Sir, this gentleman
Steps in to Cassio and entreats his pause;

230   Myself the crying fellow did pursue,
Lest by his clamor (as it so fell out)
The town might fall in fright. He, swift of foot,
Outran my purpose; and I return'd [the] rather
For that I heard the clink and fall of swords,

235   And Cassio high in oath; which till to-night
I ne'er might say before. When I came back
(For this was brief), I found them close together
At blow and thrust, even as again they were
When you yourself did part them.

240   More of this matter cannot I report.
But men are men; the best sometimes forget.
Though Cassio did some little wrong to him,
As men in rage strike those that wish them best,
Yet surely Cassio, I believe, receiv'd

245   From him that fled some strange indignity
Which patience could not pass.

Othello   I know, Iago,
Thy honesty and love doth mince this matter,
Making it light to Cassio. Cassio, I love thee,
But never more be officer of mine.

Enter **Desdemona** *attended.*

250   Look if my gentle love be not rais'd up!
I'll make thee an example.

[*as if reconsidering*] Yet I'm persuaded that telling the truth will not injure him. Here is what happened, general. Montano and I were talking when a fellow came running, calling for help, with Cassio following him, determined to attack him with his sword. This gentleman [**Iago** *points to* **Montano**.] detained Cassio and begged him to stop; I followed the man who was calling for help to prevent his outcry from alarming the city—which it did. He, a fast runner, got away from me, and I hurried back because I heard the clashing of swords and Cassio cursing loudly, which I've never heard him do before tonight. When I returned I found them all fighting together, just as they were when you separated them. I can't tell you anything more. But men are men; even the best sometimes forget themselves. Although Cassio did slightly injure Montano, angry men are prone to lash out even at those who are their well-wishers, and I'm sure Cassio must have been somehow insulted past endurance by the one who ran off.

Othello   I'm convinced, Iago, that you are trying to make light of this matter because of your decency and your friendship with Cassio.

[*to* **Cassio**] Cassio, I care about you, but you can no longer be an officer of mine.

[**Desdemona** *enters with* **Attendants**.]

[*angrily, to the brawlers*] Look, my sweet love has been awakened!

[*to* **Cassio**] I'll make an example of you.

Desdemona   What is the matter, dear?

Othello   All's well [now], sweeting;
Come away to bed. [*To Montano.*] sir, for your hurts,
Myself will be your surgeon.—Lead him off.

[*Some lead Montano off.*]

255   Iago, look with care about the town,
And silence those whom this vild brawl distracted.
Come, Desdemona, 'tis the soldiers' life
To have their balmy slumbers wak'd with strife.

Exit [*with Desdemona, Gentlemen, and Attendants*].

Iago   What, are you hurt, lieutenant?

260   **Cassio**   Ay, past all surgery.

Iago   Marry, [God] forbid!

Cassio   Reputation, reputation, reputation! O, I have
lost my reputation! I have lost the immortal part of
myself, and what remains is bestial. My reputation,
265   Iago, my reputation!

Iago   As I am an honest man, I had thought you had
receiv'd some bodily wound; there is more sense in that
than in reputation. Reputation is an idle and most false
imposition; oft got without merit, and lost without
270   deserving. You have lost no reputation at all,
unless you repute yourself such a loser. What, man,
there are more ways to recover the general again. You
are but now cast in his mood, a punishment more in
policy than in malice, even so as one would beat his
offenseless dog to affright an imperious lion. Sue to
276   him again, and he's yours.

Cassio   I will rather sue to be despis'd than to deceive
so good a commander with so slight, so drunken, and
so indiscreet an officer. Drunk? and speak parrot? and

Desdemona   [*to* **Othello**] What is the matter, dear?

Othello   [*tenderly*] All is well now, sweetheart. Come back to bed.
[*to* **Montano**] Sir, I will personally bind your wounds.
[*to* **Attendants**] Escort him away. [*Some* **Attendants** *carry*
Montano *offstage.*]
[*to* **Iago**] Iago, look carefully throughout the town and calm
those who have been upset by this miserable brawl.
[*to* **Desdemona**] Come, Desdemona, it's normal for soldiers to
have their pleasant slumbers disturbed by violence.

[**Othello** *leaves with* **Desdemona, Gentlemen,** *and* **Attendants.**]

Iago   [*to* **Cassio,** *who is visibly upset*] What, are you injured,
lieutenant?

Cassio   [*groaning*] Yes, beyond the help of medical aid.

Iago   [*in apparent horror*] God forbid!

Cassio   [*in great distress*] Reputation, reputation, reputation! Oh,
I have lost my reputation! I have lost the immortal part of myself,
and what is left is an animal! My reputation, Iago, my reputation!

Iago   [*feigning relief*] I swear as an honest man, I thought you
had been physically wounded; there is more pain in that than
in losing your reputation. Reputation is only a foolish and false
notion. It's often gotten without earning it and lost
undeservedly. You haven't lost your reputation at all unless
you consider yourself to have lost it. Why, man, there are
many ways to regain the general's good opinion. He has
dismissed you in anger, a punishment inflicted more to satisfy
public policy than from genuine ill will, much as a person
would beat his innocent dog in order to frighten a fierce lion.
Plead with him again, and he'll come around.

Cassio   I would rather beg him to despise me than to disappoint
so worthy a commander as Othello with such a worthless,
drunken, foolish officer as I. Drunk and talking nonsense? And

280   squabble? swagger? swear? and discourse fustian
        with one's own shadow? O thou invisible spirit of
        wine, if thou hast no name to be known by, let us call
        thee devil!

        Iago   What was he that you follow'd with your
285   sword? What had he done to you?

        Cassio   I know not.

        Iago   Is't possible?

        Cassio   I remember a mass of things, but nothing
        distinctly; a quarrel, but nothing wherefore. O [God],
290   that men should put an enemy in their mouths to
        steal away their brains! that we should, with joy,
        pleasance, revel, and applause, transform ourselves
        into beasts!

        Iago   Why, but you are now well enough. How
295   came you thus recover'd?

        Cassio   It hath pleas'd the devil drunkenness to give
        place to the devil wrath: one unperfectness shows me
        another, to make me frankly despise myself.

        Iago   Come, you are too severe a moraler. As the
300   time, the place, and the condition of this country
        stands, I could heartily wish this had not befall'n; but
        since it is as it is, mend it for your own good.

        Cassio   I will ask him for my place again, he shall tell
        me I am a drunkard! Had I as many mouths as Hydra,
305   such an answer would stop them all. To be now a
        sensible man, by and by a fool, and presently a beast!
        O strange! Every inordinate cup is unbless'd, and the
        ingredient is a devil.

        Iago   Come, come; good wine is a good familiar
        creature, if it be well us'd; exclaim no more against it.
311   And, good lieutenant, I think you think I love you.

fighting? Swaggering? Cursing? And babbling at my own shadow? Oh, you invisible spirit of wine, if you are known by no other name we should call you "Devil."

Iago   Who was it that you chased after with your sword? What had he done to you?

Cassio   [*groaning*] I don't know.

Iago   [*appearing shocked*] Is this possible?

Cassio   I remember many things but nothing clearly. A quarrel, but not why it happened. Oh God, that men should swallow a thing that steals their sanity! That we, in joy, merriment, revelry, and celebration, should turn ourselves into beasts!

Iago   Yes, but you are better now. How did you recover?

Cassio   The demon drunkenness has been displaced by the demon anger; one fault in me shows me another and makes me despise myself.

Iago   Come now, you are too hard on yourself. Considering the time, the place, and the current condition of this country, I certainly wish this hadn't happened, but, since it has, turn it to your own advantage.

Cassio   [*despairingly*] If I ask him for my position again, he'll tell me I'm a drunkard! If I had as many mouths as Hydra [*in Greek mythology, a nine-headed serpent that was killed by Hercules*] to plead my cause, such an answer from him would silence them all. To be at one moment a sober man, and the next moment a beast! Unbelievable! Every immoderate drink is cursed, and one of the ingredients in it is the devil.

Iago   Come, come, good wine is a useful thing if it's not abused. Don't continue to find fault with it. Now, good lieutenant, I believe you know I care about you.

Cassio I have well approv'd it, sir. I drunk!

Iago You, or any man living, may be drunk at a
time, man. [I'll] tell you what you shall do. Our
general's wife is now the general—I may say so in this
316 respect, for that he hath devoted and given up
himself to the contemplation, mark, and [denotement]
of her parts and graces. Confess yourself freely to her;
importune her help to put you in your place again. She
is of so free, so kind, so apt, so bless'd a disposition,
321 she holds it a vice in her goodness not to do more
than she is requested. This broken joint between you
and her husband entreat her to splinter; and my fortunes against any lay worth naming, this crack of your
325 love shall grow stronger than it was before.

Cassio You advise me well.

Iago I protest, in the sincerity of love and honest
kindness.

Cassio I think it freely; and betimes in the morning
I will beseech the virtuous Desdemona to undertake
for me. I am desperate of my fortunes if they check
332 me [here].

Iago You are in the right. Good night, lieutenant,
I must to the watch.

Cassio Good night, honest Iago.

Exit Cassio.

336 **Iago** And what's he then that says I play the villain,
When this advice is free I give, and honest,
Probal to thinking, and indeed the course
To win the Moor again? For 'tis most easy
340 Th' inclining Desdemona to subdue
In any honest suit; she's fram'd as fruitful

Cassio   I have learned that is true, sir. I, a drunk!

Iago   You or any other living man may become drunk at some time, man. I'll tell you what you should do. The general's wife is now his "general"—that is, in the sense that he has devoted himself entirely to dwelling on, obsessing about, and noting her merits and virtues. Tell her everything. Ask her to help restore you to your rank. She has such a generous, kind, helpful, and saintly disposition that she considers it a sin not to do even more than she's asked to do. Ask her to heal this rift between you and her husband, and I'd take any bet that your relationship with Othello will be restored to greater strength than it had before.

Cassio   You give me good advice.

Iago   I tell you this in genuine concern and honest kindness.

Cassio   I'm sure of it. And, first thing in the morning, I will beg the good Desdemona to take up my cause. I am worried about my future if I remain stuck where I am.

Iago   You're right. Good night, lieutenant. I must go stand watch.

Cassio   Good night, Iago.

[**Cassio** *leaves.*]

Iago   [*to himself*] And how could anyone say I play the part of a villain when I give this generous, honest, sensible advice, and, indeed, tell him how to regain the Moor's friendship? For it's easy to enlist the kindly Desdemona's help in any good cause; she's as generous as the elements are abundant. And then, his soul is so enslaved by her love that she may do anything or

As the free elements. And then for her
To win the Moor, were['t] to renounce his baptism,
All seals and symbols of redeemed sin,
345   His soul is so enfetter'd to her love,
That she may make, unmake, do what she list,
Even as her appetite shall play the god
With his weak function. How am I then a villain,
To counsel Cassio to this parallel course,
350   Directly to his good? Divinity of hell!
When devils will the blackest sins put on,
They do suggest at first with heavenly shows,
As I do now; for whiles this honest fool
Plies Desdemona to repair his fortune,
355   And she for him pleads strongly to the Moor,
I'll pour this pestilence into his ear—
That she repeals him for her body's lust,
And by how much she strives to do him good,
She shall undo her credit with the Moor.
360   So will I turn her virtue into pitch,
And out of her own goodness make the net
That shall enmesh them all.

Enter **Roderigo**.

How now, Roderigo?

Roderigo   I do follow here in the chase, not like a hound
that hunts, but one that fills up the cry. My money is
almost spent; I have been to-night exceedingly well
366   cudgell'd; and I think the issue will be, I shall have
so much experience for my pains; and so, with no
money at all and a little more wit, return again to
Venice.

Iago   How poor are they that have not patience!
371   What wound did ever heal but by degrees?

undo it—whatever she wants. She could even convince the
Moor to renounce his baptism with all the official marks and
symbols of his redemption. Her desires, whatever they may
be, dictate to his weak will. Then how can I be a villain to
advise Cassio to do this thing which will directly benefit him?
[*He laughs wickedly.*] This is advice from hell itself. When
devils perform the blackest sins, they appear at first to be
from heaven as I do now. For while this honest fool Cassio
begs Desdemona to help repair his situation and she
urgently pleads with the Moor on his behalf, I'll pour an
infection into Othello's ear, telling him that she is trying to
have Cassio reinstated because she lusts after him. And
the more she tries to help him, the more it will destroy the
Moor's trust in her. In this way, I'll turn her virtue into filth
and make a net from Desdemona's goodness that will
ensnare them all.

[**Roderigo** *enters.*] How are you doing, Roderigo?

Roderigo   [*glumly*] I'm like a dog that runs after the pack of
hounds—not like one of the dogs hot on the trail, but only as
one that barks a lot. [*He is describing the futility of his pursuit
of* **Desdemona**.] My money is almost gone, I have been
horribly beaten, and I think that all I will have gained for my
pains is considerable experience. And so, with no money at all
and only a little more sense, I will return to Venice.

Iago   People like you who have no patience are pathetic! What
wound doesn't take time to heal? You know we're working

Thou know'st we work by wit, and not by witchcraft,
And wit depends on dilatory time.
Does't not go well? Cassio hath beaten thee,
And thou by that small hurt [hast] cashier'd Cassio.
376 Though other things grow fair against the sun,
Yet fruits that blossom first will first be ripe.
Content thyself a while. [By the mass], 'tis morning;
Pleasure and action make the hours seem short.
380 Retire thee, go where thou art billeted.
Away, I say, thou shalt know more hereafter.
Nay, get thee gone. (*Exit Roderigo.*) Two things are to be done:
My wife must move for Cassio to her mistress—
I'll set her on—
385 Myself a while to draw the Moor apart,
And bring him jump when he may Cassio find
Soliciting his wife. Ay, that's the way;
Dull not device by coldness and delay.

Exit.

with our wits, not using magic, and schemes such as these take time. Isn't everything progressing well? Cassio has beaten you, and because of that little bit of pain you have gotten Cassio cashiered from the service. [*He recites a proverb.*] "Although other things may grow well in the sunshine, it is the fruit of the plant that blossoms first which will ripen soonest." [**Iago** *looks at the slowly brightening sky.*] By the mass, it's morning. Pleasure and activity make time pass quickly. Go to bed. Go back to your rooms. [**Roderigo** *hesitates so* **Iago** *persists.*] Go on, I say. You'll know more soon. [*As* **Roderigo** *still hesitates,* **Iago** *urges him along.*] No, get going. [**Roderigo** *leaves.*]

[**Iago,** *speaking to himself*] There are two things that must be done. My wife must intercede for Cassio with her mistress, Desdemona—I'll put her up to it. Meanwhile, I'll take the Moor aside and see that he is watching when Cassio asks Desdemona for help. Yes, that's how to do it. I won't give my plots time to cool off.

[*He leaves.*]

Act three

Scene 1

Enter **Cassio** [*with*] **Musicians**.

Cassio   Masters, play here, I will content your pains;
  Something that's brief; and bid "Good morrow, general."

  [*They play, and enter the*] **Clown**.

Clown   Why, masters, have your instruments been in
  Naples, that they speak i' th' nose thus?

5 **1ˢᵗ Musician**   How, sir? how?

Clown   Are these, I pray you, wind instruments?

1ˢᵗ Musician   Ay, marry, are they, sir.

Clown   O, thereby hangs a tail.

9 **1ˢᵗ Musician**   Whereby hangs a tale, sir?

Clown   Marry, sir, by many a wind instrument that I
  know. But, masters, here's money for you; and the
  general so likes your music, that he desires you for
  love's sake to make no more noise with it.

Act three

Scene 1

The following day, outside the castle.

*[**Cassio** enters with **Musicians**.]*

Cassio Men, play your music here, and I will pay you for your efforts. Play something lively; and say, "Good day, general."

*[The **Musicians** play their instruments. The **Clown** enters.]*

Clown *[to the **Musicians**]* Why, men, have your instruments been in Naples that they sound so nasal? *[The **Clown** is referring to the belief that syphilis originated in Naples; syphilis is a venereal disease which, in advanced cases, could at that time result in amputation of the nose.]*

First Musician *[highly insulted]* What, sir? What?

Clown Tell me, are these wind instruments? *[The **Clown**, referring to flatulence, means that he knows many who make wind come out their "tails." The **First Musician** misses the joke and looks puzzled.]*

First Musician Yes, indeed they are, sir.

Clown *[with feigned seriousness]* Oh, there hangs a tail.

First Musician *[The **First Musician** thinks the **Clown** means "tale."]* What story do you mean, sir?

Clown Indeed, sir, by many a wind instrument I know. *[Again referring to the musicians themselves, the **Clown** implies that the **Musicians** are jackasses and therefore have tails.]* But, men, here's money for you, and the general likes your music so well that he asks you to kindly make no more noise with it.

14 **1ˢᵗ Musician**   Well, sir, we will not.

Clown   If you have any music that may not be heard,
to't again; but (as they say) to hear music the general
does not greatly care.

1ˢᵗ Musician   We have none such, sir.

Clown   Then put up your pipes in your bag, for I'll
away. Go, vanish into air, away!

Exeunt Musicians.

21 **Cassio**   Dost thou hear, mine honest friend?

Clown   No, I hear not your honest friend; I hear you.

Cassio   Prithee keep up thy quillets. There's a poor
piece of gold for thee. If the gentlewoman that attends
25   the [general's wife] be stirring, tell her there's one
Cassio entreats her a little favor of speech. Wilt thou
do this?

Clown   She is stirring, sir. If she will stir hither, I
shall seem to notify unto her.

Cassio   [Do, good my friend.]

Exit Clown.

Enter **Iago**.

30   In happy time, Iago.

Iago   You have not been a-bed then?

Cassio   Why, no; the day had broke
Before we parted. I have made bold, Iago,

First Musician   [*deeply offended that the* **Clown** *doesn't want them to play their instruments*] Well, sir, we will not.

Clown   If you have any music that can't be heard, start playing again, since it's said that the general doesn't really like to hear music.

First Musician   [*looking puzzled*] We don't have any like that, sir.

Clown   Then put your horns in your bags [*the* **Clown** *is making another bawdy joke which the* **First Musician** *fails to understand*], for I am leaving. Go, vanish into the air, [*The* **Clown** *makes shooing gestures.*] go on! [*The* **Musicians** *leave in a huff.*]

Cassio   [*to the* **Clown**] Do you hear, my honest friend?

Clown   [*deliberately misunderstanding* **Cassio**] No, I don't hear your honest friend. I hear you.

Cassio   Please stop your puns. Here's a small piece of gold for you. [**Cassio** *gives the* **Clown** *coin.*] If the lady that attends the general's wife is awake, tell her that Cassio asks to speak with her. Will you do this?

Clown   She's awake, sir. If she'll come here, I'll seem to tell her.

Cassio   Do so, my good friend. [*The* **Clown** *leaves.*]

[**Iago** *enters.*]

[*to* **Iago**] It's good that you've arrived, Iago.

Iago   You haven't been to bed then?

Cassio   Why, no. The sun was up before we parted.
I've gone ahead, Iago, and sent for your wife. I'm going

To send in to your wife. My suit to her
35   Is that she will to virtuous Desdemona
Procure me some access.

Iago   I'll send her to you presently;
And I'll devise a mean to draw the Moor
Out of the way, that your converse and business
May be more free.

Cassio   I humbly thank you for't.

Exit [Iago].

40   I never knew a Florentine more kind and honest.

Enter **Emilia.**

Emilia   Good morrow, good lieutenant. I am sorry
For your displeasure; but all will sure be well.
The general and his wife are talking of it,
And she speaks for you stoutly. The Moor replies
45   That he you hurt is of great fame in Cyprus,
And great affinity; and that in wholesome wisdom
He might not but refuse you. But he protests he loves you,
And needs no other suitor but his likings
[To take the safest occasion by the front]
To bring you in again.

50 **Cassio**   Yet I beseech you,
If you think fit, or that it may be done,
Give me advantage of some brief discourse
With Desdemon alone.

Emilia   Pray you come in.
54   I will bestow you where you shall have time
To speak your bosom freely.

Cassio   I am much bound to you.

[Exeunt.]

to ask her to help me gain access to the virtuous
Desdemona.

Iago   I'll send her to you soon, and I'll think of an excuse to draw
the Moor aside so that your conversation and dealings with
her may be more free.

Cassio   I humbly thank you for it. [**Iago** *exits.*]
[*to himself*] I never have known a more kind and honest
Florentine than Iago.

[**Emilia** *enters.*]

Emilia   Good day, good lieutenant. I am sorry about your loss of
favor with Othello, but all will surely be well. The general and
his wife are discussing it, and she speaks strongly on your
behalf. The Moor replies that the man you wounded is well
known in Cyprus and is from a powerful family, and therefore
it's only wise to refuse to reinstate you. But he protests that he
cares about you and needs no other plea than his regard for
you—and only the smallest excuse—to reinstate you.

Cassio   Yet I beg of you, if you don't mind and you think it can
be done, allow me to have a brief conversation with
Desdemona alone.

Emilia   Please come in. I'll leave you where you'll have time to
confide your private concerns to Desdemona.

Cassio   I am deeply indebted to you.

[**Cassio** *and* **Emilia** *exit.*]

Scene 2

Enter **Othello**, **Iago**, *and* **Gentlemen**.

Othello   These letters give, Iago, to the pilot,
And by him do my duties to the Senate.
That done, I will be walking on the works;
Repair there to me.

4 **Iago**   Well, my good lord, I'll do't.

Othello   This fortification, gentlemen, shall we see't?

Gentlemen   We'll wait upon your lordship.

Exeunt.

Scene 3

Enter **Desdemona**, **Cassio**, *and* **Emilia**.

Desdemona   Be thou assur'd, good Cassio, I will do
All my abilities in thy behalf.

Emilia   Good madam, do. I warrant it grieves my husband
As if the cause were his.

Desdemona   O, that's an honest fellow. Do not doubt,
5   Cassio,
But I will have my lord and you again
As friendly as you were.

Cassio   Bounteous madam,
What ever shall become of Michael Cassio,
He's never any thing but your true servant.

Scene 2

A room in the castle.

[Othello, Iago, *and* **Gentlemen** *enter.*]

Othello [*to* **Iago**] Give these letters to the pilot, Iago, and bring my greetings to the senate. When you're finished, I'll be walking on the fortifications. Come to me there.

Iago [**Iago** *salutes.*] Of course, my lord. I'll do it.

Othello [*to* **Gentlemen**] This fortification, gentlemen—shall we see it?

Gentlemen We're at your lordship's disposal.

[*They all exit.*]

Scene 3

The garden of the castle, a short time later.

[Desdemona, Cassio, *and* **Emilia** *enter.*]

Desdemona I promise you, good Cassio, I'll do all I can for you.

Emilia Good madam, do. I'm sure it upsets my husband as if the problem were his.

Desdemona Oh, Iago is an honest fellow. Don't doubt, Cassio, that I'll see to it that you and my husband are once again as friendly as you were.

Cassio [*fervently*] Generous madam, whatever happens to me, I will never be anything but your devoted servant.

Desdemona   I know't; I thank you. You do love my lord;
  You have known him long, and be you well assur'd
12   He shall in strangeness stand no farther off
  Than in a politic distance.

Cassio   Ay, but, lady,
  That policy may either last so long,
15   Or feed upon such nice and waterish diet,
  Or breed itself so out of circumstances,
  That I being absent and my place supplied,
  My general will forget my love and service.

Desdemona   Do not doubt that; before Emilia here,
20   I give thee warrant of thy place. Assure thee,
  If I do vow a friendship, I'll perform it
  To the last article. My lord shall never rest,
  I'll watch him tame, and talk him out of patience;
  His bed shall seem a school, his board a shrift,
25   I'll intermingle every thing he does
  With Cassio's suit. Therefore be merry, Cassio,
  For thy solicitor shall rather die
  Than give thy cause away.

  Enter **Othello** *and* **Iago**.

Emilia   Madam, here comes my lord.

30 **Cassio**   Madam, I'll take my leave.

Desdemona   Why, stay, and hear me speak.

Cassio   Madam, not now; I am very ill at ease,
  Unfit for mine own purposes.

Desdemona   Well, do your discretion.

                                        Exit Cassio.

Desdemona I know it, thank you. You care about my husband, you have known him a long time, and you may be very sure he shall maintain no greater distance than policy requires.

Cassio Yes, but, lady, that policy may either last so long, or it may require such scant "food" to survive, or it may increase because of some unexpected event, that, because I am absent and my post taken by another, my general may forget my devotion and service.

Desdemona Don't be afraid of that. With Emilia as my witness, I guarantee your reinstatement. Be assured that if I promise this as your friend, I will carry it out in full. [*jokingly*] My husband shall have no rest from the subject. I'll pester him and talk about it until he loses patience. When he's in bed, he'll be lectured. When he's eating, he'll feel like a priest hearing a long confession. I'll interrupt everything he does with your problem. Therefore, be cheerful, Cassio, for as your advocate I would rather die than give up on your cause.

[**Othello** and **Iago** *enter a little way off.*]

Emilia Madam, here comes your husband.

Cassio I'll leave you now, madam.

Desdemona Why, stay and hear what I say.

Cassio Madam, not now. I am very uncomfortable and in no state to further my cause.

[**Cassio** *leaves. From a short distance,* **Othello** *and* **Iago** *have been observing the conversation between* **Cassio** *and* **Desdemona**.]

Iago Hah? I like not that.

Othello   What dost thou say?

36 **Iago** Nothing, my lord; or if—I know not what.

Othello Was not that Cassio parted from my wife?

Iago Cassio, my lord? No, sure, I cannot think it,
That he would steal away so guilty-like,
Seeing your coming.

40 **Othello**   I do believe 'twas he.

Desdemona How now, my lord?
I have been talking with a suitor here,
A man that languishes in your displeasure.

44 **Othello** Who is't you mean?

Desdemona Why, your lieutenant, Cassio. Good my lord,
If I have any grace or power to move you,
His present reconciliation take;
For if he be not one that truly loves you,
That errs in ignorance and not in cunning,
50 I have no judgment in an honest face.
I prithee call him back.

Othello   Went he hence now?

Desdemona [Yes, faith]; so humbled
That he hath left part of his grief with me
54 To suffer with him. Good love, call him back.

Othello Not now, sweet Desdemon, some other time.

Desdemona But shall't be shortly?

Othello   The sooner, sweet, for you.

Iago [*as if unaware that he is speaking out loud*] Humph? I don't like the looks of that.

Othello What did you say?

Iago [*appearing startled and guilty, as if uncomfortable about having been overheard*] Nothing, my lord. Or if . . . [*He hesitates.*] I don't know.

Othello Wasn't that Cassio who just left my wife?

Iago [*acting as if he's trying to hide something*] Cassio, my lord? No, surely . . . [*He hesitates again.*] I can't believe that he would steal away so guiltily at seeing your approach.

Othello I do believe it was he.

Desdemona [*approaching, addresses* **Othello**] How are you, my lord? I have been talking to a man who is very upset by your displeasure with him.

Othello Whom do you mean?

Desdemona Why, your lieutenant, Cassio. My kind husband, if I have any favor with you or influence over you, accept his apologies, for, if he is not one who is truly devoted to you, whose error arose from poor judgment and not from an intention to do wrong, I am unable to judge an honest face. I beg you to call him back.

Othello Did he just leave?

Desdemona Yes, indeed. He is so humbled that he left me feeling very upset on his behalf. My love, call him back.

Othello Not now, sweet Desdemona. Some other time.

Desdemona But will it be soon?

Othello [*indulgently*] The sooner, sweetheart, for you.

Desdemona   Shall't be to-night at supper?

Othello   No, not to-night.

Desdemona   To-morrow dinner then?

Othello   I shall not dine at home;
I meet the captains at the citadel.

60 **Desdemona**   Why then to-morrow night, [or] Tuesday morn;
On Tuesday noon, or night; on We'n'sday morn.
I prithee name the time, but let it not
Exceed three days. In faith, he's penitent;
And yet his trespass, in our common reason
65 (Save that they say the wars must make example
Out of her best), is not almost a fault
T' incur a private check. When shall he come?
Tell me, Othello. I wonder in my soul
What you would ask me that I should deny,
70 Or stand so mamm'ring on. What? Michael Cassio,
That came a-wooing with you, and so many a time,
When I have spoke of you dispraisingly,
Hath ta'en your part—to have so much to do
74 To bring him in! [By'r lady], I could do much—

Othello   Prithee no more; let him come when he will;
I will deny thee nothing.

Desdemona   Why, this is not a boon;
'Tis as I should entreat you wear your gloves,
Or feed on nourishing dishes, or keep you warm,
Or sue to you to do a peculiar profit
80 To your own person. Nay, when I have a suit
Wherein I mean to touch your love indeed,
It shall be full of poise and difficult weight,
And fearful to be granted.

Othello   I will deny thee nothing;
Whereon, I do beseech thee, grant me this,
85 To leave me but a little to myself.

Desdemona   Shall it be tonight at supper?

Othello   No, not tonight.

Desdemona   At dinner tomorrow, then?

Othello   I shall not dine at home. I am meeting the captains at the citadel.

Desdemona   Why then, tomorrow night, or Tuesday morning, or Tuesday noon or night, [**Othello** *shakes his head in the negative after each suggested time.*] or on Wednesday morning. I beg you to tell me when, but don't let it be more than three days. Truly, he's very sorry. And yet—except for the fact that in wartimes, the best must serve as examples— according to our customs what Cassio did is hardly enough to incur even a private rebuke. [*As* **Desdemona** *speaks,* **Othello** *shows signs of increasing irritation.*] When shall he come to you? Tell me, Othello. [*gently chiding*] I wonder what you could ask of me that I would refuse or even be so hesitant about. What? Michael Cassio, who came with you when you were wooing me, and many times, if I said something negative about you, he spoke up for you. How can it be such a great problem to restore him to your good graces? My goodness, I could do much—

Othello   [*clearly annoyed*] Please say no more. Let him come when he chooses. I can refuse nothing you ask.

Desdemona   Why, this isn't even a favor! It's as if I should urge you to wear your gloves, or eat nourishing food, or keep you warm, or ask you to do something to benefit yourself. No, when I have a request which shall depend upon your love for me to see that it's granted, I shall ask carefully and weigh my words and be fearful about its being granted.

Othello   [*resignedly*] I'll refuse nothing you request. Therefore, I beg you to grant me this, that you leave me alone for a while.

143

Desdemona Shall I deny you? No. Farewell, my lord.

Othello Farewell, my Desdemona, I'll come to thee straight.

Desdemona Emilia, come.—Be as your fancies teach you;
What e'er you be, I am obedient.

Exit [with Emilia].

90 **Othello** Excellent wretch! Perdition catch my soul
But I do love thee! and when I love thee not,
Chaos is come again.

Iago My noble lord—

Othello   What dost thou say, Iago?

Iago Did Michael Cassio, when [you] woo'd my lady,
95 Know of your love?

Othello He did, from first to last. Why dost thou ask?

Iago But for a satisfaction of my thought,
No further harm.

Othello   Why of thy thought, Iago?

Iago I did not think he had been acquainted with her.

100 **Othello** O yes, and went between us very oft.

Iago Indeed!

Othello Indeed? ay, indeed. Discern'st thou aught in that?
Is he not honest?

Iago   Honest, my lord?

Othello Honest? ay, honest.

Iago   My lord, for aught I know.

Desdemona   [*playfully*] Shall I refuse you anything? No.
Farewell, my lord.

Othello   Farewell, my Desdemona. I'll come to you soon.

Desdemona   Come, Emilia.
[*to* **Othello**] You may be as you wish [*that is, either alone or with
her*]. Whatever you are, I will obey you.

[**Desdemona** *and* **Emilia** *leave.*]

Othello   [*unheard by the departing* **Desdemona**] Excellent
wretch! Hell may take my soul, but I do love you. And when I do
not love you, Chaos has come again. [*According to ancient
Greek mythology, Chaos was the dark and silent abyss which
gave birth to Night and to Erebus, the fathomless dwelling place
of death. The ordered universe was later created out of Chaos.*]

Iago   My noble lord . . .

Othello   What did you say, Iago?

Iago   [*hesitantly*] Did Michael Cassio, when you wooed my lady
Desdemona, know about your love?

Othello   He did, from beginning to end. Why do you ask?

Iago   [*shrugging and appearing reluctant to say more*] Merely to
satisfy my curiosity, nothing else.

Othello   What makes you curious about it?

Iago   I didn't think he was acquainted with her.

Othello   Oh yes, and he very often carried messages between us.

Iago   [*appearing startled and concerned*] Indeed!

Othello   [*becoming slightly annoyed*] Indeed? Yes, indeed. Do
you see something suspicious in that? Isn't Cassio trustworthy?

Iago   Trustworthy?

Othello   Trustworthy? Yes, trustworthy.

Iago   [*with a slight hesitation, as if unsure*] For all I know, my lord.

Othello   What dost thou think?

105 **Iago**   Think, my lord?

Othello   Think, my lord? [By heaven], thou echo'st me,
As if there were some monster in thy thought
Too hideous to be shown. Thou dost mean something.
I heard thee say even now, thou lik'st not that,
110 When Cassio left my wife. What didst not like?
And when I told thee he was of my counsel
[In] my whole course of wooing, thou criedst, "Indeed!"
And didst contract and purse thy brow together,
As if thou then hadst shut up in thy brain
115 Some horrible conceit. If thou dost love me,
Show me thy thought.

Iago   My lord, you know I love you.

Othello   I think thou dost;
And for I know thou'rt full of love and honesty,
And weigh'st thy words before thou giv'st them breath,
Therefore these stops of thine fright me the more;
121 For such things in a false disloyal knave
Are tricks of custom; but in a man that's just
They're close dilations, working from the heart,
That passion cannot rule.

Iago   For Michael Cassio,
125 I dare be sworn I think that he is honest.

Othello   I think so too.

Iago   Men should be what they seem,
Or those that be not, would they might seem none!

Othello   Certain, men should be what they seem.

Iago   Why then I think Cassio's an honest man.

Othello   What do you think?

Iago   Think, my lord?

Othello   [*repeating for Iago as before and becoming exasperated*] Think, my lord? By heaven, you repeat me as if there were some monster in your mind too hideous to be revealed. You must mean something. I heard you say just now that you didn't like it when Cassio left my wife. What did you not like? And when I told you he was in my confidence during the entire course of my wooing, you exclaimed, "Indeed!" and you wrinkled your brow as if you had locked away some horrible notion in your brain. If you are my friend, reveal your thoughts to me.

Iago   [*appearing very uncomfortable and reluctant to speak*] My lord, you know I am your friend.

Othello   I believe you are. And because I know you are care about me and are very trustworthy, and you weigh your words before saying them, therefore, these hesitations of yours frighten me all the more, for in a dishonest and disloyal rogue such things are tricks of the trade, but in a man who is upright, they indicate hidden thoughts coming from the heart which are so strong that they can't be suppressed.

Iago   Concerning Michael Cassio, I would swear he is trustworthy.

Othello   I think so, too.

Iago   Men should be what they appear to be, or, if they aren't, I wish they would cease to exist!

Othello   Of course, men should be what they appear to be.

Iago   Why, then I think Cassio is a trustworthy man.

130 **Othello**   Nay, yet there's more in this.
         I prithee speak to me as to thy thinkings,
         As thou dost ruminate, and give thy worst of thoughts
         The worst of words.

    Iago   Good my lord, pardon me:
         Though I am bound to every act of duty,
135   I am not bound to that all slaves are free [to].
         Utter my thoughts? Why, say they are vild and false,
         As where's that palace whereinto foul things
         Sometimes intrude not? Who has that breast so pure
         [But some] uncleanly apprehensions
140   Keep leets and law-days and in sessions sit
         With meditations lawful?

    Othello   Thou dost conspire against thy friend, Iago,
         If thou but think'st him wrong'd, and mak'st his ear
         A stranger to thy thoughts.

    Iago   I do beseech you,
145   Though I perchance am vicious in my guess
         (As I confess it is my nature's plague
         To spy into abuses, and [oft] my jealousy
         Shapes faults that are not), that your wisdom [then],
         From one that so imperfectly [conjects],
150   Would take no notice, nor build yourself a trouble
         Out of his scattering and unsure observance.
         It were not for your quiet nor your good,
         Nor for my manhood, honesty, and wisdom,
         To let you know my thoughts.

    Othello   ['Zounds,] what dost thou mean?

    Iago   Good name in man and woman, dear my lord,
156   Is the immediate jewel of their souls.
         Who steals my purse steals trash; 'tis something, nothing;
         'Twas mine, 'tis his, and has been slave to thousands;

Othello   No, there's still more to this. I ask you to tell me what you are thinking, what you are dwelling on, and to tell me the very worst of your thoughts.

Iago   [*appearing reluctant and very uncomfortable*] Good my lord, excuse me from answering you. Although I am required to fulfill all my duties, I am not required to do what even a slave is free from. Speak my thoughts? Why, suppose they are low and false. For what palace exists into which disgusting things do not, now and then, creep? Who has a heart so pure that, in addition to innocent thoughts, no unclean thoughts ever hold court or convene meetings.

Othello   [*sternly*] You conspire against me, Iago, if you suspect I've been wronged and refuse to tell me your thoughts.

Iago   I beg you to use wisdom. Ignore what I've said and don't create a problem for yourself based on my sketchy and uncertain observations, since I am merely guessing. Perhaps my suppositions are wrong—I admit that I have a weakness for investigating corruption, and often my suspicions create problems that don't exist. It will neither help your peace of mind nor benefit you, nor will it enhance my manhood, honesty, and wisdom to tell you my thoughts.

Othello   [*now seriously alarmed*] My God, what do you mean?

Iago   A man's or woman's reputation, my lord, is the true jewel of their soul. He who steals my money steals only trash; it's something, it's nothing. It was mine; now it's his, and has

But he that filches from me my good name
160   Robs me of that which not enriches him,
And makes me poor indeed.

Othello   [By heaven,] I'll know thy thoughts.

Iago   You cannot, if my heart were in your hand,
Nor shall not, whilst 'tis in my custody.

Othello   Ha?

165 **Iago**   O, beware, my lord, of jealousy!
It is the green-ey'd monster which doth mock
The meat it feeds on. That cuckold lives in bliss
Who, certain of his fate, loves not his wronger;
But O, what damned minutes tells he o'er
Who dotes, yet doubts; suspects, yet [strongly] loves!

171 **Othello**   O misery!

Iago   Poor and content is rich, and rich enough,
But riches fineless is as poor as winter
To him that ever fears he shall be poor.
175   Good [God], the souls of all my tribe defend
From jealousy!

Othello   Why? why is this?
Think'st thou I'ld make a life of jealousy?
To follow still the changes of the moon
With fresh suspicions? No! to be once in doubt
180   Is [once] to be resolv'd. Exchange me for a goat,
When I shall turn the business of my soul
To such [exsufflicate] and [blown] surmises,
Matching thy inference. 'Tis not to make me jealious
To say my wife is fair, feeds well, loves company,
185   Is free of speech, sings, plays, and dances [well];
Where virtue is, these are more virtuous.
Nor from mine own weak merits will I draw

formerly been the servant to thousands of others. But he who
steals my reputation robs me of something which doesn't
make him richer, yet makes me poor indeed.

Othello   [*becoming increasingly angry*] By heaven, I demand to
know your thoughts.

Iago   You cannot nor shall you know them, even if my life were
in your hands, as long as I live.

Othello   [*threateningly*] Indeed?

Iago   Oh beware, my lord, of jealousy! It's a green-eyed monster
that laughs at the person who is devoured by it. The one who
is betrayed is perfectly happy, certain that he knows what lies
ahead, as long as he doesn't know his beloved has wronged
him. But, oh, what tortuous moments are spent by the one
who loves, yet doubts; who suspects, yet loves deeply!

Othello   [*He groans, recognizing the truth of what Iago says.*]
Oh, misery!

Iago   He who is poor and content to be so is rich, quite rich
enough, but he who has unlimited wealth is as barren as a
winter field if he lives always fearing poverty. Good God, may
all my ancestors' souls protect me from jealousy!

Othello   [*anguished and fearful*] Why? Why do you say this? Do
you think I want to live a life of jealousy? That I want to have
new suspicions with every new phase of the moon? No! To
doubt once is to doubt always. You may turn me into a goat on
the day I allow myself to worry about such contemptible and
inflated suspicions like those you suggest. The fact that my
wife is beautiful, well mannered, loves company, converses
well, sings, plays musical instruments, and dances well is not
enough to make me jealous; when a person has virtue, these
abilities only increase her virtue. Nor shall my own lack of
accomplishments cause me to feel the smallest fear or doubt

The smallest fear or doubt of her revolt,
For she had eyes, and chose me. No, Iago,
190 I'll see before I doubt; when I doubt, prove;
And on the proof, there is no more but this—
Away at once with love or jealousy!

    Iago   I am glad of this, for now I shall have reason
To show the love and duty that I bear you
195 With franker spirit; therefore (as I am bound)
Receive it from me. I speak not yet of proof.
Look to your wife, observe her well with Cassio,
Wear your eyes thus, not jealous nor secure.
I would not have your free and noble nature,
200 Out of self-bounty, be abus'd; look to't.
I know our country disposition well:
In Venice they do let [God] see the pranks
They dare not show their husbands; their best conscience
Is not to leave't undone, but keep't unknown.

205 **Othello**   Dost thou say so?

    Iago   She did deceive her father, marrying you,
And when she seem'd to shake and fear your looks,
She lov'd them most.

    Othello   And so she did.

    Iago   Why, go to then.
She that so young could give out such a seeming
210 To seel her father's eyes up, close as oak,
He thought 'twas witchcraft—but I am much to blame;
I humbly do beseech you of your pardon
For too much loving you.

    Othello   I am bound to thee for ever.

    Iago   I see this hath a little dash'd your spirits.

about her fidelity, for she had the ability to see, and still she chose me. No, Iago, I'll have to see something suspicious before I suspect, and when I do suspect I'll require proof, and if there is proof, there's nothing to be done but this—I'll immediately eliminate either love or jealousy!

Iago   I'm glad of this, for I now shall be able to demonstrate my friendship and my loyalty to you more fully. Therefore, since you insist, hear what I think. I don't yet speak of something which can be proven. [**Iago** *lowers his voice conspiratorially.*] Watch your wife. Closely observe her with Cassio, and see things this way: neither jealously nor securely. I wouldn't want your free and noble nature, because of your innate goodness, to be taken advantage of. [**Othello** *looks doubtful, so* **Iago** *urges him.*] Do it. I know the customs of Venice well. There women let God see the tricks they don't dare show their husbands. Their highest morals don't say that they shouldn't do it [*that is, commit adultery*] but only to make sure it isn't discovered.

Othello   [*horrified*] Are you serious?

Iago   She deceived her father when she married you, and when she seemed to be trembling and afraid of your looks, she loved them most.

Othello   [*thoughtfully*] So she did.

Iago   Why, there you have it. Although she is so young, yet she could so convincingly give a false appearance that her father was so deceived that he thought you had bewitched her. [**Iago** *pauses, appearing to regret having spoken.*] But this is wrong of me. I beg you to pardon me for being so concerned for you.

Othello   I am in your debt forever.

Iago   I see that hearing this has depressed you a little.

Othello   Not a jot, not a jot.

Iago   [I' faith], I fear it has.
216   I hope you will consider what is spoke
Comes from [my] love. But I do see y' are mov'd.
I am to pray you not to strain my speech
To grosser issues nor to larger reach
220   Than to suspicion.

Othello   I will not.

Iago   Should you do so, my lord,
My speech should fall into such vild success
Which my thoughts aim'd not. Cassio's my worthy friend—
My lord, I see y' are mov'd.

Othello   No, not much mov'd:
225   I do not think but Desdemona's honest.

Iago   Long live she so! and long live you to think so!

Othello   And yet how nature erring from itself—

Iago   Ay, there's the point; as (to be bold with you)
Not to affect many proposed matches
230   Of her own clime, complexion, and degree,
Whereto we see in all things nature tends—
Foh, one may smell in such, a will most rank,
Foul disproportions, thoughts unnatural.
But (pardon me) I do not in position
235   Distinctly speak of her, though I may fear
Her will, recoiling to her better judgment,
May fall to match you with her country forms,
And happily repent.

Othello   Farewell, farewell!
If more thou dost perceive, let me know more;
240   Set on thy wife to observe. Leave me, Iago.

Iago   [*Going.*] My lord, I take my leave.

Othello   [*with false heartiness*] Not a bit, not a bit.

Iago   Truly, I'm afraid it has. I hope you'll realize that what I've just said springs from my concern for you. Please don't let what I've said make you jump to conclusions or go beyond being suspicious.

Othello   I won't.

Iago   If you should, my lord, my speech would have a terrible effect, which I hadn't intended. Cassio is my good friend . . . [**Iago** *pauses and looks intently at* **Othello** *who is deeply troubled.*] My lord, I see that you're upset.

Othello   [*Although* **Othello** *clearly is perturbed, he denies it.*] No, not very upset. I can't believe that Desdemona isn't faithful.

Iago   Long may she be so! And long may you live to think so. [**Iago** *is well aware of the ambiguity of his second statement and aware that* **Othello** *has noted it.*]

Othello   And yet, that someone should act so contrary to nature [*as Desdemona had in falling in love with Othello*] . . .

Iago   Yes, that's the point! That she did not—if I may speak openly with you—desire any of the proposed suitors she could have had of her own country, race, and social rank, as we see all creatures in nature tend to do. . . . Phew! It reeks of an uncontrolled lust, a corrupt deviation, unnatural ideas. But, pardon me, I'm not referring specifically to Desdemona, although I worry that she, having second thoughts, may begin to compare you to those of her own country and perhaps regret her choice.

Othello   [*to himself*] Farewell, farewell!
[*to* **Iago**] If you observe anything else, let me know. Have your wife observe Desdemona. Leave me, Iago.

Iago   [*with veiled self-satisfaction*] My lord, I take my leave. [*He starts to walk away.*]

Othello   Why did I marry? This honest creature, doubtless,
Sees and knows more, much more, than he unfolds.

Iago   [*Returning.*] My lord, I would I might entreat your honor
245   To scan this thing no farther; leave it to time.
Although 'tis fit that Cassio have his place—
For sure he fills it up with great ability—
Yet if you please to [hold] him off awhile,
You shall by that perceive him and his means.
250   Note if your lady strain his entertainment
With any strong or vehement importunity;
Much will be seen in that. In the mean time,
Let me be thought too busy in my fears
(As worthy cause I have to fear I am)
255   And hold her free, I do beseech your honor.

Othello   Fear not my government.

Iago   I once more take my leave.

Exit.

Othello   This fellow's of exceeding honesty,
And knows all [qualities], with a learned spirit,
260   Of human dealings. If I do prove her haggard,
Though that her jesses were my dear heart-strings,
I'ld whistle her off, and let her down the wind
To prey at fortune. Haply, for I am black,
And have not those soft parts of conversation
265   That chamberers have, or for I am declin'd
Into the vale of years (yet that's not much),
She's gone. I am abus'd, and my relief
Must be to loathe her. O curse of marriage!
That we can call these delicate creatures ours,
270   And not their appetites! I had rather be a toad
And live upon the vapor of a dungeon
Than keep a corner in the thing I love
For others' uses. Yet 'tis the plague [of] great ones,

Othello   [*despairingly, to himself*] Why did I marry? This honest
creature, Iago, sees and knows more, much more, than he is
revealing.

Iago   [*He returns.*] My lord, I'd like to beg you to think no more
about this. Wait and see. Although it's appropriate that Cassio
be reinstated—for he certainly performs his duties very ably—
yet if you would put him off for a while, you will be able to
observe him and his intentions. See if your wife pressures
you to reinstate him with any particular or extreme urgency;
that will reveal much. In the meantime, assume that I'm
unnecessarily worried (although I fear I have reason to be),
and, I do beg of you, honored sir, to believe her to be
innocent.

Othello   Don't worry about my ability to control myself.

Iago   Once again I'll leave you. [**Iago** *exits.*]

Othello   [*to himself*] This fellow, Iago, is extremely honest, and
he's very wise about the various ways people behave. If I
discover that Desdemona is like a wild, untamed hawk, even
though the binding straps [*that metaphorically force her to
stay with him*] were my very heart-strings, I'll whistle her off
and release her to her own fortunes. Perhaps because I am
black and don't have the refined manners that courtiers have,
or because I am somewhat older—although I'm not yet so very
old!—she has betrayed me. I've been wronged, and it will
make me feel better if I hate her. Oh, the curse of marriage!
That we can call these lovely women ours, yet not be able to
control their lusts! I would rather be a toad and live in the
sewage of a dungeon than set aside even a portion of the thing
I love for others to use. Yet this is the curse of honorable

157

Prerogativ'd are they less than the base;
275 'Tis destiny unshunnable, like death.
Even then this forked plague is fated to us
When we do quicken. Look where she comes:

Enter **Desdemona** *and* **Emilia**.

If she be false, [O then] heaven [mocks] itself!
I'll not believe't.

Desdemona   How now, my dear Othello?
280 Your dinner, and the generous islanders
By you invited, do attend your presence.

Othello   I am to blame.

Desdemona   Why do you speak so faintly?
Are you not well?

Othello   I have a pain upon my forehead, here.

285 **Desdemona**   [Faith], that's with watching, 'twill away again.
Let me but bind it hard, within this hour
It will be well.

Othello   Your napkin is too little;

[*He puts the handkerchief from him, and it drops.*]

Let it alone. Come, I'll go in with you.

Desdemona   I am very sorry that you are not well.

Exit [*with Othello*].

290 **Emilia**   I am glad I have found this napkin;
This was her first remembrance from the Moor.
My wayward husband hath a hundred times
Woo'd me to steal it; but she so loves the token
(For he conjur'd her she should ever keep it)
295 That she reserves it evermore about her

people; they are worse off than those who are dishonorable. It is their inescapable destiny, just as death is. We're fated to be betrayed from the day we're born.

[*He sees* **Desdemona** *and* **Emilia** *approaching.*] Look, here she comes.

[**Desdemona** *and* **Emilia** *enter.*]

[*The sight of* **Desdemona** *causes* **Othello**'s *love and trust to reassert itself.* **Othello** *continues speaking to himself.*] If she's unfaithful, then heaven is faithless to itself! I won't believe it.

Desdemona   How are you, my dear Othello? Your dinner, as well as the noble people of this island whom you invited to the celebration, await you.

Othello   [*to himself*] I am wrong.

Desdemona   [*concernedly*] Why are you speaking so faintly? Are you ill?

Othello   I have a pain here in my forehead.

Desdemona   Truly, that's from lack of sleep. It will leave soon. Let me just bandage it securely and it will be well in no time. [*She tries to tie her handkerchief around his forehead.*]

Othello   [*harshly*] Your handkerchief is too small. [*He thrusts the handkerchief away, and it falls to the ground.*] Never mind. Come, I'll go in with you.

Desdemona   [*She looks wounded by his sharpness. She replies in a subdued voice.*] I'm very sorry that you aren't well.

[**Desdemona** *and* **Othello** *leave.* **Emilia** *remains behind. She quickly picks up the handkerchief after they leave.*]

Emilia   I'm glad I've found this handkerchief; it was her first keepsake from the Moor. That stubborn husband of mine has asked me a hundred times to steal it, but she loves the memento so—for Othello made her solemnly promise to

To kiss and talk to. I'll have the work ta'en out,
And give't Iago. What he will do with it
Heaven knows, not I;
I nothing but to please his fantasy.

Enter **Iago**.

300 **Iago**   How now? what do you here alone?

Emilia   Do not you chide; I have a thing for you.

Iago   You have a thing for me? It is a common thing—

Emilia   Hah?

Iago   To have a foolish wife.

Emilia   O, is that all? What will you give me now
For that same handkerchief?

306 **Iago**   What handkerchief?

Emilia   What handkerchief?
Why, that the Moor first gave to Desdemona,
That which so often you did bid me steal.

310 **Iago**   Hast stol'n it from her?

Emilia   No, [faith]; she let it drop by negligence,
And to th' advantage, I, being here, took't up.
Look, here 'tis.

Iago   A good wench, give it me.

Emilia   What will you do with't, that you have been
so earnest
To have me filch it?

Iago   [*Snatching it*].   Why, what is that to you?

316 **Emilia**   If it be not for some purpose of import,
Give't me again. Poor lady, she'll run mad
When she shall lack it.

always keep it—that she always carries it with her, kissing it and talking to it. I'll have it copied and give it to Iago. Heaven knows what he'll do with it; I certainly don't. I only want to keep him happy by gratifying his whim.

[**Iago** *enters.*]

Iago   What? Are you alone here?

Emilia   [*She swiftly hides the handkerchief.*] Don't scold me. I have something for you.

Iago   You have something for me? [*mockingly*] It's a common thing . . .

Emilia   What?

Iago   To have a foolish wife.

Emilia   [*disappointed and annoyed*] Oh, is that all? What will you give me now for that handkerchief?

Iago   [*suddenly on the alert*] What handkerchief?

Emilia   [*She repeats his question, mockingly.*] What handkerchief? Why, the one the Moor gave to Desdemona, which you have so often told me to steal.

Iago   Have you stolen it from her?

Emilia   No, indeed. She dropped it carelessly and, taking advantage of the opportunity, I picked it up. Look, here it is. [*She shows the handkerchief to* **Iago**.]

Iago   You're a good woman. Give it to me.

Emilia   [*She withholds it teasingly.*] What do you plan to do with it, that you've been so urgent to have me steal it?

Iago   [*He snatches it from her.*] Why? What do you care?

Emilia   If you don't have some particular plan for it, give it back to me. The poor lady, she'll be frantic when she discovers it's gone.

Iago   Be not acknown on't; I have use for it.
320   Go, leave me.

Exit Emilia.

I will in Cassio's lodging lose this napkin,
And let him find it. Trifles light as air
Are to the jealous confirmations strong
As proofs of holy writ; this may do something.
325   The Moor already changes with my poison:
Dangerous conceits are in their natures poisons,
Which at the first are scarce found to distaste,
But with a little act upon the blood
Burn like the mines of sulphur.

Enter **Othello**.

I did say so.
Look where he comes! Not poppy, nor mandragora,
331   Nor all the drowsy syrups of the world
Shall ever medicine thee to that sweet sleep
Which thou ow'dst yesterday.

Othello   Ha, ha, false to me?

Iago   Why, how now, general? No more of that.

Othello   Avaunt, be gone! thou hast set me on the rack.
336   I swear 'tis better to be much abus'd
Than but to know't a little.

Iago   How now, my lord?

Othello   What sense had I in her stol'n hours of lust?
I saw't not, thought it not; it harm'd not me.
340   I slept the next night well, fed well, was free and merry;
I found not Cassio's kisses on her lips.

Iago   Act as if you know nothing about it. I need it. Go. Leave me. [*As* **Emilia** *hesitates, hoping for some sign of gratitude or affection,* **Iago** *pushes her, sending her on her way. She departs huffily.*]

[*to himself*] I will lose this handkerchief in Cassio's lodging and let him find it. Little things as light as air, to the jealous, are proofs as strong as words of scripture. The Moor already is feeling the effects of my "poison"—dangerous thoughts are like poisons which at first can hardly be tasted, but after a while they burn in the blood like sulfur mines.

[**Othello** *enters, looking deeply worried.*]

[**Iago** *continues, to himself.*] Just as I said. Here he comes. [*to* **Othello**, *but not with the intention of being heard*] Neither sleeping potions made from poppies, nor mandragora [*a drug made from the mandrake*], nor any of the sleeping potions in the world shall ever help you regain the untroubled sleep you had yesterday.

Othello   [*to himself*] Humph! Humph! Unfaithful to me?

Iago   Why, what's this, general? You must stop this.

Othello   [*enraged*] Leave! Be gone! You have put me on the torturer's rack. I swear that it's better to be betrayed much than to know of it even a little.

Iago   What, my lord?

Othello   What knowledge did I have of her stolen hours of lust? I didn't see it, didn't think about it; it didn't harm me. I slept well at night, ate well, was carefree and merry. I didn't taste Cassio's kisses on her lips. When one is robbed, if he doesn't miss what

He that is robb'd, not wanting what is stol'n,
Let him not know't, and he's not robb'd at all.

Iago   I am sorry to hear this.

345 **Othello**   I had been happy, if the general camp,
Pioners and all, had tasted her sweet body,
So I had nothing known. O now, for ever
Farewell the tranquil mind! farewell content!
Farewell the plumed troops and the big wars
350 That makes ambition virtue! O, farewell!
Farewell the neighing steed and the shrill trump,
The spirit-stirring drum, th' ear-piercing fife,
The royal banner, and all quality,
Pride, pomp, and circumstance of glorious war!
355 And O you mortal engines, whose rude throats
Th' immortal Jove's dread clamors counterfeit,
Farewell! Othello's occupation's gone.

Iago   Is't possible, my lord?

Othello   Villain, be sure thou prove my love a whore;

[*Taking him by the throat.*]

360 Be sure of it. Give me the ocular proof,
Or by the worth of mine eternal soul,
Thou hadst been better have been born a dog
Than answer my wak'd wrath!

Iago   Is't come to this?

Othello   Make me to see't; or (at the least) so prove it
365 That the probation bear no hinge nor loop
To hang a doubt on; or woe upon thy life!

Iago   My noble lord—

Othello   If thou dost slander her and torture me,
Never pray more; abandon all remorse;

164

is stolen and doesn't know about the theft, he hasn't been
robbed at all.

Iago [*pretending sympathy and concern*] I'm sorry to hear this.

Othello   I would have been happy if the entire army, even down
to the common soldier and the manual laborers, had tasted
her sweet body so long as I knew nothing about it. But now,
farewell to a tranquil mind, farewell to contentment, farewell to
the finely attired troops and magnificent battles that make it a
virtue to be ambitious. Oh, farewell! Farewell to the neighing
steed and the loud trumpet, the spirit-stirring drum, the shrill
fife, the royal banner, and all the attributes, proud display,
dignity, and ceremonial splendor of glorious war! And, you
deadly cannons, whose harsh throats mimic the terrifying
clamor of the immortal Jove, farewell! Othello's profession is
gone.

Iago   Is this possible, my lord?

Othello   [*glaring at* **Iago**] Villain, you had better have solid proof
that my love is a whore. [**Othello** *takes* **Iago** *by the throat.*]
Have solid proof. Give me proof I can see with my own eyes,
or, by the worth of my eternal soul, you would have been
better off to have been born a dog than to face my awakened
wrath.

Iago   Has it come to this?

Othello   Show it to me, or at least prove it so fully that the proof
may have no hinge or hook on which a doubt could hang, or
your life is in deadly peril.

Iago   [*gasping for breath*] My noble lord . . .

Othello   [*interrupts* **Iago**] If you're slandering her and torturing
me, don't bother to pray, don't hope for mercy. Horrors are

370   On horror's head horrors accumulate;
       Do deeds to make heaven weep, all earth amaz'd;
       For nothing canst thou to damnation add
       Greater than that.

       Iago   O grace! O heaven forgive me!
374   Are you a man? Have you a soul? or sense?
       God buy you; take mine office. O wretched fool,
       That lov'st to make thine honesty a vice!
       O monstrous world! Take note, take note, O world,
       To be direct and honest is not safe.
       I thank you for this profit, and from hence
380   I'll love no friend, sith love breeds such offense.

       Othello   Nay, stay. Thou shouldst be honest.

       Iago   I should be wise—for honesty's a fool
       And loses that it works for.

       Othello   By the world,
       I think my wife be honest, and think she is not;
385   I think that thou art just, and think thou art not.
       I'll have some proof. [Her] name, that was as fresh
       As Dian's visage, is now begrim'd and black
       As mine own face. If there be cords, or knives,
       Poison, or fire, or suffocating streams,
390   I'll not endure it. Would I were satisfied!

       Iago   I see, [sir], you are eaten up with passion;
       I do repent me that I put it to you.
       You would be satisfied?

       Othello   Would? nay, and I will.

       Iago   And may; but how? How satisfied, my lord?
395   Would you, the [supervisor], grossly gape on?
       Behold her topp'd?

       Othello   Death and damnation! O!

heaped on the head of the one who causes horror. Do things that make heaven weep and all the earth appalled, for you can do nothing more to add to your soul's damnation.

Iago   Oh, grace of God! Oh, heaven forgive me. Are you a man? Do you have a soul? Or a mind? Good-bye. Strip me of my rank. [*as if speaking to himself, but intending for* **Othello** *to hear every word*] Oh, you stupid fool, that you must be honest to a fault! Oh, monstrous world! See this, see this, oh world; it isn't safe to be open and honest.
[*to* **Othello,** *with false bitterness*] Thank you for this lesson, and from now on I'll never care about a friend, as caring only results in trouble.

Othello   [*slowly releasing his grip on* **Iago**] No, wait. You should be honest.

Iago   [*bitterly*] I should be wise—honesty is a fool and it loses the friend it tries to help.

Othello   I swear by the entire world, I think my wife is faithful, and yet I think she isn't. I think you are truthful, and yet I think you aren't. I must have proof. Her name, which once was as spotless as Diana's face [*in Roman mythology, Diana was the virgin goddess of the moon and the hunt*], is now filthy and as black as my own. If there are ropes or knives, poison or fire or suffocating streams [*with which to kill* **Desdemona** *and* **Cassio**], I won't stand for it. I wish I could be sure!

Iago   I see, sir, that you are eaten up with suffering. I'm sorry I mentioned it to you. [**Iago** *hesitates as if unsure whether to continue.*] Would you like to be certain?

Othello   [*explosively*] Like to be? No, I will be!

Iago   And you may be . . . but how? How can you be certain, my lord? Would you, as a spectator, obscenely watch? See her mounted?

Othello   [*enraged*] Death and damnation! [*deeply pained*] Oh!

Iago   It were a tedious difficulty, I think,
To bring them to that prospect; damn them then,
If ever mortal eyes do see them bolster
400   More than their own. What then? How then?
What shall I say? Where's satisfaction?
It is impossible you should see this,
Were they as prime as goats, as hot as monkeys,
As salt as wolves in pride, and fools as gross
405   As ignorance made drunk. But yet, I say,
If imputation and strong circumstances
Which lead directly to the door of truth
Will give you satisfaction, you might have't.

Othello   Give me a living reason she's disloyal.

410 **Iago**   I do not like the office;
But sith I am ent'red in this cause so far
(Prick'd to't by foolish honesty and love),
I will go on. I lay with Cassio lately,
And being troubled with a raging tooth,
415   I could not sleep.
There are a kind of men, so loose of soul,
That in their sleeps will mutter their affairs;
One of this kind is Cassio.
In sleep I heard him say, "Sweet Desdemona,
420   Let us be wary, let us hide our loves";
And then, sir, would he gripe and wring my hand;
Cry, "O sweet creature!" then kiss me hard,
As if he pluck'd up kisses by the roots
424   That grew upon my lips; [then] laid his leg
[Over] my thigh, and [sigh'd], and [kiss'd], and then
[Cried], "Cursed fate that gave thee to the Moor!"

Othello   O monstrous! monstrous!

Iago   Nay, this was but his dream.

Othello   But this denoted a foregone conclusion.

Iago It would be very difficult, I think, to catch them in the act. You must condemn them as guilty, then, only if someone other than they themselves should see them in bed together. [**Iago** *pretends to think aloud.*] What can be done then? How can it be accomplished? What shall I suggest? Where can proof be found? It's impossible for you to actually watch them even if they were as lustful as goats, as hot as monkeys, as lecherous as wolves in heat, and as obscene as stupid, drunken fools. [*As* **Iago** *speaks,* **Othello** *becomes increasingly distraught and furious.*] But still, if a judgment may be founded on strong circumstantial evidence leading straight to the door of truth, you might be able to have proof.

Othello Give me an actual incident to show she's unfaithful.

Iago [*pretending to speak reluctantly*] I don't like to perform this task, but since I'm this deeply involved already—driven to it by unwise honesty and concern—I'll go on with it. I shared a bed with Cassio recently and was kept awake by a terrible toothache. There are certain men who have little self-control, who mutter about their affairs while sleeping; Cassio is one of this type. I heard him say in his sleep, "Sweet Desdemona, let's be careful. Let's hide our love." And then, sir, he would grip and wring my hand, cry out, "Sweet creature!" and then kiss me hard, as if he plucked kisses up by the roots as they grew on my lips. And then he laid his leg over my thigh and sighed and kissed me and then cried out, "Curse the fate that gave you to the Moor!"

Othello [*in an agony of jealous, impotent fury*] Oh, horrible, horrible!

Iago [*pretending to try to reassure* **Othello**] No, but that was only his dream.

Othello But it represented something that had already happened.

[**Iago**]   'Tis a shrewd doubt, though it be but a dream,
430   And this may help to thicken other proofs
     That do demonstrate thinly.

Othello   I'll tear her all to pieces.

Iago   Nay, yet be wise; yet we see nothing done;
     She may be honest yet. Tell me but this,
     Have you not sometimes seen a handkerchief
435   Spotted with strawberries in your wive's hand?

Othello   I gave her such a one; 'twas my first gift.

Iago   I know not that; but such a handkerchief
     (I am sure it was your wive's) did I to-day
     See Cassio wipe his beard with.

Othello   If it be that—

440 **Iago**   If it be that, or any [that] was hers,
     It speaks against her with the other proofs.

Othello   O that the slave had forty thousand lives!
     One is too poor, too weak for my revenge.
     Now do I see 'tis true. Look here, Iago,
445   All my fond love thus do I blow to heaven.
     'Tis gone.
     Arise, black vengeance, from the hollow hell!
     Yield up, O love, thy crown and hearted throne
     To tyrannous hate! Swell, bosom, with thy fraught,
     For 'tis of aspics' tongues!

450 **Iago**   Yet be content.

Othello   O blood, blood, blood!

Iago   Patience, I say; your mind [perhaps] may change.

Othello   Never, Iago. Like to the Pontic Sea,
     Whose icy current and compulsive course

Iago   There's reason to be suspicious. Although it was merely a dream, it may help reinforce other proofs that only weakly indicate Cassio's and Desdemona's guilt.

Othello   I'll tear her all to pieces!

Iago   No, reserve your judgment. As yet we haven't seen any real proof. She may still prove to be virtuous. Tell me one thing. Have you not occasionally seen a handkerchief with a pattern of strawberries in your wife's hand?

Othello   I gave her one like that. It was my first gift to her.

Iago   I don't know about that, but today I saw Cassio wipe his beard with just such a handkerchief. I'm sure it was you wife's.

Othello   [*threateningly*] If it was hers . . .

Iago   [*interrupting* **Othello**] If it was hers or any other belonging to her, added to the other evidence, it convicts her.

Othello   Oh, that Cassio had 40,000 lives! One life is not enough, not enough for my revenge. Now I see it is true. Look here, Iago, all my deep love I cast to the winds. It's gone. Come, black vengeance, from the depths of hell. Give your crown and your throne within my heart, my love for Desdemona, to vicious hatred. Grow furious, my heart, with your burden, for it [*Othello's heart*] is filled with snakes' venom.

Iago   Calm down.

Othello   Oh, blood! Blood! Blood!

Iago   Be patient, I tell you! You may perhaps change your mind.

Othello   Never, Iago. Like the Pontic Sea whose icy current and unchanging waves never ebb but keep heading to the

455 Nev'r [feels] retiring ebb, but keeps due on
    To the Propontic and the Hellespont,
    Even so my bloody thoughts, with violent pace,
    Shall nev'r look back, nev'r ebb to humble love,
459 Till that a capable and wide revenge
    Swallow them up. [*He kneels.*] Now by yond marble heaven,
    In the due reverence of a sacred vow
    I here engage my words.

Iago   Do not rise yet. [*Iago kneels.*]
    Witness, you ever-burning lights above,
    You elements that clip us round about,
465 Witness that here Iago doth give up
    The execution of his wit, hands, heart,
    To wrong'd Othello's service! Let him command,
    And to obey shall be in me remorse,
    What bloody business ever.

                                        [*They rise.*]

Othello   I greet thy love,
    Not with vain thanks, but with acceptance bounteous,
471 And will upon the instant put thee to't:
    Within these three days let me hear thee say
    That Cassio's not alive.

Iago   My friend is dead; 'tis done at your request.
    But let her live.

476 **Othello**   Damn her, lewd minx! O, damn her, damn her!
    Come go with me apart, I will withdraw
    To furnish me with some swift means of death
    For the fair devil. Now art thou my lieutenant.

Iago   I am your own for ever.

                                        Exeunt.

Propontic and the Hellespont, my bloodthirsty thoughts, violently surging forward, shall never look back, never return to their former gentle love, until they are swallowed up by my all-encompassing and comprehensive revenge.
[**Othello** *kneels.*] I now swear by the changeless heavens above, and in the true reverence of a sacred vow I hereby give my word.

Iago   Don't arise yet. [**Iago** *also kneels.*] You stars above, you heavens that encircle the earth, I call you to witness that Iago hereby devotes his mind, hands, and heart to serve the betrayed Othello! Let him give me orders, and I will perform even the cruelest acts as if they were gentle and prompted by compassion.

[*They rise.*]

Othello   I welcome your affection, not with pointless words of thanks, but with heartfelt appreciation, and I will immediately give you a task. Within the next three days, I want to hear you say that Cassio is dead.

Iago   My friend, Cassio, is as good as dead. I will do as you ask. But let Desdemona live.

Othello   [*explosively*] Damn her, the lustful whore! Oh, damn her! Damn her! [*to* **Iago**] Come with me. I will contrive some way to speedily kill the beautiful devil. You are now my lieutenant.

[*They leave.*]

Scene 4

Enter **Desdemona**, **Emilia**, *and* **Clown**.

Desdemona   Do you know, sirrah, where Lieutenant
Cassio lies?

Clown   I dare not say he lies any where.

Desdemona   Why, man?

Clown   He's a soldier, and for me to say a solider lies,
6   'tis stabbing.

Desdemona   Go to! where lodges he?

Clown   To tell you where he lodges, is to tell you
where I lie.

10 **Desdemona**   Can any thing be made of this?

Clown   I know not where he lodges, and for me to devise a lodging and say he lies here, or he lies there,
were to lie in mine own throat.

Desdemona   Can you inquire him out, and be edified by
15   report?

Clown   I will catechize the world for him, that is,
make questions, and by them answer.

Desdemona   Seek him, bid him come hither. Tell him I
have mov'd my lord on his behalf, and hope all will be
20   well.

Clown   To do this is within the compass of man's wit,
and therefore I will attempt the doing it.

Exit Clown.

Desdemona   Where should I lose the handkerchief,
Emilia?

Emilia   I know not, madam.

Scene 4

A short time later outside the castle.

[**Desdemona, Emilia**, *and the* **Clown** *enter.*]

Desdemona   [*to the* **Clown**] Do you know, fellow, where Cassio lies [*that is, lives*]?

Clown   I wouldn't dare say he lies anywhere.

Desdemona   Why not?

Clown   [*making a pun on the word "lies"*] Because he's a soldier, and if I say a soldier lies, I'll get stabbed for it.

Desdemona   [*laughing*] Oh, stop! Where does he live?

Clown   If I tell you where he lives, I'll be telling you where I lie.

Desdemona   [*still laughing but becoming exasperated*] Could anyone make any sense out of this?

Clown   [*explains*] I don't know where he lives, and, if I were to make up a location and say he lies here or he lies there, I would be telling a lie.

Desdemona   Could you ask around and find out where he lives?

Clown   I'll inquire everywhere for him. That is, I'll ask questions, and then I'll answer you.

Desdemona   Find him and tell him to come here. Tell him I have persuaded my husband to see him, and I hope that everything will soon be all right.

Clown   A man should be able to figure out how to do this, and, therefore, being a man, I will try to do it. [*He leaves.*]

Desdemona   [*returning to the topic of an earlier discussion with* **Emilia**] Where did I lose the handkerchief, Emilia?

Emilia   [*pretending not to know*] I don't know, madam.

25 **Desdemona**   Believe me, I had rather have lost my purse
Full of crusadoes; and but my noble Moor
Is true of mind, and made of no such baseness
As jealous creatures are, it were enough
To put him to ill thinking.

Emilia   Is he not jealous?

Desdemona   Who, he? I think the sun where he was born
Drew all such humors from him.

31 **Emilia**   Look where he comes.

Enter **Othello**.

Desdemona   I will not leave him now till Cassio
Be call'd to him.—How is't with you, my lord?

Othello   Well, my good lady. [*Aside*.] O, hardness to
dissemble!—
How do you, Desdemona?

35 **Desdemona**   Well, my good lord.

Othello   Give me your hand. This hand is moist, my lady.

Desdemona   It [yet] hath felt no age nor known no sorrow.

Othello   This argues fruitfulness and liberal heart;
Hot, hot, and moist. This hand of yours requires
40 A sequester from liberty: fasting and prayer,
Much castigation, exercise devout,
For here's a young and sweating devil here
That commonly rebels. 'Tis a good hand,
A frank one.

Desdemona   You may, indeed, say so;
45 For 'twas that hand that gave away my heart.

Othello   A liberal hand. The hearts of old gave hands;
But our new heraldry is hands, not hearts.

Desdemona   [*worriedly*] Believe me, I would rather I had lost a purse full of money. If it weren't for the fact that my noble Moor trusts me and isn't a jealous man, it would be enough to make him suspicious.

Emilia   Isn't he jealous?

Desdemona   Who, Othello? I think that the hot sun of his native land must have baked any jealous thoughts right out of him.

Emilia   [*seeing* **Othello** *approach*] Here he comes.

[**Othello** *enters.*]

Desdemona   [*to* **Emilia**] I'm not going to leave him alone until he lets Cassio come see him.
[*to* **Othello**] How are you, my lord?

Othello   Fine, my good lady.
[*to himself*] How hard it is to pretend!
[*to* **Desdemona**] How are you, Desdemona.

Desdemona   Fine, my lord.

Othello   Give me your hand. [*She does so.*] Your hand is moist, my lady.

Desdemona   Because it hasn't yet grown old or experienced sorrow.

Othello   A hand like this indicates generosity and a giving heart. It's hot, hot and moist. Your hand needs to lose its freedom. It needs fasting and prayer, many acts of penance, and righteous deeds, for your hand is a young and sweaty devil that often rebels. [*He adds involuntarily.*] It's a good hand. An open hand.

Desdemona   You may certainly say so, for it was this hand that gave away my heart.

Othello   A giving hand. In the old days, people gave their hearts when they married, but our new customs permit people to marry without giving their hearts.

Desdemona   I cannot speak of this. Come now, your
    promise.

Othello   What promise, chuck?

Desdemona   I have sent to bid Cassio come speak with you.

51 **Othello**   I have a salt and sorry rheum offends me;
    Lend me thy handkerchief.

Desdemona   Here, my lord.

Othello   That which I gave you.

Desdemona   I have it not about me.

Othello   Not?

Desdemona   No, [faith], my lord.

55 **Othello**   That's a fault. That handkerchief
    Did an Egyptian to my mother give;
    She was a charmer, and could almost read
    The thoughts of people. She told her, while she kept it,
    'Twould make her amiable, and subdue my father
60   Entirely to her love; but if she lost it,
    Or made a gift of it, my father's eye
    Should hold her loathed, and his spirits should hunt
    After new fancies. She, dying, gave it me,
    And bid me, when my fate would have me wiv'd,
65   To give it her. I did so; and take heed on't,
    Make it a darling like your precious eye.
    To lose't or give't away were such perdition
    As nothing else could match.

Desdemona   Is't possible?

Othello   'Tis true; there's magic in the web of it.
70   A sibyl, that had numb'red in the world
    The sun to course two hundred compasses,

Desdemona   I don't know about that custom. Come now, keep your promise.

Othello   What promise, sweetheart?

Desdemona   I have sent for Cassio to come talk to you.

Othello   [*He stiffens at the mention of* **Cassio**.] My eyes are watering badly. Give me your handkerchief.

Desdemona   Here you are, my lord. [*She hands him a handkerchief.*]

Othello   The one I gave to you.

Desdemona   [*pausing*] I don't have it with me.

Othello   No?

Desdemona   No, honestly, my lord.

Othello   [*sternly*] That's very wrong of you. An Egyptian gave it to my mother. The Egyptian was a magician and could almost read people's minds. She told my mother that as long as she had it, it would make her desirable and would enslave my father to her love. But if she lost it or gave it away, my father would look on her with hatred, and he would pursue other women. When she died, my mother gave it to me and told me, when it would be my fate to get married, to give it to my wife. I did so, and you—pay close attention—must cherish it as greatly as you do your ability to see. To lose it or give it away would be terrible beyond anything.

Desdemona   [*turning pale with fear*] Can this be possible?

Othello   It's true. There's magical power woven into it. A sorceress who was more than two hundred years old, while in

In her prophetic fury sew'd the work;
The worms were hallowed that did breed the silk,
And it was dy'd in mummy which the skillful
Conserv'd of maidens' hearts.

75 **Desdemona**   [I' faith]! is't true?

Othello   Most veritable, therefore look to't well.

Desdemona   Then would to [God] that I had never seen't!

Othello   Ha? wherefore?

Desdemona   Why do you speak so startingly and rash?

80 **Othello**   Is't lost? Is't gone? Speak, is't out o' th' way?

Desdemona   [Heaven] bless us!

Othello   Say you?

Desdemona   It is not lost; but what and if it were?

Othello   How?

Desdemona   I say, it is not lost.

85 **Othello**   Fetch't, let me see't.

Desdemona   Why, so I can, [sir,] but I will not now.
This is a trick to put me from my suit.
Pray you let Cassio be receiv'd again.

Othello   Fetch me the handkerchief, my mind misgives.

90 **Desdemona**   Come, come;
You'll never meet a more sufficient man.

Othello   The handkerchief!

[**Desdemona**   I pray talk me of Cassio.

a mystical frenzy, made it. The silk worms that spun the silk were sacred, and it was dyed in the fluid skillfully extracted from the hearts of embalmed virgins.

Desdemona   [*looking even more frightened*] Really! Is this true?

Othello   Absolutely. So take good care of it.

Desdemona   Then I wish to God I'd never seen it!

Othello   [*startled and offended*] Humph! Why?

Desdemona   Why do you speak so haltingly and abruptly?

Othello   [*seizing* **Desdemona** *and shouting*] Is it lost? Is it gone? Tell me! Have you mislaid it?

Desdemona   [*seriously alarmed*] Heaven help us!

Othello   What is your answer?

Desdemona   [*lying because of her fear of* **Othello**'s *anger*] It isn't lost, but what if it were?

Othello   How did you lose it?

Desdemona   I'm telling you, it isn't lost.

Othello   Go get it. Let me see it.

Desdemona   [*with false bravado*] Why, I could, sir, but I'm not going to right now. This is merely a trick to try to make me forget my request. Please let Cassio come see you again.

Othello   [*He stiffens once again at her mention of* **Cassio**.] Bring me the handkerchief. I'm very worried.

Desdemona   Come, come. You'll never find a more capable man.

Othello   The handkerchief!

Desdemona   Please answer me about Cassio.

Othello   The handkerchief!]

Desdemona   A man that all his time
Hath founded his good fortunes on your love,
95   Shar'd dangers with you—

Othello   The handkerchief!

Desdemona   [I' faith], you are to blame.

Othello   ['Zounds!]

Exit Othello.

Emilia   Is not this man jealous?

100 **Desdemona**   I nev'r saw this before.
Sure, there's some wonder in this handkerchief;
I am most unhappy in the loss of it.

Emilia   'Tis not a year or two shows us a man:
They are all but stomachs, and we all but food;
105   They eat us hungerly, and when they are full
They belch us.

Enter **Iago** *and* **Cassio**.

Look you, Cassio and my husband!

Iago   There is no other way: 'tis she must do't;
And lo the happiness! Go, and importune her.

Desdemona   How now, good Cassio, what's the news with you?

110 **Cassio**   Madam, my former suit. I do beseech you
That by your virtuous means I may again
Exist, and be a member of his love
Whom I, with all the office of my heart,
Entirely honor. I would not be delay'd.

Othello   The handkerchief!

Desdemona   He has always depended on your support, shared dangers with you . . .

Othello   [*He interrupts her.*] The handkerchief!

Desdemona   Truly, you are in the wrong about Cassio.

Othello   [*giving up in anger, frustration, and despair*] My God!

[*He stalks off.*]

Emilia   Is he jealous?

Desdemona   I've never seen him like this before. There must be some great power in this handkerchief. I'm very upset about losing it.

Emilia   You don't learn everything about a man in just a year or two. [*bitterly*] Men are all like stomachs, and we women are all like food. They devour us when they're hungry, and when they're full, they belch us out.

[**Iago** *and* **Cassio** *enter.*]

Look, here are Cassio and my husband.

Iago   There's no other way. Desdemona must do it, and [*He sees her.*] what luck, here she is.

Desdemona   Hello, Cassio. What has been happening with you?

Cassio   [*glumly*] Still the same problem, madam. I beg you to be so kind as to make every effort to give me back my life and enable me to regain the respect of your husband, a man I honor from the bottom of my heart. I can't stand this waiting!

115 If my offense be of such mortal kind
That nor my service past, nor present sorrows,
Nor purpos'd merit in futurity,
Can ransom me into his love again,
But to know so must be my benefit;
120 So shall I clothe me in a forc'd content,
And shut myself up in some other course,
To fortune's alms.

Desdemona   Alas, thrice-gentle Cassio,
My advocation is not now in tune.
My lord is not my lord; nor should I know him
125 Were he in favor as in humor alter'd.
So help me every spirit sanctified,
As I have spoken for you all my best,
And stood within the blank of his displeasure
For my free speech! You must awhile be patient.
130 What I can do, I will; and more I will
Than for myself I dare. Let that suffice you.

Iago Is my lord angry?

Emilia   He went hence but now;
And certainly in strange unquietness.

Iago Can he be angry? I have seen the cannon
135 When it hath blown his ranks into the air,
And like the devil from his very arm
Puff'd his own brother—and is he angry?
Something of moment then. I will go meet him.
There's matter in't indeed, if he be angry.

Desdemona I prithee do so.

Exit [*Iago*].

Something sure of state,
141 Either from Venice, or some unhatch'd practice

184

If I have done something so unforgivable that neither my past service, nor my present repentance, nor anything I may do in the future can restore me to his favor, I'm better off knowing it. If that's the case, I would just resign myself and decide to pursue some other career, hoping that fortune will see fit to toss a few crumbs of luck my way.

Desdemona   [*regretfully*] I'm afraid, Cassio, that it's not a good time for me to be your advocate with Othello. My husband is not himself. In fact, I wouldn't even recognize him if his appearance were as altered as his temperament is. I swear by all that is holy, I have said everything I could in your defense, and for my efforts I've become the target of his anger.

Iago   [*swiftly concealing his satisfaction at the news*] Is Othello angry?

Emilia   He just left here, and he was upset for some strange reason.

Iago   Is he really angry? I've seen the ranks of his soldiers thrown into the air by cannon fire, and even when his own brother was shot as he held him in his arms . . . and he's angry now? Something important has happened. I'll go find him. It must be something serious if he's angry.

Desdemona   Please do so.

[**Iago** *leaves.*]

[*to* **Cassio** *and* **Emilia**] He must have received some official news from Venice, or he has learned of some plot here in

Made demonstrable here in Cyprus to him,
Hath puddled his clear spirit; and in such cases
Men's natures wrangle with inferior things,
145   Though great ones are their object. 'Tis even so;
For let our finger ache, and it endues
Our other healthful members even to a sense
Of pain. Nay, we must think men are not gods,
Nor of them look for such observancy
150   As fits the bridal. Beshrew me much, Emilia,
I was (unhandsome warrior as I am)
Arraigning his unkindness with my soul;
But now I find I had suborn'd the witness,
And he's indicted falsely.

Emilia   Pray heaven it be state matters, as you think,
156   And no conception nor no jealous toy
Concerning you.

Desdemona   Alas the day, I never gave him cause.

Emilia   But jealous souls will not be answer'd so;
They are not ever jealous for the cause,
160   But jealous for they're jealous. It is a monster
Begot upon itself, born on itself.

Desdemona   Heaven keep the monster from Othello's mind!

Emilia   Lady, amen.

Desdemona   I will go seek him. Cassio, walk hereabout;
166   If I do find him fit, I'll move your suit
And seek to effect it to my uttermost.

Cassio   I humbly thank your ladyship.

Exeunt [Desdemona and Emilia].

Enter **Bianca**.

Cyprus that hasn't yet been carried out which is troubling him greatly. When such things happen, men pick quarrels over trivialities although it's the serious matters that really concern them. That's how it is; if nothing more than our finger hurts, even the uninjured parts of our bodies seem to hurt, too. No, we must remember that men aren't gods, nor should we expect them always to treat us as if they were newlyweds. Honestly, Emilia, clumsy "soldier" that I am, I was condemning his harshness in my heart, but now I realize I've misinterpreted his actions and that he's been falsely accused.

Emilia   [*looking ill at ease*] I pray that it is affairs of state as you suspect, and not suspicion or a jealous notion concerning you.

Desdemona   Alas the day, I never gave him reason to be jealous.

Emilia   But people who are jealous aren't satisfied with that. They're not jealous only because they have reason to be; they're jealous because they're jealous. Jealousy is like a monster that gives birth to itself.

Desdemona   May heaven keep that monster far from Othello's mind!

Emilia   Amen, lady.

Desdemona   I'll go look for him.
[*to* **Cassio**] Cassio, you wait here. If Othello is in a reasonable frame of mind, I'll bring up your cause and do everything I can to promote it.

Cassio   I humbly thank you, your ladyship.

[**Desdemona** *and* **Emilia** *leave.* **Bianca** *enters.*]

Bianca   'Save you, friend Cassio!

Cassio   What make you from home?
170   How is't with you, my most fair Bianca?
       [I'faith], sweet love, I was coming to your house.

Bianca   And I was going to your lodging, Cassio.
       What? keep a week away? seven days and nights?
       Eightscore eight hours? and lovers' absent hours,
175   More tedious than the dial eightscore times?
       O weary reck'ning!

Cassio   Pardon me, Bianca.
       I have this while with leaden thoughts been press'd,
       But I shall in a more continuate time
       Strike off this score of absence. Sweet Bianca,

       [*Giving her Desdemona's handkerchief.*]

       Take me this work out.

Bianca   O Cassio, whence came this?
181   This is some token from a newer friend;
       To the felt absence now I feel a cause.
       Is't come to this? Well, well.

Cassio   Go to, woman!
184   Throw your vild guesses in the devil's teeth,
       From whence you have them. You are jealious now
       That this is from some mistress, some remembrance;
       No, [by my faith], Bianca.

Bianca   Why, whose is it?

Cassio   I know not, neither; I found it in my chamber.
       I like the work well; ere it be demanded
190   (As like enough it will) I would have it copied.
       Take it, and do't, and leave me for this time.

Bianca   God save you, dear Cassio!

Cassio   What brings you away from your home? How are you, my beautiful Bianca? Actually sweetheart, I was about to come see you.

Bianca   And I was going to your place, Cassio. [*She speaks with a flirtatious pout.*] How could I stay away from you for a whole week? Seven days and nights? One hundred sixty-eight hours? And the hours lovers spend apart are much longer than the hours on the clock. Oh, what a dismal number!

Cassio   Forgive me, Bianca. I've been weighed down for some time now with heavy thoughts, but when things are more settled I will make it up to you. Sweet Bianca,

[*He gives her* **Desdemona**'s *handkerchief.*]

copy this embroidery for me.

Bianca   [*with jealousy and suspicion*] Cassio, where did this come from? This belongs to some new girlfriend! Now I know why you've stayed away. Is that it? Well? Well?

Cassio   [*impatiently*] Oh, stop it, woman! Go throw your evil guesses back into the devil's mouth where you got them. Now you're jealous that this is a keepsake from some lover. I swear it isn't, Bianca.

Bianca   Then whose is it?

Cassio   I don't know, either. I found it in my bedroom. I like the pattern very much, so before it is claimed by someone—as it very likely will be—I'd like to have it copied. [*coaxingly*] Take it and copy it. And run along for now.

Bianca   Leave you? Wherefore?

Cassio   I do attend here on the general,
194   And think it no addition, nor my wish,
To have him see me woman'd.

Bianca   Why, I pray you?

Cassio   Not that I love you not.

Bianca   But that you do not love me.
I pray you bring me on the way a little,
And say if I shall see you soon at night.

Cassio   'Tis but a little way that I can bring you,
200   For I attend here; but I'll see you soon.

Bianca   'Tis very good; I must be circumstanc'd.

Exeunt omnes.

Bianca   [*Her suspicions, which had begun to subside, are rekindled at his request.*] Leave you? Why?

Cassio   I'm waiting here for the general, and it isn't going to look good if you're here. I don't want him to find me with a woman.

Bianca   [*indignantly*] And why not?

Cassio   [*putting his arms around her and kissing her*] It's not that I don't love you.

Bianca   [*pouting*] You don't love me. [*She suddenly relents and returns his embrace.*] Please walk with me part of the way and tell me if I'll see you one night soon.

Cassio   I can only come a little way with you because I must wait here, but I'll see you soon.

Bianca   All right, I'll just have to put up with the circumstances.

[*They exit.*]

Act four

Scene 1

Enter **Othello** *and* **Iago**.

Iago Will you think so?

Othello   Think so, Iago?

Iago   What,
To kiss in private?

Othello   An unauthoriz'd kiss!

Iago Or to be naked with her friend in bed
An hour, or more, not meaning any harm?

5 **Othello**   Naked in bed, Iago, and not mean harm?
It is hypocrisy against the devil.
They that mean virtuously, and yet do so,
The devil their virtue tempts, and they tempt heaven.

Iago If they do nothing, 'tis a venial slip;
10   But if I give my wife a handkerchief—

Othello What then?

Iago Why then 'tis hers, my lord, and being hers,
She may, I think, bestow't on any man.

Othello She is protectress of her honor too;
15   May she give that?

Iago Her honor is an essence that's not seen;
They have it very oft that have it not.
But for the handkerchief—

Act four

Scene 1
Shortly thereafter, in front of the castle.

[**Othello** *and* **Iago** *enter.*]

Iago   Do you think so?

Othello   Think what, Iago?

Iago   That they've kissed secretly?

Othello   [*in an agony of jealousy*] An illicit kiss!

Iago   [*watching* **Othello**'s *reactions closely*] Or that she could have been naked in bed with her friend, Cassio, and not intended to do anything wrong?

Othello   [*explosively*] Naked in bed and not intend to do anything wrong? It's a devilish sham! Those who intend to behave virtuously and yet would do such a thing invite the devil to tempt them, and they themselves tempt heaven to damn them.

Iago   If they don't do anything, it's only a very minor slip up. However, if I give my wife a handkerchief . . . [**Iago** *hesitates.*]

Othello   What then?

Iago   Why then, it's hers, my lord, and because it's hers she may, I think, give it to any man.

Othello   She is the guardian of her chastity? Can she give that away as well?

Iago   Her chastity is something that can't be seen. Women often seem to have it who don't. But as for the handkerchief . . .

Othello   By heaven, I would most gladly have forgot it.
20   Thou saidst (O, it comes o'er my memory,
        As doth the raven o'er the infectious house,
        Boding to all) he had my handkerchief.

Iago   Ay; what of that?

Othello   That's not so good now.

Iago   What
        If I had said I had seen him do you wrong?
25   Or heard him say—as knaves be such abroad,
        Who having by their own importunate suit,
        Or voluntary dotage of some mistress,
        Convinced or supplied them, cannot choose
        But they must blab—

29 **Othello**   Hath he said any thing?

Iago   He hath, my lord, but be you well assur'd,
        No more than he'll unswear.

Othello   What hath he said?

Iago   [Faith], that he did—I know not what he did.

33 **Othello**   What? what?

Iago   Lie—

Othello   With her?

Iago   With her? On her; what you will.

Othello   Lie with her? lie on her? We say lie on her,
        when they belie her. Lie with her! ['Zounds,] that's
        fulsome! Handkerchief—confessions—handkerchief!
        To confess, and be hang'd for his labor—first to be

Othello By heaven, I wish I could forget about it. What you said about Cassio having my handkerchief hovers over my memory like a raven over a house infested with disease, an evil omen to all.

Iago Yes, what of it?

Othello That's not good.

Iago What if I said I had seen him wrong you? Or heard him say . . . [**Iago** *pauses as if considering what to say.*] There are scoundrels who, because they have some urgent matter or because they are infatuated with some woman who controls them or who keeps their lust satisfied, who can't keep from blabbing . . .

Othello [*urgently*] Has he said anything?

Iago [*pretending to be reluctant to answer*] He has, my lord . . . [*emphatically, as if intending to take revenge on Cassio for* **Othello**'s *sake,* **Iago** *adds*] but you may be sure he'll be forced to take it back.

Othello What has he said?

Iago Well, that he did . . . [*He pretends to change his mind about saying anything further.*] I don't know what he said.

Othello What? What?

Iago [*pretending reluctance*] Lie . . . [*He hesitates.*]

Othello [*clearly beside himself with grief and jealousy*] With her?

Iago [*shrugging*] With her. On her. Whatever.

Othello Lie with her? Lie on her? We would say "lie on her" when someone tells lies about her. Lie with her! My God, that's revolting! Handkerchief . . . confessions . . . handkerchief! [**Othello** *paces to and fro in impotent fury.*] He shall confess this and be hanged for what he's done. [**Othello** *pauses to think.*] The most important thing is for him to be hanged;

hang'd, and then to confess. I tremble at it. Nature
40   would not invest herself in such shadowing passion
without some instruction. It is not words that shakes
me thus. Pish! Noses, ears, and lips. Is't possible?
Confess? Handkerchief? O devil!

Falls in a trance.

Iago   Work on,
45   My medicine, [work]! Thus credulous fools are caught,
And many worthy and chaste dames even thus
(All guiltless) meet reproach.—What ho! my lord!
My lord, I say! Othello!

Enter **Cassio**.

How now, Cassio?

Cassio   What's the matter?

50 **Iago**   My lord is fall'n into an epilepsy.
This is his second fit; he had one yesterday.

Cassio   Rub him about the temples.

Iago   [No, forbear,]
The lethargy must have his quiet course;
If not, he foams at mouth, and by and by
55   Breaks out to savage madness. Look, he stirs.
Do you withdraw yourself a little while,
He will recover straight. When he is gone,
I would on great occasion speak with you.

[*Exit Cassio.*]

How is it, general? Have you not hurt your head?

making him confess is secondary. [**Othello** *looks at his hand, which is trembling.*] I am shaking. I would not be shaking like this if nothing had happened between them to cause me to do so. It can't be that just hearing about it makes me shake so. Pish! Noses, ears, and lips! [**Othello** *is saying that he would like to punish* **Desdemona** *and* **Cassio** *by cutting off their noses, ears, and lips.*] Can this be possible? Confess? Handkerchief? Oh damn!

[*He has an epileptic seizure from his overwhelming emotions and falls to the ground, unconscious.*]

Iago   [*to himself, with great satisfaction*] Keep on working, my "medicine," keep on! This is how gullible fools are tricked, and many good and faithful wives, although innocent, are accused. [*He bends over* **Othello** *and tries to restore him to consciousness.*] My lord, do you hear me? Othello! [**Cassio** *enters.* **Iago** *addresses* **Cassio.**] How are you, Cassio?

Cassio   [*alarmed at seeing* **Othello** *lying unconscious*] What's the matter?

Iago   Othello has fallen into a coma. This is the second one; he had one yesterday.

Cassio   Rub his temples to bring him around.

Iago   No, don't. This condition must run its course. If it doesn't, he foams at the mouth and then becomes extremely violent. [*He notices that* **Othello** *is beginning to recover.*] Look, he's coming to. You'd better leave for now. He'll be better soon. When Othello leaves, I have something important to discuss with you.

[**Cassio** *leaves.*]

How are you, general? Have you hurt your head?

Othello   Dost thou mock me?

60 **Iago**   I mock you not, by heaven.
Would you would bear your fortune like a man!

Othello   A horned man's a monster and a beast.

Iago   There's many a beast then in a populous city,
And many a civil monster.

Othello   Did he confess it?

65 **Iago**   Good sir, be a man;
Think every bearded fellow that's but yok'd
May draw with you. There's millions now alive
That nightly lie in those unproper beds
Which they dare swear peculiar; your case is better.
70 O, 'tis the spite of hell, the fiend's arch-mock,
To lip a wanton in a secure couch,
And to suppose her chaste! No, let me know,
And knowing what I am, I know what she shall be.

Othello   O, thou art wise; 'tis certain.

Iago   Stand you a while apart,
75 Confine yourself but in a patient list.
Whilst you were here o'erwhelmed with your grief
(A passion most [unsuiting] such a man),
Cassio came hither. I shifted him away,
And laid good 'scuses upon your ecstasy;
80 Bade him anon return and here speak with me,
The which he promis'd. Do but encave yourself,
And mark the fleers, the gibes, and notable scorns
That dwell in every region of his face,
For I will make him tell the tale anew:
85 Where, how, how oft, how long ago, and when

Othello [*groggily but angrily*] Are you making fun of me?
[**Othello** *suspects that* **Iago** *is referring to "cuckolding," the folk custom in which, in a public ceremony of ridicule, an animal's horns were tied to the head of a man—the "cuckold"—whose wife had betrayed him, after which he was paraded through the streets of the town.*]

Iago [*hiding his amusement*] I swear I wouldn't make fun of you. You should endure your bad luck like a man.

Othello [*getting to his feet unsteadily*] A man wearing the cuckold's horns is a monster and a beast.

Iago [*sardonically*] There are many beasts in a large city, then, and many a monster, too.

Othello Did Cassio confess it?

Iago Dear sir, be a man. Probably every other grown man that's married is in the same situation as you. There are millions who sleep in beds that don't really belong to them, yet they're convinced that they do. Your situation is actually better than theirs. It's a humiliation from hell itself, the devil's worst trick on a man when he unsuspectingly kisses an unfaithful woman in his own bed and believes that she's true to him. No, I'd rather know about it, and, knowing what kind of man I am, I know what she'll be [*when he pays her back by being unfaithful to her*].

Othello [*heavily*] You are truly wise.

Iago Wait for a time and try to exercise patience and self-control. While you were unconscious from your grief—in an emotional state in which no man should permit himself to be—Cassio came by. I sent him away and made excuses for your condition. I told him to return soon to talk to me, which he promised to do. You go hide yourself and observe his sneers, his mockery, and the obvious contempt on his face, for I will make him tell me again about his affair with Desdemona: where they did it, how they did it, how often, how long ago,

He hath, and is again to cope your wife.
I say, but mark his gesture. Marry, patience,
Or I shall say y' are all in all in spleen,
And nothing of a man.

Othello   Dost thou hear, Iago,
90   I will be found most cunning in my patience;
But (dost thou hear) most bloody.

Iago   That's not amiss,
But yet keep time in all. Will you withdraw?

                                   [*Othello withdraws.*]

Now will I question Cassio of Bianca,
A huswife that by selling her desires
95   Buys herself bread and [clothes]. It is a creature
That dotes on Cassio (as 'tis the strumpet's plague
To beguile many and be beguil'd by one);
He, when he hears of her, cannot restrain
From the excess of laughter. Here he comes.

Enter **Cassio.**

100   As he shall smile, Othello shall go mad;
And his unbookish jealousy must [conster]
Poor Cassio's smiles, gestures, and light behaviors
Quite in the wrong. How do you [now], lieutenant?

Cassio   The worser that you give me the addition
105   Whose want even kills me.

Iago   Ply Desdemona well, and you are sure on't.
[*Speaking lower.*] Now, if this suit lay in Bianca's [pow'r],
How quickly should you speed!

Cassio   Alas, poor caitiff!

and on what occasions he has done it and is again going to sleep with your wife. Listen, just watch how he acts. Indeed, have patience, or I'll think you have no self-control at all and aren't much of a man.

Othello   Hear me, Iago. I will be cunning and have patience but—hear me—I am out for blood.

Iago   There's nothing wrong with that, but wait for the proper time. You'd better go hide now.

[**Othello** *leaves.*]

[**Iago,** *speaking to himself*] Now I'll ask Cassio about Bianca, a slut who sells her sexual favors to buy herself food and clothing. She's wild about Cassio—it's a curse on whores that they drive men wild, yet they themselves can be wild about someone—yet when someone mentions her, Cassio can't stop laughing. [**Iago** *seeing* **Cassio** *approaching, speaks to himself.*] Here he comes. When Cassio smiles, it will drive Othello mad, and his foolish jealousy will completely misinterpret Cassio's smiles, gestures, and lighthearted attitude.
[*to* **Cassio**] How are you now, lieutenant?

Cassio   [*glumly*] It makes me feel even worse when you address me by that title. Not having it just about kills me.

Iago   Keep on working on Desdemona, and you'll be sure to get it back.
[**Iago** *lowers his voice.*] Now, if it were in Bianca's power to help you, you'd get what you want very quickly.

Cassio   [*chuckling and shaking his head ruefully*] Alas, the poor fool.

Act four   Scene 1

Othello   Look how he laughs already!

110 **Iago**   I never knew woman love man so.

Cassio   Alas, poor rogue, I think, [i' faith], she loves me.

Othello   Now he denies it faintly, and laughs it out.

Iago   Do you hear, Cassio?

Othello   Now he importunes him
To tell it o'er. Go to, well said, well said.

Iago   She gives it out that you shall marry her.
116   Do you intend it?

Cassio   Ha, ha, ha!

Othello   Do [you] triumph, Roman? do you triumph?

Cassio   I marry [her]! What? a customer! Prithee
bear some charity to my wit, do not think it so un-
121   wholesome. Ha, ha, ha!

Othello   So, so, so, so; they laugh that wins.

Iago   [Faith], the cry goes that you marry her.

Cassio   Prithee say true.

125 **Iago**   I am a very villain else.

Othello   Have you scor'd me? Well.

Othello   [**Othello**, *watching from a distance, cannot hear what is being said and assumes that* **Iago** *and* **Cassio** *are discussing* **Desdemona**. *He mutters angrily to himself.*]
Look at how he's laughing already!

Iago   I've never known a woman who loved a man so much.

Cassio   [*laughing and shaking his head again*] Alas, poor thing, I think she actually does love me.

Othello   [*continuing throughout the conversation to misinterpret what is being discussed*] Now he's trying to deny it halfheartedly and laughing it off.

Iago   Have you heard, Cassio?

Othello   Now Iago is asking Cassio to tell him again about his affair with Desdemona. [*urging Iago on, although not with the intention of being heard*] Go on, yes, yes.

Iago   She's telling people you're going to marry her. Do you intend to?

Cassio   [*laughs uproariously*] Ha, ha, ha!

Othello   [*to* **Cassio**, *but not with the intention of being heard*] You think you're winning, soldier? You think you're winning?

Cassio   [*breathless from laughter*] Marry her? A prostitute? Please don't insult my intelligence. I'm not that crazy. [*laughing again*] Ha, ha, ha!

Othello   [*furiously*] So, so, so, so. The winner is the one who gets to laugh.

Iago   [*joining* **Cassio** *in laughing uproariously*] No, really, everyone says you're going to marry her.

Cassio   [*still laughing*] You must be joking.

Iago   I'm a liar if it isn't so.

Othello   [*to* **Cassio**, *still not with the intention of being heard*] Do you think you've fooled me? Good.

Cassio   This is the monkey's own giving out. She is
persuaded I will marry her, out of her own love and
flattery, not out of my promise.

Othello   Iago [beckons] me; now he begins the
131   story.

Cassio   She was here even now; she haunts me in
every place. I was the other day talking on the
seabank with certain Venetians, and thither comes
the bauble, and [by this hand,] falls me thus about
136   my neck—

Othello   Crying, "O dear Cassio!" as it were; his
gesture imports it.

Cassio   So hangs, and lolls, and weeps upon me; so
140   [hales] and pulls me. Ha, ha, ha!

Othello   Now he tells how she pluck'd him to my
chamber. O, I see that nose of yours, but not that dog
I shall throw it to.

Cassio   Well, I must leave her company.

145 **Iago**   Before me! look where she comes.

Enter **Bianca**.

Cassio   'Tis such another fitchew! marry, a perfum'd
one!—What do you mean by this haunting of me?

Cassio   This is some busybody's rumor. Bianca believes I'm going to marry her because she has such a high opinion of herself and is so vain—not because I've proposed.

Othello   [*to himself*] Iago is beckoning to me [*to come closer*]. Now Cassio is talking about it.

Cassio   She was here just now. She follows me everywhere. The other day I was down by the seashore talking to some men from Venice, and here comes my little plaything and, I swear it, she throws her arms around my neck, like this . . . [**Cassio** *pantomimes the gesture.*]

Othello   [*still assuming* **Cassio** *is speaking about* **Desdemona**] Crying out, "Oh, dear Cassio!" or something. I can tell by his gestures.

Cassio   She hangs on me, and clings, and weeps all over me, like this. [**Cassio**, *still laughing, pantomimes* **Bianca**'s *actions again.*] Ha, ha, ha!

Othello   [*to himself*] Now he's telling how Desdemona urged him to our bedroom. [*venomously, but not intending to be heard by* **Cassio**] Oh yes, Cassio, I see your nose, but not the dog I'm going to throw it to.

Cassio   Well, I must stop seeing her.

Iago   Look over there. She's coming.

[**Bianca** *enters.*]

Cassio   [*to* **Iago**, *before* **Bianca** *is within earshot*] She's a smelly little polecat [*the polecat, a small mammal of the weasel family, not only has a strong odor but also was believed to be very lascivious*]. She hides it with perfume, of course! [**Cassio** *and* **Iago** *stifle their laughter about* **Bianca** *as she draws near.*]
[*disdainfully, to* **Bianca**] Why do you keep bothering me?

Bianca   Let the devil and his dam haunt you! What
did you mean by that same handkerchief you gave me
150   even now? I was a fine fool to take it. I must take
out the work? A likely piece of work, that you should
find it in your chamber, and know not who left it
there! This is some minx's token, and I must take out
the work? There, give it your hobby-horse. Where-
155   soever you had it, I'll take out no work on't.

Cassio   How now, my sweet Bianca? how now? how
now?

Othello   By heaven, that should be my handkerchief!

Bianca   [An'] you'll come to supper to-night, you
may; [an'] you will not, come when you are next pre-
161   par'd for.

Exit.

Iago   After her, after her.

Cassio   [Faith,] I must, she'll rail in the streets clse.

Iago   Will you sup there?

165   **Cassio**   [Faith], I intend so.

Iago   Well, I may chance to see you; for I would
very fain speak with you.

Cassio   Prithee come; will you?

Iago   Go to; say no more.

[Exit Cassio.]

Othello   [*Advancing.*] How shall I murther him, Iago?

Iago   Did you perceive how he laugh'd at his vice?

Bianca   [*furiously*] May the devil and his wife bother you! Why did you give me that handkerchief just now? I was a big fool to accept it. I should copy the pattern for you? A likely story that you found it in your room and don't know who left it there. This is some other woman's gift, and you want me to copy it? There, give it to your tramp. [*She flings the handkerchief at him.*] Wherever you got it, I'm not going to copy it for you.

Cassio   [*relenting*] What's the matter, sweetheart? What's wrong? What's wrong? [**Cassio** *hugs and kisses her.*]

Othello   My God, that's my handkerchief!

Bianca   [*responding to* **Cassio**'s *lovemaking*] If you want to come to dinner tonight, you may. If you can't come tonight, come as soon as you can.

   [**Bianca** *leaves.*]

Iago   [*continuing to laugh*] Follow her, follow her!

Cassio   Honestly, I'd better, or she'll be shouting in the streets about our "love."

Iago   Are you going there for dinner?

Cassio   [*shrugging and grinning ruefully*] Honestly, I do intend to.

Iago   Well, maybe I'll see you there. I very much want to talk to you.

Cassio   Please come. Will you?

Iago   [*shrugging and sending* **Cassio** *on his way*] Go ahead. Don't say anything.

   [**Cassio** *leaves.*]

Othello   [*comes out of hiding*] How shall I murder him, Iago?

Iago   [*feigning indignation*] Did you see how he laughed at his lechery?

172 **Othello**   O Iago!

Iago   And did you see the handkerchief?

Othello   Was that mine?

Iago   Yours, by this hand. And to see how he
prizes the foolish woman your wife! She gave it him,
177   and he hath giv'n it his whore.

Othello   I would have him nine years a-killing. A fine
woman! a fair woman! a sweet woman!

180 **Iago**   Nay, you must forget that.

Othello   Ay, let her rot, and perish, and be damn'd to-
night, for she shall not live. No, my heart is turn'd to
stone; I strike it, and it hurts my hand. O, the world
hath not a sweeter creature! she might lie by an
185   emperor's side and command him tasks.

Iago   Nay, that's not your way.

Othello   Hang her, I do but say what she is. So delicate with her needle! an admirable musician! O, she
will sing the savageness out of a bear. Of so high and
190   plenteous wit and invention!

Iago   She's the worse for all this.

Othello   O, a thousand, a thousand times. And then
of so gentle a condition!

194 **Iago**   Ay, too gentle.

Othello   Nay, that's certain. But yet the pity of it,
Iago! O Iago, the pity of it, Iago!

Iago   If you are so fond over her iniquity, give her
patent to offend, for if it touch not you, it comes near
nobody.

Othello   I will chop her into messes. Cuckold me!

Othello   [*in anguish*] Oh, Iago!

Iago   Did you see the handkerchief?

Othello   Was it mine?

Iago   Yours, I swear it. And to see how little he values your wife! She gave it to him, and he has given it to his whore.

Othello   [*venomously*] I'd like to take nine years to kill him. Desdemona is a wonderful woman! A beautiful woman! A sweet woman!

Iago   No, you mustn't think about that.

Othello   Yes, let her rot and die and be damned tonight, for she shall not live. No, my heart is turned to stone. When I strike it, it hurts my hand. [**Othello** *momentarily softens toward* **Desdemona**.] Oh, there isn't a sweeter creature in the world! She is worthy to lie beside an emperor and order him about.

Iago   No, don't dwell on that.

Othello   Hang her, I'm just saying what she is. So skilled in needlework! A wonderful musician! Oh, she could calm the savage bear with her singing. So intelligent and witty and clever!

Iago   Which only makes her worse.

Othello   Oh yes, a million times worse. And then so nobly born and bred.

Iago   She's too generous with her favors.

Othello   No, that's true. But what a shame, Iago! Oh Iago, what a shame, Iago!

Iago   [*shrugging*] If you love her so much that her sin is all right with you, let her keep on cheating on you, for, if it doesn't bother you, then no one else is affected by it.

Othello   I'll chop her to bits! Cheat on me!

201 **Iago**   O, 'tis foul in her.

Othello   With mine officer!

Iago   That's fouler.

Othello   Get me some poison, Iago, this night. I'll not
205   expostulate with her, lest her body and beauty
unprovide my mind again. This night, Iago.

Iago   Do it not with poison; strangle her in her bed,
even the bed she hath contaminated.

Othello   Good, good; the justice of it pleases; very
210   good.

Iago   And for Cassio, let me be his undertaker.
You shall hear more by midnight.

Othello   Excellent good. [*A trumpet.*] What trumpet
is that same?

Iago   I warrant, something from Venice.

Enter **Lodovico**, **Desdemona**, *and* **Attendants.**

214   'Tis Lodovico—
This comes from the Duke. See, your wife's with him.

Lodovico   [God] save you, worthy general!

Othello   With all my heart, sir.

Lodovico   The Duke and the senators of Venice greet you.

                                    [*Gives him a letter.*]

Othello   I kiss the instrument of their pleasures.

                                    [*Opens the letter and reads.*]

Desdemona   And what's the news, good cousin Lodovico?

Iago   Oh, she's disgusting.

Othello   With my own officer!

Iago   Even worse.

Othello   Get some poison for me tonight, Iago. I won't try to confront her with it, or her great beauty will weaken my will again. Tonight, Iago.

Iago   Don't use poison. Strangle her in her bed, the very one she has polluted.

Othello   Good, good. I like the justice of it.

Iago   And as for Cassio, let me be his undertaker [*that is, his murderer*]. You'll hear more about this from me by midnight.

Othello   Very good.
[*A trumpet sounds in the distance.*] What is that trumpet about?

Iago   Some news from Venice, I suppose.

[**Lodovico, Desdemona,** *and* **Attendants** *enter.*]

It's Lodovico. This message must be from the Duke. See, your wife is with him.

Lodovico   [*to* **Othello**] God save you, worthy general!

Othello   With all my heart, sir.

Lodovico   The Duke and the senators of Venice greet you.

Othello   I kiss the message they send. [*He opens the letter and reads it.*]

Desdemona   And what is the news, good cousin Lodovico?

220 **Iago**   I am very glad to see you, signior;
     Welcome to Cyprus.

    Lodovico   I thank you. How does Lieutenant Cassio?

    Iago   Lives, sir.

    Desdemona   Cousin, there's fall'n between him and my
       lord
225 An unkind breach; but you shall make all well.

    Othello   Are you sure of that?

    Desdemona   My lord?

    Othello   [*Reads.*] "This fail you not to do, as you
     will—"

230 **Lodovico**   He did not call; he's busy in the paper.
     Is there division 'twixt my lord and Cassio?

    Desdemona   A most unhappy one. I would do much
     T' atone them, for the love I bear to Cassio.

    Othello   Fire and brimstone!

    Desdemona   My lord?

234 **Othello**   Are you wise?

    Desdemona   What, is he angry?

    Lodovico   May be th' letter mov'd him;
     For as I think, they do command him home,
     Deputing Cassio in his government.

    Desdemona   [By my troth], I am glad on't.

    Othello   Indeed?

    Desdemona   My lord?

    Othello   I am glad to see you mad.

    Desdemona   Why, sweet Othello?

240 **Othello**   [*Striking her.*] Devil!

Iago   [*to* **Lodovico**] I'm very glad to see you again, signior. Welcome to Cyprus.

Lodovico   I thank you. How is Lieutenant Cassio?

Iago   He's well, sir.

Desdemona   Cousin Lodovico, there is a problem between him and my husband, but you can patch things up.

Othello   [*menacingly*] Are you sure about that?

Desdemona   [*confused at his tone*] My lord?

Othello   [*reads message aloud*] "Do not fail to do this, as you will . . ."

Lodovico   [*to* **Desdemona**] Othello didn't answer; he's busy with the letter. Is there a problem between Othello and Cassio?

Desdemona   A serious one. I want to do whatever I can because of the love [*that is, friendship*] I have for Cassio.

Othello   [*overhearing and misinterpreting* **Desdemona**'s *meaning, says furiously*] Fire and brimstone!

Desdemona   My lord?

Othello   [*with barely controlled anger*] Are you wise?

Desdemona   [*to* **Lodovico**] What, is Othello angry?

Lodovico   Perhaps the letter upset him. I think they're ordering him to return home and appointing Cassio as his replacement.

Desdemona   [*with genuine pleasure*] I'm very glad to hear it.

Othello   Really?

Desdemona   [*surprised at* **Othello**'s *blatant hostility*] My lord?

Othello   [*sarcastically*] I'm glad to see you've lost your mind.

Desdemona   Why do you say that, sweet Othello?

Othello   [*He hits her.*] Devil!

Desdemona   I have not deserv'd this.

Lodovico   My lord, this would not be believ'd in Venice,
Though I should swear I saw't. 'Tis very much,
Make her amends; she weeps.

Othello   O devil, devil!
245 If that the earth could teem with woman's tears,
Each drop she falls would prove a crocodile.
Out of my sight!

Desdemona   I will not stay to offend you.

[*Going.*]

Lodovico   Truly, [an] obedient lady:
249 I do beseech your lordship call her back.

Othello   Mistress!

Desdemona   My lord?

Othello   What would you with her, sir?

Lodovico   Who, I, my lord?

Othello   Ay, you did wish that I would make her turn.
Sir, she can turn, and turn; and yet go on
And turn again; and she can weep, sir, weep;
255 And she's obedient, as you say, obedient;
Very obedient.—Proceed you in your tears.—
Concerning this, sir—O well-painted passion!—
I am commanded home.—Get you away;
I'll send for you anon.—Sir, I obey the mandate,
260 And will return to Venice.—Hence, avaunt!

[*Exit Desdemona.*]

Desdemona   [*greatly shocked and upset*] I didn't deserve that.

Lodovico   [*aghast, to* **Othello**] My lord, no one in Venice will believe this happened even if I swear I saw it myself. You have overreacted. Apologize to her. She is crying.

Othello   [*furiously, to* **Desdemona**] Devil, devil! If the earth were flooded with a woman's tears, every drop that falls would be as insincere as crocodile tears. Get out of my sight!

Desdemona   [*still weeping*] I will leave before I offend you further. [*She starts to leave.*]

Lodovico   Honestly, she's an obedient lady. I beg you to call her back, my lord.

Othello   [*calls to* **Desdemona**] Mistress!

Desdemona   [*pausing*] My lord?

Othello   [*to* **Lodovico**] What would you do with her, sir?

Lodovico   Who? I, my lord?

Othello   Yes, you wanted me have her turn around. [*with bitter sarcasm*] Sir, she can turn around and turn around, and still go on and turn again. And she can cry and cry, sir. And she's obedient, just as you say, oh yes, very obedient.
[*nastily, to* **Desdemona**] Go on with your tears.
[*to* **Lodovico** *while deliberately ignoring* **Desdemona**]
Concerning this matter, sir . . .
[*sarcastically, to* **Desdemona** *as she stands weeping*] Such a convincing imitation of sorrow!
[*to* **Lodovico**] I am ordered to return home.
[*to* **Desdemona**] Go away. I'll send for you soon.
[*to* **Lodovico**] Sir, I will obey the command and return to Venice.
[*to* **Desdemona**] Go on, get out of here!

[**Desdemona** *leaves, still weeping.*]

Cassio shall have my place. And, sir, to-night
I do entreat that we may sup together.
You are welcome, sir, to Cyprus.—Goats and monkeys!

Exit.

Lodovico   Is this the noble Moor whom our full Senate
265   Call all in all sufficient? Is this the nature
Whom passion could not shake? whose solid virtue
The shot of accident nor dart of chance
Could neither graze nor pierce?

Iago   He is much chang'd.

Lodovico   Are his wits safe? Is he not light of brain?

Iago   He's that he is; I may not breathe my censure
271   What he might be. If what he might he is not,
I would to heaven he were!

Lodovico   What? strike his wife?

Iago   Faith, that was not so well; yet would I knew
That stroke would prove the worst!

Lodovico   Is it his use?
275   Or did the letters work upon his blood,
And new-create [this] fault?

Iago   Alas, alas!
It is not honesty in me to speak
What I have seen and known. You shall observe him,
And his own courses will denote him so
280   That I may save my speech. Do but go after,
And mark how he continues.

Lodovico   I am sorry that I am deceiv'd in him.

Exeunt.

[*to* **Lodovico**] Cassio shall take over my command here. And, sir, please come to dinner this evening. I welcome you to Cyprus, sir. [*to himself*] Mating like goats and monkeys!

[**Othello** *leaves.*]

Lodovico   [*to* **Iago**, *in shocked disapproval*] Can this be the noble Moor whom our senate considers to be so immeasurably able? Is he the one with such self-control? The one whose strong character is unfazed by the unexpected or by extraordinary events?

Iago   He has changed a great deal.

Lodovico   Is he in his right mind? Is he having a nervous breakdown?

Iago   [*shrugging*] He is what he is. I can't criticize what he's like. If he isn't a little strange mentally, I wish that he were!

Lodovico   What? Like his hitting his wife?

Iago   [*pretending to be worried*] Really, that wasn't good. Still, I wish I knew that he isn't going to do something worse to her.

Lodovico   Is this how he usually behaves? Or did the letters that just arrived upset him and make him act like this for the first time?

Iago   [*pretending to be torn between his duty to the state and his loyalty to* **Othello**] Alas, alas! It would be wrong for me to reveal what I have seen and know about. You will be able to observe him, and his own actions will show you what he's like better than I could tell you. Follow him and watch how he acts.

Lodovico   [*shaking his head regretfully*] I am sorry to see that I've been mistaken about him.

[*They leave.*]

Scene 2

*Enter **Othello** and **Emilia**.*

Othello   You have seen nothing then?

Emilia   Nor ever heard—nor ever did suspect.

Othello   Yes, you have seen Cassio and she together.

Emilia   But then I saw no harm, and then I heard
5   Each syllable that breath made up between them.

Othello   What? did they never whisper?

Emilia   Never, my lord.

Othello   Nor send you out o' th' way?

Emilia   Never.

Othello   To fetch her fan, her gloves, her mask, nor nothing?

10 **Emilia**   Never, my lord.

Othello   That's strange.

Emilia   I durst, my lord, to wager she is honest;
Lay down my soul at stake. If you think other,
Remove your thought; it doth abuse your bosom.
15   If any wretch have put this in your head,
Let heaven requite it with the serpent's curse!
For if she be not honest, chaste, and true,
There's no man happy; the purest of their wives
Is foul as slander.

Othello   Bid her come hither; go.

Exit Emilia.

Scene 2

A room in the castle a short time later.

[**Othello** *and* **Emilia** *enter.*]

Othello   You haven't seen anything then?

Emilia   No, and I haven't ever heard anything . . . or ever suspected it.

Othello   [*insistently*] Yes, you have seen Cassio and her together.

Emilia   But I didn't see them do anything wrong, and I've heard every single syllable they've said to one another.

Othello   [*incredulously*] What? They've never whispered?

Emilia   Never, my lord.

Othello   Nor sent you away?

Emilia   Never.

Othello   Not even to get her fan, her gloves, her mask, or anything?

Emilia   Never, my lord.

Othello   [*puzzled and frustrated*] That's strange.

Emilia   I would swear, my lord, that she is faithful to you. I'd stake my life on it. If you believe anything else, put it out of your mind. It's a wrong notion to have in your heart. If some wicked person put this idea into your head, may heaven curse him. If she isn't faithful, pure, and loyal, there is no man alive who can be secure because even the purest wife is as corrupt as a slanderous lie.

Othello   Tell her to come here.

[**Othello** *is momentarily somewhat shaken about his convictions of Desdemona's infidelity. His suspicions quickly reassert themselves, however.*]

20   She says enough; yet she's a simple bawd
      That cannot say as much. This is a subtile whore,
      A closet lock and key of villainous secrets;
      And yet she'll kneel and pray; I have seen her do't.

      Enter **Desdemona** *and* **Emilia**.

      Desdemona   My lord, what is your will?

      Othello   Pray you, chuck, come hither.

      Desdemona   What is your pleasure?

      Othello   Let me see your eyes;
      Look in my face.

26   **Desdemona**   What horrible fancy's this?

      Othello   [*To Emilia.*] Some of your function, mistress;
      Leave procreants alone, and shut the door;
      Cough, or cry "hem," if anybody come.
30   Your mystery, your mystery; [nay], dispatch.

                                          Exit Emilia.

      Desdemona   Upon my knee, what doth your speech import?
      I understand a fury in your words,
      [But not the words].

      Othello   Why? what art thou?

      Desdemona   Your wife, my lord; your true
      And loyal wife.

35   **Othello**   Come swear it, damn thyself,
      Lest being like one of heaven, the devils themselves
      Should fear to seize thee; therefore be double damn'd:
      Swear thou art honest.

      Desdemona   Heaven doth truly know it.

She defends Desdemona. Still, even a very stupid servant is smart enough to say what Emilia says. Emilia's a devious slut, concealing terrible secrets. Yet she still can kneel and pray. I've seen her do it.

[**Desdemona** *and* **Emilia** *enter.*]

Desdemona   What is it that you want, my lord?

Othello   Please come here, dear.

Desdemona   What can I do for you?

Othello   Let me see your eyes. Look me in the face.

Desdemona   [*apprehensively*] What horrible notion is this?

Othello   [*harshly, to* **Emilia**] Go about your business, woman. Leave us "lovers" [*He says the word "lovers" sarcastically.*] alone and shut the door. Cough or say "ahem" if anyone comes. See to your duties. [**Emilia** *hesitates, reluctant to leave* **Desdemona** *alone with* **Othello**.] No, go on.

[**Emilia** *leaves reluctantly.*]

Desdemona   [*desperately*] I'm begging you to tell me what you are talking about. I can tell you are furious, but I don't understand what you are saying.

Othello   Why? What are you?

Desdemona   Your wife, my lord. Your honest and faithful wife.

Othello   [*furiously*] Go on, swear that you are faithful and damn yourself, rather than have the demons be afraid to come for you because you look like an angel. So be damned twice over; swear you are faithful to me.

Desdemona   [*pleadingly*] Heaven knows it is true.

Othello   Heaven truly knows that thou art false as hell.

Desdemona   To whom, my lord? With whom? How am
40   I false?

Othello   Ah, Desdemon! Away, away, away!

Desdemona   Alas the heavy day! Why do you weep?
Am I the motive of these tears, my lord?
If happily you my father do suspect
45   An instrument of this your calling back,
Lay not your blame on me. If you have lost him,
[Why,] I have lost him too.

Othello   Had it pleas'd heaven
To try me with affliction, had they rain'd
All kind of sores and shames on my bare head,
50   Steep'd me in poverty to the very lips,
Given to captivity me and my utmost hopes,
I should have found in some place of my soul
A drop of patience; but, alas, to make me
The fixed figure for the time of scorn
55   To point his slow [unmoving] finger at!
Yet could I bear that too, well, very well;
But there, where I have garner'd up my heart,
Where either I must live or bear no life;
The fountain from the which my current runs
60   Or else dries up: to be discarded thence!
Or keep it as a cestern for foul toads
To knot and gender in! Turn thy complexion there,
Patience, thou young and rose-lipp'd cherubin—
Ay, here look grim as hell!

65 **Desdemona**   I hope my noble lord esteems me honest.

Othello   O ay, as summer flies are in the shambles,
That quicken even with blowing. O thou weed!

Othello   [*thunderously*] Heaven really knows you're as false as hell.

Desdemona   [*desperately*] To whom, my lord? With whom? How have I been untrue to you?

Othello   [*groaning and weeping*] Ah, Desdemona, go away, go away, go away!

Desdemona   Alas, what a grievous day! Why are you weeping? Am I the cause of your tears, my lord? If you perhaps suspect that it's my father who has had you called back to Venice, don't put the blame on me. If you have lost his good will, why, I have lost it, too.

Othello   If heaven had poured out great troubles on me, rained all kinds of evils and humiliations on my head, sunk me deep in poverty, put me and my best hopes in captivity, I would have been able to find some small drop of patience to endure it all, but, oh, to make me a spectacle of unceasing humiliation! Yet I could stand that too—yes, very well in fact, but there where I have hidden my heart, where I must either live or die, from the very source of my life, to have it thrown away! Or to have it be a filthy breeding ground for loathsome toads to mate and reproduce in! Let my patience, as pure as an angel, look upon that . . . Yes, and look as grim as hell!

Desdemona   [*pleadingly*] I hope my husband knows that I am faithful.

Othello   [*sarcastically*] Oh yes, as faithful as summer flies in a slum, that hatch as soon as the eggs are laid. Oh, you weed!

Who art so lovely fair and smell'st so sweet
That the sense aches at thee, would thou hadst never
69   been born!

Desdemona   Alas, what ignorant sin have I committed?

Othello   Was this fair paper, this most goodly book,
Made to write "whore" upon? What committed?
Committed? O thou public commoner,
I should make very forges of my cheeks,
75   That would to cinders burn up modesty,
Did I but speak thy deeds. What committed?
Heaven stops the nose at it, and the moon winks;
The bawdy wind, that kisses all it meets,
Is hush'd within the hollow mine of earth
80   And will not hear't. What committed?
[Impudent strumpet!]

Desdemona   By heaven, you do me wrong.

Othello   Are not you a strumpet?

Desdemona   No, as I am a Christian.
If to preserve this vessel for my lord
From any other foul unlawful touch
85   Be not to be a strumpet, I am none.

Othello   What, not a whore?

Desdemona   No, as I shall be sav'd.

Othello   Is't possible?

Desdemona   O, heaven forgive us!

Othello   I cry you mercy then.
I took you for that cunning whore of Venice
90   That married with Othello.—[*Raising his voice.*] You, mistress,

Enter **Emilia**.

You are so very beautiful and smell so sweet that the sense aches at being near you. [*harshly*] I wish you'd never been born!

Desdemona   [*desperately*] What sin have I committed without knowing it?

Othello   [*taking her chin in his hand*] Was this beautiful paper [*that is, her face*], this magnificent book made to write "whore" on? [**Othello** *abruptly releases her chin, speaking in fury and despair.*] What sin have you committed? What sin? Oh, you slut, if I were to speak about what you've done, my cheeks would burn with embarrassment. What sin? Heaven holds its nose at the stench and the moon closes its eyes. The lusty wind that kisses everyone it meets is silenced in the depths of the earth and refuses to hear about it. What sin? Shameless whore!

Desdemona   By heaven, you wrong me!

Othello   You aren't a whore?

Desdemona   No, I swear it as a Christian. If reserving my body for my husband only, permitting no one to touch me illicitly means not being a whore, then I am not one.

Othello   Is this possible?

Desdemona   Oh, heaven forgive us!

Othello   [*profoundly sarcastic*] I beg your pardon, then. I mistook you for that devious whore of Venice who is married to Othello.
[**Othello** *calls out to* **Emilia** *who is just outside the door.*]
You! Woman [**Emilia** *enters the room.*]
who has the very opposite job to Saint Peter's and keeps the gates of hell! [**Emilia** *looks puzzled at what* **Othello** *is saying.*]

> That have the office opposite to Saint Peter,
> And keeps the gate of hell! You, you! ay, you!
> We have done our course; there's money for your pains.
> I pray you turn the key and keep our counsel.

Exit.

Emilia   Alas, what does this gentleman conceive?
96   How do you, madam? how do you, my good lady?

Desdemona   Faith, half asleep.

Emilia   Good madam, what's the matter with my lord?

Desdemona   With who?

100 **Emilia**   Why, with my lord, madam.

Desdemona   Who is thy lord?

Emilia   He that is yours, sweet lady.

Desdemona   I have none. Do not talk to me, Emilia;
I cannot weep, nor answers have I none
But what should go by water. Prithee to-night
105 Lay on my bed my wedding-sheets—remember;
And call thy husband hither.

Emilia   Here's a change indeed!

Exit.

Desdemona   'Tis meet I should be us'd so, very meet.
How have I been behav'd, that he might stick
The small'st opinion on my least misuse?

Enter **Iago** *and* **Emilia**.

You, you! Yes, you! We're finished here. Here's payment for your services. [**Othello** *flings several coins at her.*] Lock the door and keep quiet about this.

[**Othello** *leaves.*]

Emilia   [*appalled at what has happened*] Alas, what does your husband have in his mind? How are you, madam? [**Desdemona** *does not answer immediately, so* **Emilia** *repeats herself.*] How are you, my good lady?

Desdemona   [*trying to pretend nothing is wrong*] Half asleep.

Emilia   Dear lady, what is the matter with my lord [*that is, with Othello*]?

Desdemona   [*sadly*] With whom?

Emilia   Why, with my lord, madam.

Desdemona   Who is your lord?

Emilia   Your husband, sweet lady.

Desdemona   I have no husband. Don't talk to me, Emilia. I cannot weep nor find answers except those that would bring on my tears. Put my wedding sheets on my bed tonight, please. Don't forget. And ask your husband to come here.

Emilia   This is a strange request, indeed.

[**Emilia** *leaves.*]

Desdemona   It's right that I should be treated in such a way, very right. What have I done, that he should find fault with even the smallest thing I do wrong?

[**Emilia** *and* **Iago** *enter.*]

110 **Iago**   What is your pleasure, madam? How is't with you?

Desdemona   I cannot tell. Those that do teach young babes
Do it with gentle means and easy tasks.
He might have chid me so; for in good faith
I am a child to chiding.

Iago   What is the matter, lady?

Emilia   Alas, Iago, my lord hath so bewhor'd her,
116 Thrown such despite and heavy terms upon her,
That true hearts cannot bear it.

Desdemona   Am I that name, Iago?

Iago   What name, fair lady?

Desdemona   Such as she said my lord did say I was.

Emilia   He call'd her whore. A beggar in his drink
121 Could not have laid such terms upon his callet.

Iago   Why did he so?

Desdemona   I do not know; I am sure I am none such.

Iago   Do not weep, do not weep. Alas the day!

Emilia   Hath she forsook so many noble matches?
126 Her father? and her country? and her friends?
To be call'd whore? Would it not make one weep?

Desdemona   It is my wretched fortune.

Iago   Beshrew him for't!
How comes this trick upon him?

Desdemona   Nay, heaven doth know.

130 **Emilia**   I will be hang'd if some eternal villain,
Some busy and insinuating rogue,
Some cogging, cozening slave, to get some office,
Have not devis'd this slander. I will be hang'd else.

Iago   What can I do for you, madam? How is everything?

Desdemona   I don't know. Those who teach young babies do it gently and give them easy things to do. He could have corrected me in that manner, because, truly, I am as teachable as a child.

Iago   [*with false sympathy*] What is the matter, lady?

Emilia   Alas, Iago, Othello has accused her of being a whore, heaped such contempt and insults upon her that loyal hearts can't bear it.

Desdemona   Do I deserve to be called that, Iago?

Iago   Called what, dear lady?

Desdemona   [*unable even to speak the word "whore"*] The thing my husband said I was.

Emilia   [*indignantly*] He called her a whore. Even a drunken beggar wouldn't have called his slut such names.

Iago   Why did he do it?

Desdemona   I don't know. I do know that I'm not one.

Iago   Don't cry, don't cry. Alas, what a terrible day!

Emilia   Has she given up all those chances to marry well? Left behind her father? Her country? And her friends? To be called a whore? Doesn't it make you want to cry?

Desdemona   It's my wretched fate.

Iago   [*feigning indignation*] Damn him for it! What has made him act so strangely?

Desdemona   Heaven knows—I don't.

Emilia   I'll bet some detestable villain, some meddling rascal who wants to get on Othello's good side, some cheating, lying wretch has made up this slander in order to get a promotion. I'll bet that's it.

Iago   Fie, there is no such man; it is impossible.

135 **Desdemona**   If any such there be, heaven pardon him!

Emilia   A halter pardon him! and hell gnaw his bones!
Why should he call her whore? Who keeps her company?
What place? what time? what form? what likelihood?
The Moor's abus'd by some most villainous knave,
140   Some base notorious knave, some scurvy fellow.
O [heaven], that such companions thou'dst unfold,
And put in every honest hand a whip
To lash the rascals naked through the world
Even from the east to th' west!

Iago   Speak within door.

Emilia   O fie upon them! Some such squire he was
146   That turn'd your wit the seamy side without,
And made you to suspect me with the Moor.

Iago   You are a fool; go to.

Desdemona   Alas, Iago,
What shall I do to win my lord again?
Good friend, go to him; for by this light of heaven,
151   I know not how I lost him. Here I kneel:
If e'er my will did trespass 'gainst his love,
Either in discourse of thought or actual deed,
Or that mine eyes, mine ears, or any sense
Delighted them [in] any other form;
155   Or that I do not yet, and ever did,
And ever will (though he do shake me off
To beggarly divorcement) love him dearly,
Comfort forswear me! Unkindness may do much,
And his unkindness may defeat my life,
160   But never taint my love. I cannot say "whore."
It does abhor me now I speak the word;
To do the act that might the addition earn,
Not the world's mass of vanity could make me.

Iago   Bah! There's no one like that. It's impossible.

Desdemona   If there is such a man, may heaven forgive him.

Emilia   [*furiously*] Let a hangman's noose forgive him! And let the demons of hell gnaw his bones! Why should he call her a whore? Who comes to see her? Where? When? How? What is the evidence? The Moor has been deceived by some wicked scoundrel, some low miserable scoundrel, some contemptible fellow. Oh heaven, expose such men and give every honest hand a whip to beat the rascals naked across the entire world, from the east to the west.

Iago   Keep your voice down.

Emilia   [*refusing to quiet down*] Oh, shame on them! It must have been just such a person that turned your mind inside out and made you suspect I'd slept with the Moor.

Iago   You're a fool. Stop it.

Desdemona   Alas, Iago, what can I do to regain my husband's favor? Good friend, go to him, for I swear by the sun in the heavens that I don't know how I lost him. I swear on my knees that I never did anything either in my thoughts or my actions to betray his love. Neither my eyes, my ears, or any of my senses have ever taken pleasure in anyone else. If ever, either now or in the past or in the future—even if he divorces me and leaves me a beggar—I stop loving him dearly, may happiness abandon me. Unkindness may do a great deal, and his unkindness may destroy my life, but it cannot affect my love. I cannot even say the word "whore." It revolts me to even speak the word. Nothing in the entire world could make me do that which would earn me the name.

Iago   I pray you be content; 'tis but his humor.
166   The business of the state does him offense,
[And he does chide with you].

Desdemona   If 'twere no other—

Iago   It is but so, I warrant.

[*Trumpets within.*]

Hark how these instruments summon to supper!
170   The messengers of Venice stays the meat.
Go in, and weep not; all things shall be well.

Exeunt Desdemona and Emilia.

Enter **Roderigo.**

How now, Roderigo?

Roderigo   I do not find that thou deal'st justly with me.

174   **Iago**   What in the contrary?

Roderigo   Every day thou daff'st me with some device,
Iago, and rather, as it seems to me now, keep'st from
me all conveniency than suppliest me with the least
advantage of hope. I will indeed no longer endure it;
nor am I yet persuaded to put up in peace what already
180   I have foolishly suff'red.

Iago   Will you hear me, Roderigo?

Roderigo   [Faith,] I have heard too much; [for] your
words and performances are no kin together.

184   **Iago**   You charge me most unjustly.

Roderigo   With nought but truth. I have wasted myself
out of my means. The jewels you have had from me to
deliver Desdemona would half have corrupted a votar-
ist. You have told me she hath receiv'd them and

Iago   Please calm down. It's only a passing mood. The affairs of state have upset him, and he is taking it out on you.

Desdemona   If only it were nothing more . . .

Iago   That's all it is, I'm sure.

[*Trumpets sound offstage.*]

Listen, these trumpets summon us to dinner. The messengers from Venice are waiting to dine. Go along to dinner and don't cry. Everything will be all right.

[**Desdemona** *and* **Emilia** *leave*]

[**Roderigo** *enters.*]

How is everything, Roderigo?

Roderigo   [*sulkily*] I think you've been cheating me.

Iago   [*pretending to be greatly surprised*] In what way?

Roderigo   Every day you put me off with some excuse, Iago, and, as it seems to me, you keep me away from Desdemona rather than arranging any meeting that could further my hopes. In fact, I won't put up with it any longer, nor am I convinced that I should keep silent about what I've already been put through at your hands.

Iago   [*cajolingly*] Will you listen to me, Roderigo?

Roderigo   Indeed, I've listened to you too much, for what you say and what you do are two different things.

Iago   You accuse me very unjustly.

Roderigo   With nothing but the truth. I've wasted my money until I've none left. The jewels I've given you to take to Desdemona would just about have corrupted a nun. You've told me she received them and sent me messages to give me

return'd me expectations and comforts of sudden
190   respect and acquaintance, but I find none.

Iago   Well, go to; very well.

Roderigo   Very well! go to! I cannot go to, man, nor
'tis not very well. [By this hand,] I think it is scurvy,
and begin to find myself fopp'd in it.

195 **Iago**   Very well.

Roderigo   I tell you 'tis not very well. I will make
myself known to Desdemona. If she will return me my
jewels, I will give over my suit and repent my unlawful
solicitation; if not, assure yourself I will seek satis-
200   faction of you.

Iago   You have said now.

Roderigo   Ay; and said nothing but what I protest
intendment of doing.

Iago   Why, now I see there's mettle in thee, and
205   even from this instant do build on thee a better
opinion than ever before. Give me thy hand, Roderigo.
Thou hast taken against me a most just exception; but
yet I protest I have dealt most directly in thy affair.

209 **Roderigo**   It hath not appear'd.

Iago   I grant indeed it hath not appear'd; and your
suspicion is not without wit and judgment. But,
Roderigo, if thou hast that in thee indeed, which I have
greater reason to believe now than ever (I mean
purpose, courage, and valor), this night show it. If thou
the next night following enjoy not Desdemona, take
me from this world with treachery and devise engines
217   for my life.

Roderigo   Well; what is it? Is it within reason and
compass?

Iago   Sir, there is especial commission come from
221   Venice to depute Cassio in Othello's place.

hope and encouragement of a more intimate relationship, but nothing has changed.

Iago   Well, go ahead. Very well.

Roderigo   [*incredulously*] Very well! Go ahead! I can't go ahead, man, and it's not very well. I swear I think it's a rotten deal, and I'm beginning to think I've been tricked.

Iago   Very well.

Roderigo   I tell you it's not very well! I'm going to introduce myself to Desdemona. If she'll give me back my jewels, I'll give up my plans and repent my attempts to seduce her. If not, you may be sure I'll come looking for you.

Iago   Whatever you say.

Roderigo   Yes, and I've said nothing but what I fully intend to do.

Iago   [*pretending admiration*] Why, I see now that you have courage, and from this moment forward I will have a higher opinion of you. Let me shake your hand, Roderigo. [**Iago** *shakes* **Roderigo**'s *hand;* **Roderigo** *looks confused, but tentatively pleased.*] You have every reason to be upset with me, but still I protest that I have done exactly as I said I would do about this affair.

Roderigo   There's no evidence of it.

Iago   I admit there is no evidence, and you aren't unjustified in your suspicions. But, Roderigo, if you do indeed have in you the determination, courage, and bravery which I now have greater proof of than ever, demonstrate it tonight. If you aren't enjoying Desdemona the following night, use whatever treacherous or clever schemes you can think of to kill me.

Roderigo   Well, what is it? Is it something reasonable and possible?

Iago   Sir, there is a special order that has come from Venice making Cassio Othello's replacement here.

Roderigo Is that true? Why then Othello and
Desdemona return again to Venice.

Iago O no; he goes into Mauritania and taketh
225 away with him the fair Desdemona, unless his
abode be ling'red here by some accident; wherein none
can be so determinate as the removing of Cassio.

Roderigo How do you mean, removing him?

Iago Why, by making him uncapable of Othello's
230 place: knocking out his brains.

Roderigo And that you would have me to do?

Iago Ay; if you dare do yourself a profit and a
right. He sups to-night with a harlotry, and thither
will I go to him—he knows not yet of his honorable
235 fortune. If you will watch his going thence
(which I will fashion to fall out between twelve and
one), you may take him at your pleasure. I will be
near to second your attempt, and he shall fall between
us. Come, stand not amaz'd at it, but go along with
240 me; I will show you such a necessity in his death
that you shall think yourself bound to put it on him.
It is now high supper-time, and the night grows to
waste. About it.

Roderigo I will hear further reason for this.

245 **Iago** And you shall be satisfied.

Exeunt.

Scene 3

Enter **Othello**, **Lodovico**, **Desdemona**, **Emilia**, *and*
Attendants.

Lodovico I do beseech you, sir, trouble yourself no further.

Othello O, pardon me; 'twill do me good to walk.

Roderigo Is that true? Why then Othello and Desdemona will return to Venice.

Iago Oh, no. He is going to Mauritania and taking the beautiful Desdemona there with him unless his stay is prolonged by some unexpected event. And nothing could be so effective at detaining them than getting Cassio out of the way.

Roderigo What do you mean, "getting Cassio out of the way"?

Iago Why, by making him unable to take over for Othello. [**Roderigo** *looks puzzled, so* **Iago** *explains.*] By knocking out his brains.

Roderigo And you want me to do that?

Iago Yes, if you have the guts to do something to get yourself that which you deserve. He's having dinner tonight with a whore, and I'm going there to see him. He doesn't know about his good luck yet. If you'll watch for when he leaves—I'll see that it occurs between twelve and one—you can do what you want to him. I'll be nearby to help you out, and between us, we'll do him in. Come, don't look so shocked. Come with me, and I'll show you such a reason for killing him that you'll feel you ought to do it. It's nearly time for dinner now, and the night is being wasted. Come on.

Roderigo I want to hear more reasons for doing this.

Iago And you will be convinced.

[*They leave.*]

Scene 3

Another room in the castle after dinner that evening.

[**Othello, Lodovico, Desdemona, Emilia,** *and* **Attendants** *enter.*]

Lodovico I beg you, sir, to escort me no farther.

Othello Permit me to do so. It will do me good to walk.

Lodovico   Madam, good night; I humbly thank your
ladyship.

Desdemona   Your honor is most welcome.

Othello   Will you walk, sir?
5   O, Desdemona!

Desdemona   My lord?

Othello   Get you to bed on th' instant, I will be return'd forthwith. Dismiss your attendant there.
Look't be done.

10 **Desdemona**   I will, my lord.

Exeunt [Othello, Lodovico, and Attendants].

Emilia   How goes it now? He looks gentler than he did.

Desdemona   He says he will return incontinent,
And hath commanded me to go to bed,
And bid me to dismiss you.

14 **Emilia**   Dismiss me?

Desdemona   It was his bidding; therefore, good Emilia,
Give me my nightly wearing, and adieu.
We must not now displease him.

18 **Emilia**   I would you had never seen him!

Desdemona   So would not I. My love doth so approve him,
That even his stubbornness, his checks, his frowns—
Prithee unpin me—have grace and favor [in them].

Emilia   I have laid those sheets you bade me on the bed.

Desdemona   All's one. Good [faith], how foolish are our
minds!

Lodovico [*bowing courteously to* **Desdemona**] Madam, good
    night. I humbly thank you, your ladyship.

Desdemona   You are very welcome, honored sir.

Othello [*to* **Lodovico**] Shall we go, sir?
    [*to* **Desdemona**] Oh, Desdemona.

Desdemona   My lord?

Othello   Get yourself to bed immediately. I'll return very soon.
    Dismiss your attendant Emilia. [*sternly*] See that you do as I say.

Desdemona   I will, my lord.

    [**Othello, Lodovico,** *and* **Attendants** *leave.*]

Emilia [*to* **Desdemona**] How are things now? He looks calmer
    than he did.

Desdemona   He says he'll return right away and has
    commanded that I go to bed. And he said that I should tell you
    to leave.

Emilia [*greatly surprised and somewhat perturbed*] Tell me to
    leave?

Desdemona   Those were his orders. So, good Emilia, get my
    night clothes, and then good night to you. We mustn't
    displease him now.

Emilia [*vehemently*] I wish you'd never met him!

Desdemona   I don't wish that. My love makes me think so
    highly of him that even his harshness, his rebukes, his
    frowns—[*She interrupts herself to give* **Emilia** *instructions.*]
    Please undo my dress—[*She resumes her earlier remarks.*] are
    pleasing and attractive.

Emilia   I've put those sheets you asked for on the bed.

Desdemona [*indifferently*] It's all the same to me.
    [*trying to laugh at herself*] Honestly, how foolish our thoughts

24   If I do die before [thee], prithee shroud me
      In one of these same sheets.

Emilia   Come, come; you talk.

Desdemona   My mother had a maid call'd Barbary;
      She was in love, and he she lov'd prov'd mad,
      And did forsake her. She had a song of "Willow,"
      An old thing 'twas, but it express'd her fortune,
30   And she died singing it. That song to-night
      Will not go from my mind; I have much to do
      But to go hang my head all at one side
      And sing it like poor Barbary. Prithee dispatch.

Emilia   Shall I go fetch your night-gown?

Desdemona   No, unpin me here.
35   This Lodovico is a proper man.

Emilia   A very handsome man.

Desdemona   He speaks well.

Emilia   I know a lady in Venice would have walk'd
      barefoot to Palestine for a touch of his nether lip.

Desdemona   [*Singing.*]
40   "The poor soul sat [sighing] by a sycamore tree,
          Sing all a green willow;
      Her hand on her bosom, her head on her knee,
          Sing willow, willow, willow.
      The fresh streams ran by her, and murmur'd her moans,
45   Sing willow, willow, willow;
      Her salt tears fell from her, and soft'ned the stones,
          Sing willow"—
      Lay by these—
      [*Singing.*] "—willow, willow"—
50   Prithee hie thee; he'll come anon—
      [*Singing.*]

240

are! If I should die before you do, please bury me wrapped in these very bed sheets.

Emilia [*Shocked at* **Desdemona's** *morbidity,* **Emilia** *gently scolds her.*] Come, come, the things you say!

Desdemona My mother had a maid named Barbary. She was in love, but the man she loved was unfaithful and deserted her. She knew a song called "Willow" [*The willow was considered to be symbolic of disappointment in love.*]; it was an old song, but it told of her fate and she died singing it. I can't get that song out of my head tonight. I can barely keep myself from hanging my head over to one side and singing the song like poor Barbary. Please go now.

Emilia [*looking worried*] Shall I bring you your nightgown?

Desdemona No, undo me here. This Lodovico is a fine man.

Emilia [*unfastening* **Desdemona's** *gown*] A very handsome man.

Desdemona He converses well.

Emilia I know a lady in Venice who would have walked barefoot all the way to Palestine for a kiss from him.

Desdemona [*singing sadly*] "The poor soul sat sighing by a sycamore tree,
Sing all a green willow;
Her hand on her breast, her head on her knee;
Sing willow, willow, willow.
The fresh streams ran by her and echoed her moans.
Sing willow, willow, willow.
Her salty tears fell from her and softened the stones;
Sing willow"—
[*to* **Emilia**] Put these away—[**Desdemona** *points toward several articles of clothing*]
[*singing*]—"willow, willow"—
[*to* **Emilia**] Please go quickly. He'll be here soon—
[*singing*] "Sing all a green willow must be my garland;

"Sing all a green willow must be my garland.
Let nobody blame him, his scorn I approve"—
Nay, that's not next. Hark, who is't that knocks?

Emilia   It's the wind.

Desdemona   [*Singing.*]
55   "I call'd my love false love; but what said he then?
Sing willow, willow, willow;
If I court moe women, you'll couch with moe men."—
So get thee gone, good night. Mine eyes do itch;
Doth that bode weeping?

Emilia   'Tis neither here nor there.

60 **Desdemona**   I have heard it said so. O, these men, these men!
Dost thou in conscience think—tell me, Emilia—
That there be women do abuse their husbands
In such gross kind?

Emilia   There be some such, no question.

64 **Desdemona**   Wouldst thou do such a deed for all the world?

Emilia   Why, would not you?

Desdemona   No, by this heavenly light!

Emilia   Nor I neither by this heavenly light;
I might do't as well i' th' dark.

Desdemona   Wouldst thou do such a deed for all the world?

Emilia   The world's a huge thing; it is a great price
For a small vice.

70 **Desdemona**   [Good] troth, I think thou wouldst not.

Emilia   [By my] troth, I think I should, and undo't
when I had done ['t]. Marry, I would not do such a
thing for a joint-ring, nor for measures of lawn, nor for
gowns, petticoats, nor caps, nor any petty exhibition;

Let nobody blame him, his contempt I accept"—
[*to herself*] No, that's not what comes next.
[*with anxiety, to* **Emilia**] Listen. Who's knocking?

Emilia   It's the wind.

Desdemona   [*singing*] "I called my love untrue but what did he say?
Sing willow, willow, willow.
'If I chase more women, you'll sleep with more men.' "—
[*to* **Emilia**] Go on now, good night. My eyes are itching. Is that
a sign that I'm going to have sorrow?

Emilia   [*gruffly, her concern for* **Desdemona** *evident*] It doesn't
mean anything.

Desdemona   I've heard that it does.
[*to herself, despairingly*] Oh, these men, these men!
[*to* **Emilia**] Tell me, Emilia, do you honestly think there are
women who are unfaithful to their husbands?

Emilia   There are some like that, without a doubt.

Desdemona   Would you do such a thing for the whole world?

Emilia   Why? Wouldn't you?

Desdemona   [*vehemently*] No, I swear it by the sun in the sky!

Emilia   [*ironically, making a play on words*] I wouldn't do it by
sunlight, but I might do it in the dark.

Desdemona   [*insisting on a serious answer*] Would you do such
a thing for the whole world?

Emilia   The world is a huge thing. It would be a large payment
for such a small sin.

Desdemona   Honestly, I don't think you would.

Emilia   Honestly, I think I would, and then undo the damage
after I'd done it. Really, I wouldn't do such a thing for a cheap
little ring, or a few yards of cloth, or for new dresses,

75   but, for all the whole world—['ud's pity], who
would not make her husband a cuckold to make him a
monarch? I should venture purgatory for't.

Desdemona   Beshrew me, if I would do such a wrong
79   For the whole world.

    Emilia   Why, the wrong is but a wrong i' th' world;
and having the world for your labor, 'tis a wrong in
your own world, and you might quickly make it right.

Desdemona   I do not think there is any such woman.

    Emilia   Yes, a dozen; and as many to th' vantage as
85   would store the world they play'd for.
But I do think it is their husbands' faults
If wives do fall. Say that they slack their duties,
And pour our treasures into foreign laps;
Or else break out in peevish jealousies,
90   Throwing restraint upon us; or say they strike us,
Or scant our former having in despite:
Why, we have galls; and though we have some grace,
Yet have we some revenge. Let husbands know
Their wives have sense like them; they see, and smell,
95   And have their palates both for sweet and sour,
As husbands have. What is it that they do
When they change us for others? Is it sport?
I think it is. And doth affection bread it?
I think it doth. Is't frailty that thus errs?
100   It is so too. And have not we affections,
Desires for sport, and frailty, as men have?
Then let them use us well; else let them know,
The ills we do, their ills instruct us so.

Desdemona   Good night, good night. [God] me such uses
104   send,
Not to pick bad from bad, but by bad mend.

Exeunt.

undergarments, or hats, or for any mere trifle. But for the whole world? My God, who wouldn't cheat on her husband in order to make him a king? I'd risk purgatory for it.

Desdemona   Curse me if I would do such a terrible thing even for the whole world.

Emilia   Why, the crime is only a crime on this earth, and if you owned the earth on which it's a crime, then you'd have the power to legalize it.

Desdemona   I don't think such a woman exists.

Emilia   [*snorting derisively*] Yes, dozens. And just as many more would take the place of the other women who had been unfaithful for all the world. But I think it's their husbands' fault if women stray. They probably don't keep their wives sexually satisfied because they're chasing other women. Or else they get angry because they're jealous over nothing. Or they hit us, or decrease our allowance out of spite. Why, we have every right to resent these things, and even though we make allowances, we still can take our revenge. Let husbands know that their wives have the same physical senses they have; they see, and smell, and are able to taste both sweet and sour just as husbands can. [*She becomes increasingly indignant as she speaks.*] Why do they exchange us for other women? For pleasure? I think so. And does desire cause it? I think it does. Is it weakness that yields to it? Yes, it is. And don't we wives have the same desires, the same enjoyment of pleasure, and the same weaknesses as men? Then let them treat us well or let them know that the wrongs we do are because we've learned from their wrongs against us.

Desdemona   [*Only half-listening,* **Desdemona** *dismisses* **Emilia**.] Good night, good night.
[*to herself*] May God help me to learn nothing from bad behavior except how to avoid it.

[*They leave.*]

Act five

Scene 1

Enter **Iago** *and* **Roderigo**.

Iago Here, stand behind this [bulk], straight will he come.
Wear thy good rapier bare, and put it home.
Quick, quick, fear nothing; I'll be at thy elbow.
It makes us, or it mars us, think on that,
5 And fix most firm thy resolution.

Roderigo Be near at hand, I may miscarry in't.

Iago Here, at thy hand; be bold, and take thy stand.

[*Retires.*]

Roderigo I have no great devotion to the deed,
And yet he hath given me satisfying reasons.
10 'Tis but a man gone. Forth my sword; he dies.

Iago I have rubb'd this young quat almost to the sense,
And he grows angry. Now, whether he kill Cassio,
Or Cassio him, or each do kill the other,
Every way makes my gain. Live Roderigo,
15 He calls me to a restitution large
Of gold and jewels that I bobb'd from him
As gifts to Desdemona;
It must not be. If Cassio do remain,
He hath a daily beauty in his life
20 That makes me ugly; and besides, the Moor
May unfold me to him; there stand I in much peril.
No, he must die. [Be't] so. I [hear] him coming.

Enter **Cassio**.

Act five

Scene 1

At about the same time, in a street of the city.

[**Iago** *and* **Roderigo** *enter.*]

Iago   Here, stand behind this market stall. He'll be along soon. Unsheath your sword and thrust it into him. Hurry, hurry! Don't be afraid. I'll be right beside you. This deed will either get us all we want or destroy us, remember, so be absolutely determined.

Roderigo   [*nervously*] Stay close by in case I fail to do it.

Iago   I'm right here. Be brave and stay where you are. [*He withdraws.*]

Roderigo   I really am not convinced about doing this, yet he has given me good reasons. Killing Cassio is just one less man around [*to compete for Desdemona's favors*]. I'll draw my sword. He dies.

Iago   [*to himself*] I've picked at this little pimple [*that is, Roderigo*] about as much as possible, and now he's growing angry. Now, whether he kills Cassio or Cassio kills him, I come out ahead. If Roderigo lives, he's going to demand that I repay him for the heaps of gold and jewels I've tricked him into giving me as gifts for Desdemona. I can't let that happen. If Cassio lives, his conduct is so exemplary that I look bad in comparison. And, besides, the Moor may reveal my lies to Cassio—that's a very risky situation for me. No, he must die; that's certain. I hear him [**Cassio**] coming.

[**Cassio** *enters.*]

Roderigo   I know his gait, 'tis he.—Villain, thou diest!

[*Makes a pass at Cassio.*]

Cassio   That thrust had been mine enemy indeed,
25   But that my coat is better than thou know'st.
I will make proof of thine.

[*Draws, and wounds Roderigo.*]

Roderigo   O, I am slain.

[Iago from behind wounds Cassio in the leg, and exit.]

Cassio   I am maim'd for ever. Help ho! murther, murther!

[*Falls.*]

Enter **Othello**.

Othello   The voice of Cassio! Iago keeps his word.

Roderigo   O, villain that I am!

Othello   It is even so.

30   **Cassio**   O, help ho! light! a surgeon!

Othello   'Tis he!—O brave Iago, honest and just,
That hast such noble sense of thy friend's wrong!
Thou teachest me. Minion, your dear lies dead,
And your unblest fate hies. Strumpet, I come.
35   [Forth] of my heart those charms, thine eyes, are blotted;
Thy bed, lust-stain'd, shall with lust's blood be spotted.

Exit Othello.

Enter **Lodovico** *and* **Gratiano**.

248

Roderigo   [*to himself, nervously*] I know the sound of his walk. It is he.

[*shouting to* **Cassio**] Villain, you die! [**Roderigo** *tries to stab* **Cassio** *with his sword.*]

Cassio   [*furiously*] That thrust would certainly have wounded me except that my coat deflected it. I'll see how well your coat protects you.

[*He draws his sword and wounds* **Roderigo**.]

Roderigo   [*crying out in pain and fear*] Oh, I'm going to die!

[**Iago**, *from behind, wounds* **Cassio** *in the leg and then runs away.*]

Cassio   I'm maimed for life! [*He begins shouting.*] Help! Murder! Murder! [*He falls to the ground.*]

[**Othello** *enters a short way off.*]

Othello   [*to himself, with satisfaction*] That's Cassio' voice. Iago has done as he said he would.

Roderigo   Oh, I'm a villain.

Othello   That's very true.

Cassio   [*still shouting*] Help! Bring a light! Find a doctor!

Othello   It is he.
[*to the absent* **Iago**] Oh, excellent Iago, honest and just, you feel the wrongs to your friend so deeply. You're an example to me. [*to the absent* **Desdemona**] Desdemona, you whore, your lover lies dead and your damnation approaches quickly. I'm coming, slut. Your lust-stained bed will soon be spotted with lust's blood. [**Othello** *leaves.*]

[**Lodovico** *and* **Gratiano** *enter.*]

Cassio   What ho! no watch? no passage? Murther, murther!

Gratiano   'Tis some mischance, the voice is very direful.

Cassio   O, help!

40 **Lodovico**   Hark!

Roderigo   O wretched villain!

Lodovico   Two or three groan. 'Tis heavy night;
These may be counterfeits; let's think't unsafe
To come in to the cry without more help.

Roderigo   Nobody come? Then shall I bleed to death.

Enter **Iago** [*with a light*].

46 **Lodovico**   Hark!

Gratiano   Here's one comes in his shirt, with light and
weapons.

Iago   Who's there? Whose noise is this that cries on murther?

Lodovico   We do not know.

Iago   [Did] not you hear a cry?

Cassio   Here, here! for heaven sake help me!

50 **Iago**   What's the matter?

Gratiano   This is Othello's ancient, as I take it.

Lodovico   The same indeed, a very valiant fellow.

Iago   What are you here that cry so grievously?

Cassio   Iago? O, I am spoil'd, undone by villains!
55   Give me some help.

Iago   O me, lieutenant! What villains have done this?

Cassio   [*still shouting*] Help! Is there no night watchman, no one passing by? Murder! Murder!

Gratiano   There's something wrong. That voice sounds very bad.

Cassio   [*sounding weaker from loss of blood*] Oh, help!

Lodovico   [*to* **Gratiano**] Listen!

Roderigo   [*groaning weakly to himself*] Oh, what a wretched villain.

Lodovico   Two or three cry out. It's a dark night. These people may not really be in trouble. Let's not risk helping unless we get reinforcements.

Roderigo   Will no one come? I'm bleeding to death.

[**Iago** *enters carrying a torch.*]

Lodovico   [*to* **Gratiano**] Listen!

Gratiano   [*peering at* **Iago**'s *indistinct figure as he approaches*] Here comes someone half-dressed and carrying weapons.

Iago   [*pretending to have been awakened from sleep*] Who's there? Who's yelling "murder"?

Gratiano   We don't know.

Iago   Didn't you hear a cry?

Cassio   [*calling weakly*] Here! Here! For heaven's sake, help me!

Iago   What's the matter?

Gratiano   [*recognizing* **Iago**] That's Othello's ensign, I believe.

Lodovico   Yes, it is. He's a very brave fellow.

Iago   [*calling out*] Who is crying out so piteously?

Cassio   Iago? Oh, I've been destroyed, killed by villains! Help me!

Iago   [*runs to* **Cassio**'s *side and pretends to be horrified*] Oh, lieutenant! What villains have done this?

Cassio   I think that one of them is hereabout,
And cannot make away.

Iago   O treacherous villains!
[*To Lodovico and Gratiano.*]   What are you there?
Come in, and give some help.

60 **Roderigo**   O, help me there!

Cassio   That's one of them.

Iago   O murd'rous slave! O villain!

[*Stabs Roderigo.*]

Roderigo   O damn'd Iago! O inhuman dog!

Iago   Kill men i' th' dark?—Where be these bloody
thieves?—
How silent is this town!—Ho, murther, murther!—
65   What may you be? Are you of good or evil?

Lodovico   As you shall prove us, praise us.

Iago   Signior Lodovico?

Lodovico   He, sir.

Iago   I cry you mercy. Here's Cassio hurt by villains.

70 **Gratiano**   Cassio?

Iago   How is't, brother?

Cassio   My leg is cut in two.

Iago   Marry, heaven forbid!
Light, gentlemen! I'll bind it with my shirt.

Enter **Bianca**.

Cassio   [*gasping weakly and pointing*] I think one of them is nearby and can't get away.

Iago   [*shouting in pretended fury*] Oh, treacherous villains!
[*to* **Lodovico** *and* **Gratiano**] Who are you? Come here and help us.

Roderigo   Oh, help me!

Cassio   That's one of them.

Iago   [*shouting, to* **Roderigo**] Oh, you murderous slave! You villain!

[**Iago** *stabs* **Roderigo**.]

Roderigo   [*weakly*] Damn you, Iago! You inhuman dog!

Iago   [*loudly, to ensure that* **Gratiano** *and* **Lodovico** *can hear him*] Will you kill men in the dark?—Where are these murdering thieves?—How silent this town is!—Murder! Murder!
[*to* **Gratiano** *and* **Lodovico**] Who are you? Are you good or evil?

Lodovico   See for yourself.

Iago   [*shining the light from the torch on their faces*] Signior Lodovico?

Lodovico   I am he, sir.

Iago   Forgive me. Cassio here has been wounded by villains.

Gratiano   Cassio?

Iago   [**Iago** *hands the torch to* **Gratiano** *and stoops to address* **Cassio**, *pretending to be deeply concerned.*] How are you, friend?

Cassio   [*groaning with pain*] My leg is cut in two.

Iago   Heaven forbid!
[*to* **Gratiano** *and* **Lodovico**] Bring the light, gentlemen.
[*to* **Cassio**] I'll bind it with my shirt.

[**Bianca** *enters.*]

Bianca   What is the matter ho? who is't that cried?

75 **Iago**   Who is't that cried?

Bianca   O my dear Cassio, my sweet Cassio!
O Cassio, Cassio, Cassio!

Iago   O notable strumpet! Cassio, may you suspect
Who they should be that have thus mangled you?

80 **Cassio**   No.

Gratiano   I am sorry to find you thus; I have been to seek you.

Iago   Lend me a garter. So.—O for a chair
To bear him easily hence!

Bianca   Alas, he faints! O Cassio, Cassio, Cassio!

85 **Iago**   Gentlemen all, I do suspect this trash
To be a party in this injury.—
Patience awhile, good Cassio.—Come, come;
Lend me a light. Know we this face or no?
Alas, my friend and my dear countryman
Roderigo! No—yes, sure—[O heaven,] Roderigo!

91 **Gratiano**   What, of Venice?

Iago   Even he, sir; did you know him?

Gratiano   Know him? ay.

Iago   Signior Gratiano? Cassio? I cry your gentle pardon;
These bloody accidents must excuse my manners
That so neglected you.

95 **Gratiano**   I am glad to see you.

Bianca   What is the matter? Who cried out?

Iago   [*repeats her question, feigning suspicion*] Who cried out?

Bianca   [*horrified to see* **Cassio** *lying wounded on the ground*]
Oh, my dear Cassio! My sweet Cassio! [*weeping*] Oh, Cassio,
Cassio, Cassio!

Iago   [*accusingly, to* **Bianca**] You whore!
[*to* **Cassio**] Cassio, do you know who wounded you?

Cassio   No.

Gratiano   I'm sorry to see you're wounded. I was on my way to
find you.

Iago   Lend me your garter [*that is, a piece of ribbon or string
used to hold up stockings*].
[**Iago** *ties up the wound.*] There. Oh, if only we had a sedan
chair [*that is, an enclosed chair, carried on poles by two
servants*] to carry him from here.

Bianca   Alas, he's fainted! Oh, Cassio, Cassio, Cassio!

Iago   [*to* **Gratiano** *and* **Lodovico**] Gentlemen, I suspect this
trashy woman to be partly responsible for Cassio's being
wounded.
[*to the unconscious* **Cassio**] Have patience, good Cassio.
[*to* **Gratiano** *and* **Lodovico**] Come, come, lend me the light.
Do we know who this other man is?
[**Iago** *walks over to* **Roderigo** *and shines the light on his face.*]
Alas, it's my friend and dear countryman, Roderigo!
[*pretending to be momentarily uncertain*] No . . . Yes, I'm sure
. . . Oh heavens, Roderigo!

Gratiano   What, Roderigo from Venice?

Iago   Yes, it is he, sir. Did you know him?

Gratiano   Know him? Yes.

Iago   Signior Gratiano? I beg your pardon. These bloody events
have caused me to forget my manners.

Gratiano   [*bowing formally*] I am glad to see you.

Iago   How do you, Cassio? O, a chair, a chair!

Gratiano   Roderigo!

Iago   He, he, 'tis he. [*A chair brought in.*] O, that's
     well said: the chair.
     Some good man bear him carefully from hence,
100   I'll fetch the general's surgeon. [*To Bianca.*] For you, mistress,
     Save you your labor.—He that lies slain here, Cassio,
     Was my dear friend. What malice was between you?

Cassio   None in the world; nor do I know the man.

Iago   [*To Bianca.*] What? look you pale?—O, bear
     him [out] o' th' air.

                              [*Cassio and Roderigo are borne off.*]

105   Stay you, good gentlemen.—Look you pale, mistress?—
     Do you perceive the gastness of her eye?—
     Nay, [an'] you stare, we shall hear more anon.—
     Behold her well; I pray you look upon her.
     Do you see, gentlemen? Nay, guiltiness will speak,
110   Though tongues were out of use.

     [*Enter **Emilia**.*]

Emilia   Alas, what is the matter?
     What is the matter, husband?

Iago   Cassio hath here been set on in the dark
     By Roderigo and fellows that are scap'd.
     He's almost slain, and Roderigo quite dead.

Emilia   Alas, good gentleman! alas, good Cassio!

116 **Iago**   This is the fruits of whoring. Prithee, Emilia,
     Go know of Cassio where he supp'd to-night.

     [*To Bianca.*] What, do you shake at that?

Iago   [*to the still-unconscious* **Cassio**] How are you doing?
[*Receiving no reply,* **Iago** *shouts as if greatly concerned.*]
Bring a chair, a chair!

Gratiano   [*shocked to see the body of* **Roderigo**] Roderigo!

Iago   Yes, it is he. [*A sedan chair is brought in.*] Very good.
Here's a chair to carry Cassio in. Someone trustworthy see that
he's carried carefully from here. I'll get the general's doctor.
[*to* **Bianca**] As for you, woman, don't waste your efforts.
[*to* **Cassio,** *who has regained consciousness*] The man who
lies here dead, Cassio, was my good friend. What was the
problem between you?

Cassio   None at all. I don't even know the man.

Iago   [*harshly, to* **Bianca**] What, are you looking pale?
[*to the servants*] Carry him out of the night air. [**Cassio** *and*
Roderigo *are carried off.*]
[*to* **Gratiano** *and* **Lodovico,** *as they start to leave*] Wait, gentlemen.
[*to* **Bianca**] Are you looking pale, woman?
[*to* **Gratiano** *and* **Lodovico**] Do you see the fear in her eyes?
[*to* **Bianca,** *as she looks at him fearfully*] Go on and stare. We'll
question you soon.
[*to* **Gratiano** *and* **Lodovico**] Do you see what I mean, gentlemen?
No, guilt will reveal itself even when a person says nothing.

[**Emilia** *enters.*]

Emilia   Alas, what is the matter? What is the matter, husband?

Iago   Roderigo, along with some other men who have escaped,
attacked Cassio here in the dark. Cassio is near death, and
Roderigo has been killed.

Emilia   Alas, good gentlemen! Alas, good Cassio!

Iago   This is what results from being with prostitutes. Emilia,
please go ask Cassio where he had dinner tonight.

[*to* **Bianca**] Are you trembling about that?

Bianca   He supp'd at my house, but I therefore shake not.

120 **Iago**   O, did he so? I charge you go with me.

Emilia   O fie upon thee, strumpet!

Bianca   I am no strumpet, but of life as honest
As you that thus abuse me.

Emilia   As I? [Fough,] fie upon thee!

Iago   Kind gentlemen, let's go see poor Cassio dress'd.
125   Come, mistress, you must tell's another tale.
Emilia, run you to the citadel,
And tell my lord and lady what hath happ'd.—
Will you go on afore? [*Aside.*] This is the night
That either makes me, or foredoes me quite.

Exeunt.

Scene 2

Enter **Othello** [*with a light*] *and* **Desdemona** *in her
bed* [*asleep*].

Othello   It is the cause, it is the cause, my soul;
Let me not name it to you, you chaste stars,
It is the cause. Yet I'll not shed her blood,
Nor scar that whiter skin of hers than snow,
5   And smooth as monumental alablaster.
Yet she must die, else she'll betray more men.

Bianca   He dined at my house, but I'm not trembling because of it.

Iago   Oh, did he? I order you to come with me.

Emilia   Shame on you, whore!

Bianca   [*defiantly*] I am not a whore! I'm as good a person as any of you who attack me.

Emilia   [*indignantly*] As good as me? Bah, shame on you!

Iago   [*to* **Gratiano** *and* **Lodovico**] Kind gentlemen, let's go see to it that Cassio is well cared for.
[*to* **Bianca**, *sarcastically*] Come along, woman, you can tell us another lie.
[*to* **Emilia**] Emilia, you go to the citadel and tell Othello and Desdemona what has happened.
[*to* **Gratiano** *and* **Lodovico**] Will you go ahead of us?
[*to himself*] This night will either accomplish all my goals or destroy me completely.

[*They all leave.*]

Scene 2

A bedchamber in the castle. Desdemona is in bed asleep; a candle is burning in the room.

[**Othello** *enters, carrying a candle. He locks the door behind himself.*]

Othello   [*to himself*] It is the cause, it is the cause, my soul. I cannot even speak of it to you, you uncorrupted stars; it is the cause. Yet I will not shed her blood nor scar her skin, which is whiter than snow and as smooth as the finest alabaster. Yet she must die or else she will betray more men.

Act five   Scene 2

Put out the light, and then put out the light:
If I quench thee, thou flaming minister,
I can again thy former light restore,
10   Should I repent me; but once put out thy light,
Thou cunning'st pattern of excelling nature,
I know not where is that Promethean heat
That can thy light relume. When I have pluck'd thy rose,
I cannot give it vital growth again,
15   It needs must wither. I'll smell thee on the tree.

[*Kisses her.*]

O balmy breath, that dost almost persuade
Justice to break her sword! One more, one more.
Be thus when thou art dead, and I will kill thee
And love thee after. One more, and that's the last.
20   So sweet was ne'er so fatal. I must weep,
But they are cruel tears. This sorrow's heavenly,
It strikes where it doth love. She wakes.

Desdemona   Who's there? Othello?

Othello   Ay, Desdemona.

Desdemona   Will you come to bed, my lord?

Othello   Have you pray'd to-night, Desdemon?

Desdemona   Ay, my lord.

26 **Othello**   If you bethink yourself of any crime
Unreconcil'd as yet to heaven and grace,
Solicit for it straight.

Desdemona   Alack, my lord, what may you mean by this.

30 **Othello**   Well, do it, and be brief, I will walk by.
I would not kill thy unprepared spirit,
No, [heaven] forefend! I would not kill thy soul.

Put out the light [*He extinguishes* **Desdemona**'s *candle.*], and then put out the light [*He refers symbolically to* **Desdemona**.]. [*to the candle*] If I put you out, burning candle, I can light your flame again if I should change my mind, [*to* **Desdemona**] but if I put out your light, you counterfeit of Nature's perfection, I do not know where the heavenly spark is that can rekindle your life. When I have plucked your rose, I'll smell you while you are still on the tree. [*He kisses her and groans.*] Oh, your sweet breath almost persuades me to break the sword of justice. One more kiss, one more.

[*He kisses her again.*]

Be as you are now when you are dead, and I'll kill you and love you afterwards. One more kiss, and that's the last one. [*He kisses her again.*] There has never been anything this sweet that was so deadly. I must weep, but my tears don't signify a change of heart. My sorrow is like heaven's sorrow [*that is, it grieves even as it punishes the sinner*]; it punishes out of love.

[**Desdemona** *moves restlessly.*] She is waking up.

Desdemona   [*She awakens suddenly.*] Who's there? Othello?

Othello   Yes, Desdemona.

Desdemona   Are you coming to bed, my lord?

Othello   Have you prayed tonight, Desdemona?

Desdemona   [*in confusion*] Yes, my lord.

Othello   If you remember any sin that you haven't yet confessed, ask forgiveness for it immediately.

Desdemona   What do you mean, my lord?

Othello   [*sternly*] Well, do it, and quickly. I will wait a moment. I wouldn't want to kill you before you have confessed. No, God forbid! I wouldn't want to kill your soul.

Desdemona   Talk you of killing?

Othello   Ay, I do.

Desdemona   Then heaven.
Have mercy on me!

Othello   Amen, with all my heart!

35 **Desdemona**   If you say [so], I hope you will not kill me.

Othello   Humh!

Desdemona   And yet I fear you; for you're fatal then
When your eyes roll so. Why I should fear I know not,
Since guiltiness I know not; but yet I feel I fear.

Othello   Think on thy sins.

40 **Desdemona**   They are loves I bear to you.

Othello   Ay, and for that thou di'st.

Desdemona   That death's unnatural that kills for loving.
Alas, why gnaw you so your nether lip?
Some bloody passion shakes your very frame.
45   These are portents; but yet I hope, I hope,
They do not point on me.

Othello   Peace, and be still!

Desdemona   I will so. What's the matter?

Othello   That handkerchief which I so lov'd, and gave thee,
Thou gav'st to Cassio.

Desdemona   No, by my life and soul!
Send for the man, and ask him.

50 **Othello**   Sweet soul, take heed,
Take heed of perjury, thou art on thy death-bed.

Desdemona   [*becoming fearful*] You talk of killing?

Othello   Yes, I do.

Desdemona   [*in great fear*] Then may heaven have mercy on me!

Othello   Amen, I agree with all my heart.

Desdemona   If you say that, I hope you won't kill me.

Othello   Humph!

Desdemona   And yet I am afraid of you, for you are deadly when your eyes roll like that. I don't know why I should be fearful since I am without guilt, yet still I feel afraid.

Othello   [*very sternly*] Think about your sins.

Desdemona   My sin is the love I have for you.

Othello   Yes, and for that you die.

Desdemona   [*pleadingly, trying to reason with him*] It's unnatural to kill because of love. Alas, why do you gnaw like that on your lower lip? Some violent emotion makes your whole body shake. These are evil omens, but still I hope, I hope they aren't directed toward me.

Othello   [*roars*] Peace, and be silent!

Desdemona   I will. What's the matter?

Othello   You gave Cassio that handkerchief which I loved so much and gave to you.

Desdemona   [*vehemently*] No, I swear it on my life and soul! Send for him and ask him.

Othello   Sweet soul, beware, beware of telling lies, for you are on your death bed.

Desdemona   Ay, but not yet to die.

Othello   [Yes,] presently:
Therefore confess thee freely of thy sin;
For to deny each article with oath
55   Cannot remove nor choke the strong conception
That I do groan withal. Thou art to die.

Desdemona   [Then Lord] have mercy on me!

Othello   I say, amen.

Desdemona   And have you mercy too! I never did
Offend you in my life; never lov'd Cassio
60   But with such general warranty of heaven
As I might love. I never gave him token.

Othello   By heaven, I saw my handkerchief in 's hand.
O perjur'd woman, thou dost stone my heart,
And [mak'st] me call what I intend to do
65   A murther, which I thought a sacrifice.
I saw the handkerchief.

Desdemona   He found it then;
I never gave it him. Send for him hither;
Let him confess a truth.

Othello   He hath confess'd.

69 **Desdemona**   What, my lord?

Othello   That he hath us'd thee.

Desdemona   How? unlawfully?

Othello   Ay.

Desdemona   He will not say so.

Othello   No—his mouth is stopp'd;
Honest Iago hath ta'en order for't.

Desdemona   Yes, but not to die yet. [*Deliberately misinterpreting what* **Othello** *says,* **Desdemona** *means that someday in the distant future she would be likely to die in that bed.*]

Othello   Yes, very soon. So fully confess your sin, because your denying every wrong even with an oath cannot remove or smother the strong conviction of your guilt that makes me groan. You are to die.

Desdemona   [*in great fear*] Then may the Lord have mercy on me!

Othello   I say amen.

Desdemona   [*pleadingly*] And may you have mercy, too! I've never wronged you in my life! I've never loved Cassio beyond what heaven would approve. I've never given him a token of love.

Othello   [*explosively*] By heaven, I saw my handkerchief in his hand! Oh, perjured woman, you turn my heart to stone and make me call a murder that which I intended as a sacrifice. I saw the handkerchief.

Desdemona   [*with increasing desperation*] He found it then. I never gave it to him. Send for him. Let him tell you the truth.

Othello   He has confessed.

Desdemona   [*in confusion*] What, my lord?

Othello   That he has made use of you.

Desdemona   [*in disbelief*] How? In adultery?

Othello   Yes.

Desdemona   He will not say that.

Othello   No . . . his mouth is silenced. Honest Iago has seen to it.

Desdemona   O, my fear interprets. What, is he dead?

Othello   Had all his hairs been lives, my great revenge
75   Had stomach for them all.

Desdemona   Alas, he is betray'd and I undone!

Othello   Out, strumpet! weep'st thou for him to my face?

Desdemona   O, banish me, my lord, but kill me not!

Othello   Down, strumpet!

80 **Desdemona**   Kill me to-morrow, let me live to-night!

Othello   Nay, [an'] you strive—

Desdemona   But half an hour!

Othello   Being done, there is no pause.

Desdemona   But while I say one prayer!

Othello   It is too late. *Smothers her.*

[**Desdemona** O Lord, Lord, Lord!]

Emilia   (*At the door*, [*within*].) My lord, my lord!
85   What ho! my lord, my lord!

Othello   What noise is this? Not dead? not yet quite dead?
I that am cruel am yet merciful,
I would not have thee linger in thy pain.
So, so.

Emilia   (*Within.*) What ho! my lord, my lord!

Othello   Who's there?

Desdemona   Oh, my fear interprets your meaning. Is he dead?

Othello   If he had as many lives as he has hairs, my revenge would have been strong enough to take them all.

Desdemona   [*despairingly*] Alas, he is betrayed, and I am destroyed!

Othello   Silence, whore! Do you weep for him to my face?

Desdemona   [*clinging to him and pleading desperately*] Oh, banish me, my lord, but don't kill me!

Othello   [*thrusting her away*] Down, whore!

Desdemona   Kill me tomorrow, but let me live tonight!

Othello   [*He takes her by the throat, pushing her down on the bed.*] No, if you resist . . .

Desdemona   [*with ever-increasing desperation and fear*] Just half an hour more!

Othello   Since all is at an end between us, there's no reason to wait.

Desdemona   Let me say just one prayer!

Othello   It's too late. [*He smothers her.*]

Desdemona   Oh, Lord, Lord, Lord!

Emilia   [*urgently, from outside the door*] My lord, my lord! What ho, my lord!

Othello   [*Intent upon killing* **Desdemona**, *he either ignores or doesn't hear* **Emilia** *and speaks rhetorically to* **Desdemona**.] What is this sound? Not dead? Not quite dead? Although I am harsh, I am still merciful; I wouldn't want you to linger on in pain. There. [*He strangles her again.*] There.

Emilia   [*calling urgently from outside the room*] What ho, my lord! My lord!

Othello   Who's there?

Emilia   [*Within.*] O, good my lord, I would speak
90   a word with you!

Othello   Yes.—'Tis Emilia.—By and by.—She's dead.
'Tis like she comes to speak of Cassio's death;
The noise was high. Hah, no more moving?
Still as the grave. Shall she come in? Were't good?
95   I think she stirs again. No. What's best to do?
If she come in, she'll sure speak to my wife.
My wife, my wife! what wife? I have no wife.
O insupportable! O heavy hour!
Methinks it should be now a huge eclipse
100   Of sun and moon, and that th' affrighted globe
Did yawn at alteration.

Emilia   [*Within.*]   I do beseech you
That I may speak with you. O, good my lord!

Othello   I had forgot thee. O, come in, Emilia.—
104   Soft, by and by, let me the curtains draw.—
Where art thou?

[*Unlocks the door.*]

Enter **Emilia**.

What's the matter with thee now?

Emilia   O, my good lord, yonder's foul murthers done!

Othello   What? now?

Emilia   But now, my lord.

Othello   It is the very error of the moon,
110   She comes more nearer earth than she was wont,
And makes men mad.

Emilia [*still outside the room*] My lord, I need to talk to you.

Othello [*absently, to* **Emilia**] Yes.

[*to himself*] It's Emilia.

[*to* **Emilia**] I'll be there in a minute.

[*to himself*] Desdemona is dead. Emilia has probably come to report Cassio's death. There was a great commotion about it. [*rhetorically, to* **Desdemona**] So, not moving?

[*to himself*] She's as silent as the grave. Shall I let Emilia come in? Would that be a good idea? [*He looks at* **Desdemona**'s *body.*] I think Desdemona is moving again. [*He pauses, watching her intently.*] No, she's not. What would be the best thing to do? If she comes in, she'll surely speak to my wife. [*As he says the word "wife,"* **Othello** *is overcome with grief.*] My wife, my wife! What wife? I have no wife. Oh, I can't stand this! Oh, how horrible this is! There should be a total eclipse of the sun and the moon, and the terrified earth should be racked with earthquakes because of this.

Emilia [*from outside*] Please let me speak to you. [*She calls again when he fails to answer.*] Oh, good my lord!

Othello [*to* **Emilia**] I had forgotten about you. [*He starts to unlock the door.*] Come in, Emilia . . . [*He pauses, remembering that* **Desdemona**'s *body is visible on the bed.*] Wait a moment. [*to himself*] I must close the bed curtains.

[*He does so.*]

[*to* **Emilia**] Where are you? [**Othello** *unlocks the door.* **Emilia** *rushes into the room.*] What's the matter with you now?

Emilia [*in great agitation*] Oh, my lord, terrible murders have been committed out there!

Othello What? Just now?

Emilia Just now, my lord.

Othello The moon must have gone off course. It must be nearer the earth than usual, and men are driven mad because of it.

Emilia   Cassio, my lord, hath kill'd a young Venetian
Call'd Roderigo.

Othello   Roderigo kill'd?
And Cassio kill'd?

Emilia   No, Cassio is not kill'd.

115 **Othello**   Not Cassio kill'd? Then murther's out of tune,
And sweet revenge grows harsh.

Desdemona   O, falsely, falsely murder'd!

Emilia   [O Lord], what cry is that?

Othello   That? what?

Emilia   Out, and alas, that was my lady's voice.
120   Help, help, ho, help! O lady, speak again!
Sweet Desdemona, O sweet mistress, speak!

Desdemona   A guiltless death I die.

Emilia   O, who hath done this deed?

124 **Desdemona**   Nobody; I myself. Farewell!
Commend me to my kind lord. O, farewell!

[*Dies.*]

Othello   Why, how should she be murd'red?

Emilia   Alas! who knows?

Othello   You [heard] her say herself, it was not I.

Emilia   She said so; I must needs report the truth.

Emilia Cassio, my lord, has killed a young man from Venice named Roderigo.

Othello [*greatly surprised*] Roderigo has been killed? And is Cassio dead?

Emilia No, Cassio isn't dead.

Othello [*in surprise and consternation*] Cassio isn't dead? [*to himself*] Then murder is out of tune, and sweet revenge's notes grate on the ear.

Desdemona [*cries out weakly from the bed*] Oh, murdered, wrongly murdered!

Emilia [*startled and fearful*] My lord, what is that cry?

Othello That? What?

Emilia Oh my God and alas, that was Desdemona's voice! [**Emilia** *runs to the door and cries out*] Help, help, oh help! [*pushes past* **Othello** *and runs to the bed calling in great agitation to* **Desdemona** *and flinging open the bed curtains*] Oh lady, speak again! Sweet Desdemona, oh sweet mistress, say something!

Desdemona [*very weakly*] I die a guiltless death.

Emilia [*greatly distressed, to* **Desdemona**] Who did this thing?

Desdemona Nobody. I did it myself. Farewell! Greet my husband for me. Farewell!

[*She dies.*]

Othello Why, how can she have been murdered?

Emilia [*sobbing*] Alas, who knows?

Othello You heard her say herself it wasn't I who did it.

Emilia [*looking at* **Othello** *suspiciously*] She said so. I must report the truth.

Othello   She's like a liar gone to burning hell:
'Twas I that kill'd her.

130 **Emilia**   O, the more angel she,
And you the blacker devil!

Othello   She turn'd to folly, and she was a whore.

Emilia   Thou dost belie her, and thou art a devil.

Othello   She was false as water.

Emilia   Thou art rash as fire to say
135   That she was false. O, she was heavenly true!

Othello   Cassio did top her; ask thy husband else.
O, I were damn'd beneath all depth in hell
But that I did proceed upon just grounds
To this extremity. Thy husband knew it all.

140 **Emilia**   My husband?

Othello   Thy husband.

Emilia   That she was false to wedlock?

Othello   Ay, with Cassio. [Nay,] had she been true,
If heaven would make me such another world
145   Of one entire and perfect chrysolite,
I'ld not have sold her for it.

Emilia   My husband?

Othello   Ay, 'twas he that told me on her first.
An honest man he is, and hates the slime
That sticks on filthy deeds.

Emilia   My husband?

Othello   What needs this iterance, woman? I say thy
150   husband.

272

Othello   She's like a liar gone to burning hell. It was I who killed her.

Emilia   [*in grief and helpless rage*] Oh, then she's even more an angel, and you're an even blacker devil.

Othello   She gave in to lust, and she was a whore.

Emilia   [*weeping and vehement*] You lie about her, and you're a devil.

Othello   She was as changeable as the tides.

Emilia   [*furiously*] You are as imprudent as fire to say that she was unfaithful. Oh, she was completely faithful!

Othello   Cassio slept with her. Ask your husband about it. I would be condemned to the deepest pit of hell except that I was fully justified in taking these extreme measures. Your husband knew everything.

Emilia   [*suspiciously*] My husband?

Othello   Your husband.

Emilia   Knew that she was unfaithful to her marriage?

Othello   Yes, with Cassio. No, if she'd been faithful, even if heaven itself were to make the entire world into a perfect topaz [*an expensive gemstone*], I wouldn't have traded her for it.

Emilia   My husband?

Othello   Yes, it was he who first told me about her. He's an honest man, and he hates the very slime that sticks to such filthy actions.

Emilia   My husband?

Othello   [*becoming irritated by her seeming incomprehension*] Why do you keep repeating me? I said your husband.

Emilia   O mistress, villainy hath made mocks with love!
My husband say she was false?

Othello   He, woman:
I say thy husband; dost understand the word?
My friend, thy husband, honest, honest Iago.

155 **Emilia**   If he say so, may his pernicious soul
Rot half a grain a day! He lies to th' heart.
She was too fond of her most filthy bargain.

Othello   Hah?

Emilia   Do thy worst!
160 This deed of thine is no more worthy heaven
Than thou wast worthy her.

Othello   Peace, you were best.

Emilia   Thou hast not half that pow'r to do me harm
As I have to be hurt. O gull, O dolt,
As ignorant as dirt! Thou hast done a deed—
165 I care not for thy sword, I'll make thee known,
Though I lost twenty lives. Help, help, ho, help!
The Moor hath kill'd my mistress! Murther, murther!

Enter **Montano**, **Gratiano**, *and* **Iago**, [*with others*].

Montano   What is the matter! How now, general?

Emilia   O, are you come, Iago? You have done well,
170 That men must lay their murthers on your neck.

Gratiano   What is the matter?

Emilia   Disprove this villain, if thou be'st a man.
He says thou toldst him that his wife was false.
I know thou didst not; thou'rt not such a villain.
175 Speak, for my heart is full.

Iago   I told him what I thought, and told no more
Than what he found himself was apt and true.

Emilia [*wailing, to the dead* **Desdemona**] Oh Desdemona,
villainy has made a mockery of love!
[*to* **Othello**, *still unable to believe her ears*] My husband said
she was unfaithful?

Othello [*impatiently*] He did, woman. I said your husband. Don't
you understand the word? My friend, your husband, honest,
honest Iago.

Emilia If he says so, may his soul rot in hell at the rate of a half
molecule per day! He's lying through his teeth. Desdemona
loved her disgusting marriage too much.

Othello What? [*He seizes her.*]

Emilia [*enraged and grieving*] Do your worst to me! This thing
you've done is no more worthy of heaven that you were of her.

Othello [*growling threateningly*] You'd better be silent.

Emilia You haven't got half the power to hurt me as I have to
bear the hurt. You fool, you idiot, as stupid as dirt! You have
done a deed—[**Othello** *releases her and draws his sword.*] I
don't care about your sword, I'll tell what you've done even
if I were to die twenty times!
[*She runs to the door and cries out.*] Help, help, oh help! The
Moor has killed my mistress! Murder! Murder!

[**Montano, Gratiano, Iago**, *and others enter.*]

Montano What is the matter? What is it, general?

Emilia [*sarcastically*] Oh, you're here, Iago? You've done well,
that men must say you caused them to commit murder.

Gratiano What is the matter?

Emilia [*to* **Iago**] Prove this villain [*that is,* **Othello**] to be lying,
if you're a man. Othello says you told him his wife was
unfaithful. [*pleadingly*] I know you didn't; you aren't such a
villain. Tell us, for my heart is full of grief.

Iago [*defiantly*] I told him what I thought, and it was nothing
more than he himself found to be believable and true.

Emilia   But did you ever tell him she was false?

Iago   I did.

180 **Emilia**   You told a lie, and odious, damned lie;
    Upon my soul, a lie, a wicked lie.
    She false with Cassio? did you say with Cassio?

Iago   With Cassio, mistress. Go to, charm your tongue.

Emilia   I wil not charm my tongue; I am bound to speak.
185 My mistress here lies murthered in her bed—

All   O heavens forefend!

Emilia   And your reports have set the murder on.

Othello   Nay, stare not, masters, it is true indeed.

189 **Gratiano**   'Tis a strange truth.

Montano   O monstrous act!

Emilia   Villainy, villainy, villainy!
    I think upon't, I think—I smell't—O villainy!
    I thought so then—I'll kill myself for grief—
    O villainy! villainy!

194 **Iago**   What, are you mad? I charge you get you home.

Emilia   Good gentlemen, let me have leave to speak.
    'Tis proper I obey him; but not now.
    Perchance, Iago, I will ne'er go home.

Othello   O, O, O!

[*Othello falls on the bed.*]

Emilia   Nay, lay thee down and roar;
199 For thou hast kill'd the sweetest innocent
    That e'er did lift up eye.

Othello   [*Rising.*]   O, she was foul!
    I scarce did know you, uncle; there lies your niece,

Emilia   [*insistently*] But did you ever tell him she was unfaithful?

Iago   I did.

Emilia   [*furiously*] You told a lie, a vicious, horrible lie! I swear it—a lie, a wicked lie. She cheated on him with Cassio? Did you say with Cassio?

Iago   [*in irritation*] With Cassio, woman. Enough, cast a spell on your tongue [*to silence it*].

Emilia   [*furiously*] I won't be silent! I must speak out. My mistress lies here, murdered in her bed—

All   [*horrified*] Heaven forbid!

Emilia   [*to* **Iago**] And your lies have caused the murder.

Othello   [*heavily, to all*] No, don't stare, sirs. It's true.

Gratiano   It's a strange truth.

Montano   Oh, what a monstrous thing to do!

Emilia   Villainy, villainy, villainy! I understand it, I understand—I smell it—Oh, villainy! I thought so then—I'll kill myself for grief—Oh, villainy!

Iago   [*trying to push her out of the room before she reveals what she knows*] Are you insane? I order you to go home.

Emilia   [*Pulling away from him and running back,* **Emilia** *addresses the rest of the group.*] Gentlemen, let me speak. I'm supposed to obey my husband, but not now.
[*to* **Iago**] Perhaps, Iago, I shall never go home.

Othello   Oh, oh, oh! [*Beginning to suspect the truth,* **Othello** *falls on the bed sobbing loudly in his grief.*]

Emilia   [*with bitter sarcasm*] Oh, yes, lay down and roar with grief, for you've killed the sweetest, most innocent woman that ever raised her eyes [*to look at another person*].

Othello   [*rising from the bed*] Oh, she was evil!
[*to* **Gratiano**] I hardly knew you, uncle. [**Othello** *addresses* **Gratiano** *thus because he was* **Desdemona**'s *uncle.*] There lies

277

Whose breath, indeed, these hands have newly stopp'd.
I know this act shows horrible and grim.

Gratiano   Poor Desdemon! I am glad thy father's dead
205   Thy match was mortal to him, and pure grief
Shore his old thread in twain. Did he live now,
This sight would make him do a desperate turn,
Yea, curse his better angel from his side,
And fall to reprobance.

210 **Othello**   'Tis pitiful; but yet Iago knows
That she with Cassio hath the act of shame
A thousand times committed. Cassio confess'd it,
And she did gratify his amorous works
With that recognizance and pledge of love
215   Which I first gave her. I saw it in his hand;
It was a handkerchief, an antique token
My father gave my mother.

Emilia   O [God]! O heavenly [God]!

Iago   ['Zounds], hold your peace.

Emilia   'Twill out, 'twill out! I peace.
220   No, I will speak as liberal as the north:
Let heaven and men and devils, let them all,
All, all, cry shame against me, yet I'll speak.

Iago   Be wise, and get you home.

Emilia   I will not. [Iago offers to stab Emilia.]

Gratiano   Fie,
Your sword upon a woman?

225 **Emilia**   O thou dull Moor, that handkerchief thou speak'st of
I found by fortune, and did give my husband;
For often, with a solemn earnestness

your niece, whose breathing my hands indeed have stopped.
I know this deed looks horrible and grim.

Gratiano   [*in horror and grief to the dead* **Desdemona**] Poor
Desdemona! I'm glad your father [*that is,* **Brabantio**] is dead.
Your marriage was death to him, and pure grief about it cut the
thread of his life in two. If he were now alive, seeing this sight
would make him do something desperate. Yes, he might even
send his guardian angel away and live a life of sin.

Othello   [*rising from the bed and trying to reassert the
justification for what he has done*] It's shameful, but Iago
knows that Desdemona and Cassio have committed adultery
with one another a thousand times. Cassio confessed it, and
she showed that she returned his love by giving him the love
token which I had given her. I saw it in his hand; it was a handkerchief, an antique memento my father gave to my mother.

Emilia   [*begins wailing in horrified realization of her part in*
Desdemona's death] Oh, God! Oh, heavenly God!

Iago   [*hisses angrily at her*] Damn it, be silent!

Emilia   It will come out! It will come out! I should be silent? No, I
will speak as freely as the north wind blows. Let heaven and
men and devils, let them all, all, all try to shame me into
silence, I'll still speak out.

Iago   [*threateningly*] If you're wise, you'll go home. [**Iago**
attempts to stab **Emilia**.]

Gratiano   [*intervening indignantly*] Shame on you! Would you
draw your sword on a woman?

Emilia   [*scathingly, to* **Othello**] Oh, you stupid Moor, I happened
to find that handkerchief you refer to and gave it to my
husband, for he had frequently—much more so than such an

(More than indeed belong'd to such a trifle),
He begg'd of me to steal't.

229 **Iago**   Villainous whore!

Emilia   She give it Cassio? No, alas, I found it,
And I did give't my husband.

Iago   Filth, thou liest!

Emilia   By heaven, I do not, I do not, gentlemen.
O murd'rous coxcomb, what should such a fool
Do with so good a wife?

234 **Othello**   Are there no stones in heaven
But what serves for the thunder?—Precious villain!

[*The Moor runs at Iago; Montano disarms Othello;*
Iago kills his wife.]

Gratiano   The woman falls; sure he hath kill'd his wife.

Emilia   Ay, ay! O, lay me by my mistress' side.

[*Exit Iago.*]

Gratiano   He's gone, but his wife's kill'd.

240 **Montano**   'Tis a notorious villain. Take you this weapon.
Which I have [here] recover'd from the Moor.
Come guard the door without; let him not pass,
But kill him rather. I'll after that same villain,
For 'tis a damned slave.

Exit [*with all but Othello and Emilia*]

Othello   I am not valiant neither,
But every puny whipster gets my sword.

insignificant thing would call for—begged me most urgently to steal it.

Iago   [*furiously, trying to silence her*] Villainous whore!

Emilia   You thought she gave it to Cassio? No, alas, I found it and gave it to my husband!

Iago   Filth, you lie!

Emilia   [*vehemently, to all*] By heaven, I do not, I do not, gentlemen.
[*to* **Othello**] Oh, murderous fool, how did such a fool deserve such a good wife?

Othello   Are there no thunderbolts in heaven besides those that cause thunder [*that is, with which to strike* **Iago** *down*]?
[*with bitter and contemptuous irony, to* **Iago**] You priceless villain!

[**Othello** *rushes at* **Iago** *with his sword.* **Montano** *disarms* **Othello**. *While the others are thus distracted,* **Iago** *stabs* **Emilia**.]

Gratiano   [*Seeing* **Emilia** *fall, he tries to warn the others about what* **Iago** *has done.*] The woman has fallen down. He has surely killed his wife.

Emilia   [*gasping weakly*] Yes, yes! Oh, lay me next to my mistress.

[**Iago** *runs offstage.*]

Gratiano   He's gone, but his wife is as good as dead.

Montano   [*to* **Gratiano**] He's the worst of villains.
[*to others*] Take this weapon that I took from the Moor. Guard the outer door. Don't let Othello leave, but kill him if you must. I'll go after that villain, for he's nothing but a damned slave.

[*They all exit except for* **Othello** *and the dying* **Emilia**.]

Othello   I am not so courageous, either. Even the most wretched fighter takes my sword from me. But why

245   But why should honor outlive honesty?
      Let it go all.

Emilia   What did thy song bode, lady?
      Hark, canst thou hear me? I will play the swan,
      And die in music. [*Sings.*] "Willow, willow, willow."
      Moor, she was chaste; she lov'd thee, cruel Moor;
250   So come my soul to bliss, as I speak true;
      So speaking as I think, alas, I die.

                           [*Dies.*]

Othello   I have another weapon in this chamber;
      It was a sword of Spain, the ice-brook's temper—
      O, here it is. Uncle, I must come forth.

255 **Gratiano**   [*Within.*] If thou attempt it, it will cost thee
        dear:
      Thou hast no weapon, and perforce must suffer.

Othello   Look in upon me then and speak with me,
      Or naked as I am I will assault thee.

      [*Enter* **Gratiano**.]

Gratiano   What is the matter?

Othello   Behold, I have a weapon;
260   A better never did itself sustain
      Upon a soldier's thigh. I have seen the day
      That with this little arm, and this good sword,
      I have made my way through more impediments
      Than twenty times your stop. But (O vain boast!)
265   Who can control his fate? 'tis not so now.
      Be not afraid though you do see me weapon'd;
      Here is my journey's end, here is my butt
      And very sea-mark of my utmost sail.

should my reputation survive when my honor is gone? Let it all go.

Emilia   [*to the dead* **Desdemona**] What did your song foretell, lady? Listen, can you hear me? I'll be like the dying swan and die singing.
[*weakly, she sings*] "Willow, willow, willow."
[*to* **Othello**, *growing progressively weaker*] Moor, she was faithful. She loved you, cruel Moor. I'm telling you the truth; I swear it on my dying soul. I'm telling you what I know. Alas, I die.

[**Emilia** *dies.*]

Othello   [*to himself*] I have another weapon in this room. It's a sword made in Spain, it's blade tempered in icy water. [*He looks for the sword and finds it.*] Ah, here it is. [*calls to* **Gratiano**] Uncle, I must come out there.

Gratiano   [*from outside the room*] If you try it, you'll pay dearly for it. You have no weapon, so you'll be gravely injured.

Othello   Come in then and speak to me, or unarmed though I am I will attack you.

[**Gratiano** *enters.*]

Gratiano   What is the matter?

Othello   Look, I have a weapon. [**Othello** *shows* **Gratiano** *the sword, at the sight of which* **Gratiano** *quickly draws his own sword. Othello continues contemplatively.*] No soldier ever carried a better one. I've seen when, with this puny arm of mine and this good sword, I've made my way through twenty times the resistance you could provide.
[*to himself*] But what a pointless boast. Who can control his fate? It's not possible now.
[*to* **Gratiano**] Don't be afraid although you see that I have a weapon. This is the end of my journey. I've reached the goal

Do you go back dismay'd? 'Tis a lost fear;
270   Man but a rush against Othello's breast,
And he retires. Where should Othello go?
Now—how dost thou look now? O ill-starr'd wench,
Pale as thy smock! when we shall meet at compt,
This look of thine will hurl my soul from heaven,
275   And fiends will snatch at it. Cold, cold, my girl?
Even like thy chastity. O cursed, cursed slave!
Whip me, ye devils,
From the possession of this heavenly sight!
Blow me about in winds! roast me in sulphur!
280   Wash me in steep-down gulfs of liquid fire!
O Desdemon! dead, Desdemon! dead!
O, O!

Enter **Lodovico**, **Cassio** [*in a chair*], **Montano**, *and* **Iago**
[*guarded*], *with* **Officers**.

Lodovico   Where is this rash and most unfortunate man?

284 **Othello**   That's he that was Othello; here I am.

Lodovico   Where is that viper? Bring the villain forth.

Othello   I look down towards his feet; but that's a fable.
If that thou be'st a devil, I cannot kill thee.

[*Wounds Iago.*]

Lodovico   Wrench his sword from him.

Iago   I bleed, sir, but not kill'd.

Othello   I am not sorry neither, I'ld have thee live;
290   For in my sense, 'tis happiness to die.

and final destination of my voyage. [*As* **Othello** *says this,*
Gratiano *steps cautiously back.*] Do you retreat in fear? Your
fear is groundless. Attack Othello with a piece of straw, and
he'll give up. Where could Othello go?
[*to* **Desdemona**'s *corpse*] Now . . . how do you look now?
Oh, unfortunate woman, you're as white as your nightdress.
When we meet on Judgment Day, that expression on your
face will hurl my soul from heaven and demons will catch it.
[*He reaches down and gently touches her hand.*] Are you cold,
cold, my girl? Just like your chastity.
[*to himself, groaning, raging, and weeping*] Oh, cursed, cursed
slave! Devils of hell, chase me with whips from this heavenly
sight [*that is, of* **Desdemona**]! Hurl me about with the wind!
Burn me in sulfur! Wash me in crashing waves of liquid fire!
Oh, Desdemona, you're dead, Desdemona! Dead! Oh! Oh!

[**Lodovico; Cassio,** *carried in a sedan chair;* **Montano;** *and* **Iago,**
guarded, enter, along with **Officers.**]

Lodovico   Where is that impetuous and most unfortunate man?

Othello   [*He steps forward.*] I, who once was Othello, am here.

Lodovico   Where is that serpent Iago? Bring the villain out.

Othello   [*to himself*] I see Iago's feet, but then it must be a fable
that the devil's feet are cloven hooves.
[*to* **Iago**] If you truly are the devil, I won't be able to kill you.

[**Othello** *attacks and wounds* **Iago.**]

Lodovico   [*to the* **Officers**] Get his sword away from him!

Iago   [*Clutching his wound,* **Iago** *speaks mockingly to* **Othello.**]
I'm bleeding, sir, but I'm not dead.

Othello   I'm not sorry about that. I'd rather have you live. For
anyone who feels as I do, death would be the happier state.

Lodovico   O thou Othello, that was once so good,
    Fall'n in the practice of a [damned] slave,
    What shall be said to thee?

Othello   Why, any thing:
    An honorable murderer, if you will;
295   For nought I did in hate, but all in honor.

Lodovico   This wretch hath part confess'd his villainy.
    Did you and he consent in Cassio's death?

Othello   Ay.

Cassio   Dear general, I never gave you cause.

300 **Othello**   I do believe it, and I ask your pardon.
    Will you, I pray, demand that demi-devil
    Why he hath thus ensnar'd my soul and body?

Iago   Demand me nothing; what you know, you know:
304   From this time forth I never will speak word.

Lodovico   What? not to pray?

Gratiano   Torments will ope your lips.

Othello   Well, thou dost best.

Lodovico   Sir, you shall understand what hath befall'n,
    Which, as I think, you know not. Here is a letter
    Found in the pocket of the slain Roderigo,
310   And here another. The one of them imports
    The death of Cassio to be undertook
    By Roderigo.

Othello   O villain!

Cassio   Most heathenish and most gross!

Lodovico   Now here's another discontented paper,
315   Found in his pocket too; and this it seems

Lodovico   Oh, Othello, you once were so good, yet you've fallen into the trap of that damned slave, Iago. What can be said to you?

Othello   Why, anything. Call me an honorable murderer, if you wish, for I did nothing out of hatred, but only with honorable motives.

Lodovico   [*indicates* **Iago**] This wretch has partially confessed his crimes.
[*to* **Othello**] Did you and Iago plot Cassio's death?

Othello   Yes.

Cassio   [*shocked and appalled*] Dear general, I never gave you any reason to do it.

Othello   I believe you, and I ask your forgiveness. Will you, please, demand that that demon [*that is,* **Iago**] tell you why he laid traps for my soul and body?

Iago   Demand nothing of me. You know what you know. From this time on, I won't speak a word.

Lodovico   What? Not even to pray?

Gratiano   [*threateningly*] Torture will open your mouth.

Othello   Well, you will do what is best.

Lodovico   Sir, let me explain those things that have happened of which you are unaware. Here is a letter [*He shows* **Othello** *a letter.*] that was found in the pocket of the dead Roderigo, and here is another letter. The one letter instructs Roderigo to kill Cassio.

Othello   [*to* **Iago**] You villain!

Cassio   The most barbaric and the lowest!

Lodovico   Here's another letter [*He shows* **Othello** *a second letter.*]; it's filled with complaints. It was found in his pocket,

Roderigo meant t' have sent this damned villain;
But that, belike, Iago in the [nick]
Came in and satisfied him.

Othello   O thou pernicious caitiff!—
How came you, Cassio, by that handkerchief
That was my wive's?

320 **Cassio**   I found it in my chamber:
And he himself confess'd it but even now,
That there he dropp'd it for a special purpose
Which wrought to his desire.

Othello   O fool, fool, fool!

Cassio   There is besides, in Roderigo's letter,
325   How he upbraids Iago, that he made him
Brave me upon the watch, whereon it came
That I was cast; and even but now he spake
(After long seeming dead) Iago hurt him,
329   Iago set him on.

Lodovico   You must forsake this room and go with us.
Your power and your command is taken off,
And Cassio rules in Cyprus. For this slave,
If there be any cunning cruelty
That can torment him much, and hold him long,
335   It shall be his. You shall close prisoner rest,
Till that the nature of your fault be known
To the Venetian state. Come, bring away.

Othello   Soft you; a word or two before you go.
I have done the state some service, and they know't—
340   No more of that. I pray you, in your letters,
When you shall these unlucky deeds relate,
Speak of me as I am; nothing extenuate,

too. It seems that Roderigo meant to have sent it to this damned villain, Iago, except that Iago, in the nick of time, found him and satisfied Roderigo's complaints.

Othello   [*to* **Iago**] Oh, you vicious wretch!
[*to* **Cassio**] How did you, Cassio, acquire my wife's handkerchief?

Cassio   I found it in my house. And Iago himself just confessed that he purposely dropped it there in order to further his plans.

Othello   [*bitterly, to himself*] Oh fool, fool, fool!

Cassio   In Roderigo's letter, he also rebukes Iago for forcing him [*that is,* **Roderigo**] to attack me while I was on guard duty, which resulted in my being knocked down. Just now Roderigo—although we thought he had been dead for some time—said that Iago wounded him and also put him up to the attack.

Lodovico   [*to* **Othello**] You must leave this room and come with us. Your authority and your rank are taken away from you, and Cassio is put in command of Cyprus. As for this slave, Iago, if there's any clever torture that can greatly torment him and restrain him for a very long time, he shall receive it.
[*to* **Iago**] You shall be closely guarded until the government of Venice can be informed of the crimes you have committed.
[*to the* **Officers**] Come, bring them away.

Othello   [*to* **Lodovico**] Wait. Let me speak to you before you go. I've been of service to Venice, and they know it. But never mind that. I beg you, when you tell of these unfortunate events in your reports, speak of me exactly as I am. Neither excuse anything nor write anything out of spite. Then you will have to tell of one who was not wise in his love, but who loved too much; of one not easily made jealous, but who, having been

Nor set down aught in malice. Then must you speak
Of one that lov'd not wisely but too well;
345   Of one not easily jealous, but being wrought,
Perplexed in the extreme; of one whose hand
(Like the base [Indian]) threw a pearl away
Richer than all his tribe; of one whose subdu'd eyes,
Albeit unused to the melting mood,
350   Drops tears as fast as the Arabian trees
Their medicinable gum. Set you down this;
And say besides, that in Aleppo once,
Where a malignant and a turban'd Turk
Beat a Venetian and traduc'd the state,
355   I took by th' throat the circumcised dog,
And smote him—thus.

[He stabs himself.]

Lodovico   O bloody period!

Gratiano   All that is spoke is marr'd,

Othello   I kiss'd thee ere I kill'd thee. No way but this,
359   Killing myself, to die upon a kiss.

[Falls on the bed and] dies.

Cassio   This did I fear, but thought he had no weapon,
For he was great of heart.

Lodovico   *[To Iago.]* O Spartan dog,
More fell than anguish, hunger, or the sea!
Look on the tragic loading of this bed;
365   This is thy work. The object poisons sight,
Let it be hid. Gratiano, keep the house,
And seize upon the fortunes of the Moor,
For they succeed on you. To you, Lord Governor,

provoked to it, became extremely distressed; of one who,
like the ignorant savage, held in his hand a pearl worth more
than his whole tribe and yet threw it away; of one, although
unaccustomed to the tender emotion of love, whose eyes like a
tamed beast shed tears as fast as the trees of Arabia pour out
their healing fluids. Write all this down, and say also that once,
in Aleppo, when a vicious turbaned Turk, in violation of the
laws, badly beat a man of Venice, I took that circumcised dog
by the throat and smote him . . . thus.

[*He stabs himself with a weapon he had had concealed.*]

Lodovico   [*deeply shocked*] Oh, what a violent end!

Gratiano   All that has been decided is ruined [*that is, concerning*
Othello's *trial and punishment*].

Othello   [*He staggers over to the bed and speaks to*
Desdemona's *corpse.*] I kissed you before I killed you. There's
no other way to die but this, that, killing myself, I die as I kiss
you again. [*He falls on the bed and dies.*]

Cassio   [*mournfully*] I was afraid this might happen, but I
thought he had no weapon. He was a great man.

Lodovico   [*to* **Iago**] Oh, Spartan dog [*a breed of dog, noted for*
its silence and cunning], more cruel than anguish, hunger, and
the sea! Look at the tragic burden of this bed. This is your
doing. This sight [*that is, of the dead bodies*] is like a poison to
my eyes.
[*to the* **Officers**] Hide it from view. [*The* **Officers** *draw the bed*
curtains around the bed.]
[*to* **Gratiano**] Gratiano, guard this house and take possession
of the Moor's belongings, for you are the heir.

Remains the censure of this hellish villain,
The time, the place, the torture, O, enforce it!
370   Myself will straight aboard, and to the state
This heavy act with heavy heart relate.

[Exeunt.]

[*to* **Cassio**] Lord Governor, you must decide the punishment of this hellish villain [*that is,* **Iago**]: the time, the place, the torture. I charge you to enforce it! I will return to Venice immediately and solemnly report this tragedy to the state.

[*Those still living exit.*]

Activities

Themes and Images

One of the techniques Shakespeare uses in his plays is to have characters use figurative language to reveal attitudes and emotions or to create an atmosphere. By taking note of repeated ideas or images, we can discover themes that will enhance our understanding of the play.

If the quotation given below is part of a longer speech, read the entire passage in which it appears in order to understand fully what is being said.

Jealousy

The central issue of *Othello* is jealousy. Read and think about these quotes and about which character is speaking the lines.

1   "And nothing can or shall content my soul
    Till I am even'd with him, wife for wife;
    Or failing so, yet that I put the Moor
    At least into a jealousy so strong
    That judgment cannot cure" (Act II Scene 1 lines 298–302).

2   "O, beware, my lord of jealousy!
    It is the green-ey'd monster which doth mock
    The meat it feeds on" (Act III Scene 3 lines 165–67).

3   "You are jealous now
    That this is from some mistress, some remembrance;
    No, by my faith, Bianca" (Act III Scene 4 lines 185–87).

    • Find as many other similar references as you can to jealousy.

- Which characters experience jealousy and in which cases is it or isn't it justified?
- What general ideas or attitudes about jealousy might Shakespeare be trying to convey in *Othello*?

Reputation

Another important theme in *Othello* is that of reputation. Read and think about these quotes and about which character is speaking the lines.

1   "Let housewives make a skillet of my helm,
    And all indign and base adversities
    Make head against my estimation [*that is, reputation*]" (Act I Scene 3 lines 272–74).

2   "Reputation, reputation, reputation! O, I have lost my reputation! I have lost the immortal part of myself, and what remains is bestial" (Act II Scene 3 lines 262–64).

3   "Good name [*that is, reputation*] in man or woman, dear my lord, Is the immediate jewel of their souls" (Act III Scene 3 lines 155–56).

- Find as many other similar references as you can to reputation.
- Which characters suffer a loss of reputation and in which cases is or isn't that loss justified?
- What general ideas or attitudes about reputation might Shakespeare be trying to convey in *Othello*?

Revenge

Revenge is also an important theme in *Othello*. Read and think about these quotes and about which character is speaking the lines.

1   "O, sir, content you;
    I follow him to serve my turn upon him" (Act I Scene 1 lines 41–42).

2 "And nothing can or shall content my soul
Till I am even'd with him, wife for wife" (Act II Scene 1
lines 298–99).

3 "O that the slave had forty thousand lives!
One is too poor, too weak for my revenge!" (Act III Scene
3 lines 442–43).

- Find as many other similar references as you can to
revenge or to getting even with someone.
- Which characters determine to take revenge on another
character? In which case(s) is that desire justified? To
what degree and in what ways are the plans for revenge
successful or unsuccessful?

Love

There are many references to love in *Othello*. Read and think
about these quotes and about which character is speaking the lines.

1 "I protest, in the sincerity of love and honest kindness"
(Act II Scene 3 lines 327–28).

2   "I would do much
T' atone them, for the love I bear to Cassio" (Act IV Scene
1 lines 232–33).

3   "Cassio, I love thee,
But never more be officer of mine" (Act II Scene 3 lines
249–50).

- Find as many other similar references as you can to love.
- Which characters say that they love another character?
What kinds of love are depicted in the play?
- Which characters are being honest and which are being
dishonest when they claim to love someone? Does their
love influence their behavior, and if so is the influence
positive or negative?

Justice

There are many references to justice in *Othello*. Read and think about these quotes and about which character is speaking the lines.

1   "I'm for it, lieutenant; and I'll do you justice" (Act II Scene 3 line 87).

2   "Good, good; the justice of it pleases; very good" (Act IV Scene 1 lines 209–10).

3   "O balmy breath, that dost almost persuade Justice to break her sword!" (Act V Scene 2 lines 16–17).

- Find as many other similar references as you can to justice.
- In which situations is justice referred to literally and in which situations is it referred to figuratively?
- Which characters in the play do or do not receive justice? Can you discover any patterns or anything else these situations have in common?

Appearance versus reality

A recurring theme in *Othello* is the idea that things may or may not be what they appear to be. Read and think about these quotes and about which character or situation is referred to in the lines.

1   "Of thirty sail; and now they do restem Their backward course, bearing with frank appearance Their purposes toward Cyprus" (Act I Scene 3 lines 37–39).

2   "To vouch this is no proof, Without more wider and more overt test Than these thin habits and poor likelihoods Of modern seeming do prefer against him" (Act I Scene 3 lines 106–09).

3   "Certain, men should be what they seem" (Act III Scene 3 line 128).

- Find as many other similar references as you can to behavior that appears to be false. Find as many other similar references as you can to behavior that is false even when it appears not to be.
- Which characters or groups are determined by others to be behaving falsely?
- Can you discover anything these situations have in common?

Eyes and vision

There are numerous references to eyes, sight, or vision in Othello. Read the following passages, noting who is speaking and what the circumstances are.

1 "I saw Othello's visage in his mind" (Act I Scene 3 line 252).

2 "[Desdemona's eye] sounds a parley to provocation" (Act II Scene 3 lines 21–22).

3 "Make it a darling like your precious eye" (Act III Scene 4 line 66).

- Find as many other similar references as you can to eyes or to the ability to see.
- Which of these references to eyes or sight is literal and which is figurative?
- List all the characters in the play who are unable to "see" clearly. What happens as a result of this inability?

Poison

In *Othello*, Shakespeare also often refers, either literally and figuratively, to poison. Read and think about these quotes and about which character speaks the following lines.

1 "Did you by indirect and forced courses
Subdue and poison this young maid's affections?" (Act I Scene 3 lines 111–12).

2   "The Moor already changes with my poison" (Act III Scene 3 line 325).

3   "If there be cords, or knives,
    Poison, or fire, or suffocating streams,
    I'll not endure it" (Act III Scene 3 lines 388–90).

   • Find as many other similar references as you can to poison.
   • Which references are literal and which are figurative? Who or what is being poisoned, either literally or figuratively? In which cases is the "poisoning" based on lies?
   • What might Shakespeare be implying concerning the power of lies?

Black and white

There are also many references to the colors black and white. Read and think about these quotes and about which people or situations these lines refer to.

1   "Even now, now, very now, an old black ram
    Is tupping your white ewe" (Act I Scene 1 lines 88–89).

2   "If virtue no delighted beauty lack,
    Your son-in-law is far more fair than black" (Act I Scene 3 lines 290–91).

3   "Arise, black vengeance, from the hollow hell!" (Act III Scene 3 line 447).

   • Find as many other similar references as you can to black and white.
   • How many of these references to black and white are visual or factual?
   • In what ways does Shakespeare's use of black and white act as a metaphor or symbol in the play? What are the different issues these colors represent?

- What emotions are associated with the various references to black and white in the play?

Dirt and filth

In *Othello*, Shakespeare also often refers, either literally and figuratively, to dirt or filth. Read and think about these quotes and about which character speaks the following lines.

1   "Now by heaven,
  My blood begins my safer guides to rule,
  And passion, having my best judgment collied [*that is, cast coal dust on and therefore both dirtied and darkened*],
  Assays to lead the way" (Act II Scene 3 lines 204–07).

2 "For if she be not honest, chaste, and true,
  There's no man happy; the purest of their wives
  Is foul [*that is, filthy*] as slander" (Act IV Scene 2 lines 17–19).

3 "An honest man he is, and hates the slime
  That sticks on filthy deeds" (Act V Scene 2 lines 146–47).

  - In these examples, who or what is referred to as being soiled?
  - Find as many other similar references as you can to dirt or filth.
  - Why do you think Shakespeare referred to dirt or filth so many times in *Othello*?

Characters

Search the text to find answers to the following questions. They will help you to form opinions about the principle characters in the play. Record any relevant quotations in Shakespeare's own words.

Othello

1 The audience first learns about Othello from descriptions provided by hearing him described by Iago, Roderigo, and Brabantio.
   a How do they refer to or describe him?
   b How do their descriptions compare with what we learn about him in the scene in which Brabantio and his men confront him?
   c What further impressions of Othello are created in Act I Scene 3, when he stands trial before the senate?
   d How do these impressions compare with the ones we have already formed?

2 Othello is the general of Venice's army.
   a What words are first used to describe him as a soldier?
   b What other speeches or lines are used to describe his military abilities during the course of the play?

3 Although Othello is of great value to Venice as a soldier, he is still in many ways an "outsider."
   a What specific things about Othello make him an outsider?
   b How does this status affect his relationship with Desdemona?
   c What do you think are the positive aspects of his being an outsider?
   d What do you think are the negative aspects of his being an outsider?

4 There are numerous references to Othello's race or to the color of his skin.

   a How is his race significant?

   b What implications might Shakespeare be assuming the audience will draw about either the importance or the insignificance of Othello's race?

5 Although Othello's elopement with Desdemona is the main topic of Act I Scene 1, Othello is never once referred to by name. In addition, throughout much of the play he is referred to either as "the Moor" or by his military rank.

   a Can you detect any patterns concerning which characters do or do not refer to him by name?

   b What conclusions can you draw from these patterns about the various attitudes toward Othello of the others in the play?

6 There are a number of different power structures in the play.

   a What are they?

   b In what ways is Othello a part of the power structures?

   c In what ways is Othello a victim of them?

7 a What is Othello's reaction to being told that he will have to leave Venice to lead the army on his wedding night?

   b What does that tell you about him?

8 What does Othello's decision to demote Cassio for his night of drunken brawling reveal about what Othello considers to be important?

9 When Othello becomes convinced about Desdemona's "infidelity" he gives a long speech in which he bids farewell to his "occupation." Why or how does he see the two issues as being related?

10 Othello's speeches indicate that there are at least three significant losses to him in Desdemona's supposed betrayal.

   a What are these losses?

   b Can you think of any others?

11 Othello's speech patterns change significantly during the course of the play.

    a Describe the subject matter as well as the length of the sentences and the kinds of words he uses in Act I Scene 3 lines 128–70.

    b What might Othello's tendency to use grandiose language indicate about him?

    c Othello first refers to himself in the third person when he says, "Othello's occupation's gone" (Act III Scene 3 line 357). Find other examples of his referring to himself in the third person. Explain what you can infer about his state of mind from this speech pattern.

12 Contrast his speech in Act IV Scene 1 lines 31–42 with the previous speech. What aspects of Iago's ways of speaking do you find "infecting" Othello's speeches here?

13 Othello tells Desdemona that she must carefully guard the handkerchief he gave her because "there's magic in the web of it" (Act III Scene 4 line 69). Discuss his assertions concerning the handkerchief in light of his defense before the senate in which he denied using any witchcraft or magic to ensnare Desdemona.

14 When Othello speaks to himself during the course of the play, what are the topics he talks about?

15 Othello has both strengths and weaknesses.

    a What are his strengths?

    b What are his weaknesses?

    c What aspects of Othello's personality does Iago use to further his schemes?

16 Othello is accustomed to making rapid decisions in the heat of battle.

    a When does he display this quality of military decisiveness?

    b Under what circumstances does this ability serve him well?

    c When does this quality prove to be a liability?

17 Othello initially resists Iago's attempts to convince him of Desdemona's supposed infidelity.

    a What "proofs" does Iago give Othello?

    b Why are these proofs so effective at convincing Othello?

18 Othello says that Iago told him that Desdemona and Cassio have committed adultery a "thousand times" (Act V Scene 2 line 212). What is the logical flaw in this assertion?

19 Some say that Othello yields too readily to Iago's attempts to convince him of Desdemona's infidelity.

    a Do you agree or disagree? Why or why not?

    b What might Othello's rapid loss of faith indicate about him?

20 a Do you think that Othello is describing himself accurately when he says he was "not easily jealous"?

    b Why or why not?

21 Elizabethans placed a high value on the ability to reason as a means of controlling the emotions.

    a When does Othello use reason or logic in the play?

    b When is he controlled by his emotions?

    c In what ways do both reason and emotion fail him?

22 Why is Othello unwilling to believe Emilia when she says that Desdemona and Cassio have never met secretly?

23 Compare Othello's description of Desdemona in Act III Scene 3 lines 184–86 to what he says about her in Act IV Scene 2 lines 71–81.

    a How might these descriptions be a reflection of his own personality?

    b What attitudes toward women in general do you think these lines indicate?

24 Concerning Othello's killing Desdemona, noted literary critic A. C. Bradley states, "The deed he is bound to do is

no murder, but a sacrifice. He is to save Desdemona from
herself, not in hate but in honour; in honour, and also in
love."

a What evidence can you find in the play to support
Bradley's statement?

b Do you agree with him or not?

c Why or why not?

25 Earlier in the play, Othello was determined to take revenge on both Cassio and Desdemona, yet he never
expresses any desire to take revenge on Iago after he
learns all that Iago has done. What do you think are the
reasons for Othello's apparent lack of desire for revenge on
Iago?

26 Othello refers to Desdemona as an "ill-starred wench" (Act
V Scene 2 line 272) and implies that he was unable to
"control" his "fate" (Act V Scene 2 line 265).

a Do you think these statements could be interpreted
as indicating that he is unwilling to fully accept his
guilt?

b Why or why not?

27 Othello at first appears to intend to allow Desdemona's
statement that she has killed herself to provide an alibi for
him.

a Do you think he changes his mind?

b If so, what might have caused him to do so?

c Or do you think he always intended to tell the truth?

d If so, what are your reasons for thinking this?

28 Based on what Othello says, what justification might be
found for the view that Othello's suicide is an act of cow-
ardice? Is this how he views his suicide?

29 Cassio makes the final comment about Othello's character, stating that "he was great of heart" (Act V Scene 2 line
361). Do you agree with this assessment of his character
or not? Explain your reasons for your opinion.

Iago

1   Iago claims that he hates Othello.
    a What does Iago claim are his reasons for doing so?
    b Does his resentment seem at all justified?
    c What conclusions can you draw about Iago's personality from these reasons?
    d Which of his reasons seem as if they might in fact simply be more lies?
    e What makes you think so?

2   Throughout the play, Iago is frequently referred to as "honest."
    a Why is this fact ironic?
    b What is it about Iago that makes the other characters so inclined to believe him to be honest?
    c Which of the characters do question Iago's honesty and under what circumstances?

3   How would you describe Iago's personality?
    a What are the negative aspects of his personality?
    b What positive characteristics or traits does he have?
    c What evidence can you find in the play to support your ideas?

4   In Act I Scene 1, Iago tells Roderigo, "I am not what I am" (line 65). Many scholars have commented on the similarity between Iago's assertion and God's statement to Moses, "I am that I am" (Exodus 3:14).
    a How does Iago's reversal of God's statement link him to Satan?
    b What other similarities can you find between Iago and Satan?
    c Find passages in the play in which Iago is referred to, either by himself or others, as a devil or as some demonic creature.

5   Iago deceives many people during the course of the play.
    a Whom does he deceive?

    b What are the strategies he uses to deceive people?

    c What does he gain by deceiving others?

    d Is he ever self-deceived?

6   Compare and contrast Iago's deception of Othello with his deception of Roderigo.

    a How are the situations similar?

    b How are they different?

7   a When Iago (in Act III Scene 3 lines 410–26) tells Othello about Cassio's "dream" about Desdemona, what aspects of the alleged statements by Cassio reveal that the dream must be false?

    b Why does Othello fail to realize this fact?

8   Some critics argue that Iago and Othello are reverse images of one another.

    a What justification can you find for this argument?

    b How are they different from one another?

    c How are they alike?

9   After Othello suffers his seizure, Iago exhorts him to "be a man."

    a To what other characters in the play does he give this same advice?

    b What qualities is he urging them to display?

10   Iago habitually criticizes the other men in the play behind their backs. For example, he criticizes Othello to Roderigo in order to solidify their relationship and to persuade Roderigo to continue to do as he says.

    a What other men does he criticize behind their backs?

    b To whom does he express these criticisms?

    c What does he gain by these criticisms?

11   Iago also gives advice to a number of people during the course of the play.

    a To whom does he give advice?

    b What are the results of his advice?

12　We learn a great deal about Iago's attitudes on various issues.

   a　What are his views about women?

   b　What are his views about sex?

   c　What are his views about love?

   d　What evidence can you find to support your ideas?

13　Despite his plans to destroy them, Iago sometimes says positive things about Othello, Desdemona, and Cassio.

   a　What are the positive aspects that Iago notes about these characters?

   b　By what means does Shakespeare, despite our knowing that Iago is a liar, make these statements believable?

   c　Why does Iago's recognition of the good qualities of Othello, Desdemona, and Cassio fail to keep him from enacting his plans?

14　Iago suspects that Othello and Cassio have had sex with Emilia (Iago's wife).

   a　Do his suspicions seem well-founded or not?

   b　Why or why not?

   c　What does this situation tell you about Iago's personality?

15　Shakespearean scholar Stanley Homan has described Iago as a "demonic playwright."

   a　What justification for this description can you find in the play?

   b　In which of these situations is Iago engineering events to further his schemes?

   c　What events does he make use of that arise without his having planned them?

16　Iago's speeches are frequently in the form of monologues.

   a　What are the subjects of these speeches?

   b　What conclusions can you draw about Iago's personality in connection to the fact that he speaks so frequently to himself in the play?

c What conclusions can you draw about Iago's relationships from the fact that he so often speaks in the form of monologues?

17 In the opening scene, when Iago and Roderigo inform Brabantio about the elopement, Iago says, "Even now, now, very now, an old black ram / Is tupping your white ewe" (Act I Scene 1 line 88–89). Why does Shakespeare have Iago repeat the word "now" as he does?

18 Iago tells Roderigo at the beginning of the play that he is angry with Othello for his promoting Cassio to the rank of lieutenant instead of him. However, after Othello does finally promote Iago, Iago never expresses any satisfaction over the promotion. Do you think this fact might indicate that the issue of the lieutenancy was simply an excuse? Why or why not?

19 a Do you think Iago assumes that Emilia will be willing to allow him to get away with his schemes?

b What reasons might he have for believing this?

20 Why do you suppose that Iago, at the end of the play, refuses to explain himself or his motives?

Cassio

1 Iago is the first person in the play to describe Cassio.
   a What are your impressions of him and how do they compare with what Iago says?
   b What are Cassio's good qualities?
   c What are the negative aspects of his personality?
   d Which of these attributes does Iago use to further his schemes?

2 Cassio, like Othello and Iago, is a soldier in Venice's army.
   a What words are used to describe him as a soldier?
   b What words are used to describe his manners and appearance?

    c Compare and contrast him to Othello.

    d Compare and contrast him to Iago.

3 How does Cassio describe himself to Iago immediately after the drunken brawl that results in Cassio's demotion?

4 Desdemona defends Cassio to Othello as a man "That errs in ignorance, and not in cunning" (Act III Scene 3 line 49).

    a Which other characters could also be described this way?

    b To what extent is each person's error due to a personal weakness?

    c To what extent is it due to outside influence?

5 Compare the way Cassio speaks in Act II Scene 1 lines 74–87 to the way he speaks in Act IV Scene 1 lines 111–47.

    a Who or what is the subject matter in each instance?

    b What figures of speech does he use?

    c How formal or informal is his speech in each instance?

    d Compare and contrast Cassio's speech patterns with Othello's.

6 Compare and contrast Cassio's treatment of Bianca with the way he behaves toward Desdemona.

7 Compare Cassio's attitude toward women with Othello's.

8 Compare Cassio's attitude toward women with Iago's.

Desdemona

1 During the course of the play, Desdemona is frequently described by other characters.

    a What words does Iago use to describe her to Brabantio?

    b How does Iago's description compare to the words Roderigo uses to describe her to Brabantio?

    c How does Brabantio describe her to the senate?

    d What are the last words Brabantio speaks to Othello concerning Desdemona?

    e In what way might his words have unintentionally furthered Iago's schemes?

    f What other characters describe her and in what terms?

2 Desdemona could be said to be behaving unconventionally when she elopes with Othello. What other examples of her "unconventional" behavior do we learn about or observe in the play?

3 In Act I Scene 2, Iago refers to Desdemona as "a land carrack" [*that is, a large merchant ship*].

a What other references to Desdemona reduce her to the status of an object to be acquired, traded, or given away?

b What other characters beside Iago refer to her in this manner?

c Can you detect any patterns in these types of reference?

4 There are only three female characters in the play.

a Compare and contrast Desdemona to Emilia.

b Compare and contrast Desdemona to Bianca.

5 Read Othello's greeting to Desdemona in Act II Scene 1 lines 183–93.

a Compare her response in lines 192–94 to Othello's greeting.

b What does Desdemona's response tell you about her personality?

6 Many scholars believe that Desdemona has a more healthy attitude toward sex and marriage than Othello has.

a What justification can you find in the play for this belief?

b How would you describe her attitude toward sex and marriage?

7 Desdemona's manner of speaking, even when formally addressing the senate, is never grandiose. What does this fact tell you about her personality?

8 Although Desdemona is viewed very positively by most of the characters, she behaves in a deceptive way at times.

a Whom does Desdemona deceive?

b Under what circumstances?

c In what ways do these events contribute to her destruction?

9 Describe the relationship of Desdemona and Othello at the beginning of the play.

   a How does their relationship change as the play progresses?

   b To what extent are the changes due to external forces?

   c To what extent are the changes due to forces within Othello?

10 Some scholars argue that Desdemona is too passive.

   a On what do you suppose they base this argument?

   b Do you think Desdemona is too passive?

   c What are your reasons for thinking this?

11 Cassio refers to Desdemona as "the divine Desdemona" (Act II Scene 1 line 73), and many other descriptions of her in the play link her with heaven and perfection.

   a To what extent do her actions and words live up to this image of her?

   b To what extent do they fail to do so?

   c To what extent does this perception of her make her the object of unrealistic expectations?

12 Concerning her love for Othello, Desdemona says, "My love doth so approve him, / That even his stubbornness, his checks, his frowns . . . have grace and favor in them" (Act IV Scene 3 lines 19–21).

   a What grounds does she find for excusing his anger toward her?

   b What does she blame in herself for his actions?

   c What might her blaming of herself indicate about her?

13 Desdemona tells Emilia, "Unkindness may do much, / And his unkindness may defeat my life, / But never taint my love" (Act IV Scene 2 lines 159–61).

   a To what extent does she live up to this statement?

   b Compare and contrast Desdemona's unconditional loyalty with Othello's attitude toward her.

14 Compare Desdemona's false claim that she is responsible for her own death to Othello's statement that he was unable to "control" his "fate" (Act V Scene 2 line 265).

Emilia

1 Describe Emilia's relationship with Iago.
  a What evidence can you find that their marriage is an unhappy one?
  b What evidence can you find that she cares about his opinion?
2 In what ways might her views on marriage have been considered unconventional by theatergoers of Shakespeare's time?
  a How are Emilia's views on marriage similar to Desdemona's?
  b How are they different?
3 Describe Emilia's relationship with Desdemona.
4 What evidence can you find that Emilia is class-conscious?
5 What is Emilia's attitude toward Bianca?
  a In what ways is Emilia different from Bianca?
  b In what ways is she similar to her?
6 a What examples can you find of Emilia assuming that Iago shares her views on some issue or situation?
  b Is she or is she not correct in her beliefs?
7 a What changes can you observe in Emilia during the course of the play?
  b In what way does she remain unchanged?
8 What examples of Emilia's courage can you find?
9 a What do you think Emilia means when she tells Iago, "Perchance . . . I will never go home"? (Act V Scene 2 line 97).
  b In what sense might her statement be interpreted as foreshadowing?

10 What parallels between Emilia's death and Desdemona's can you find?

Roderigo

1 We learn about Roderigo primarily through his interactions with Iago and through Iago's descriptions of him.
   a How does what Iago says to Roderigo compare to what Iago says about Roderigo behind his back?
   b What other indications of Roderigo's character, status, and possessions can you discover in the play?

2 Describe Roderigo.
   a What positive qualities does he have?
   b What negative qualities does he have?

3 Are there ways in which Roderigo is comical?

4 Is the subplot concerning Roderigo necessary to the play or could it be eliminated? What changes to the play would be required if it were eliminated?

5 At times, Roderigo tries to resist Iago's control over him. What character traits of Roderigo's does Iago play upon in order to regain his control?

6 What does the fact that Roderigo is willing to allow Iago to assist him in seducing Desdemona indicate about his love for her?

7 Roderigo could be said to have been victimized by Iago. What is it about Roderigo that tends to cause audience members to have little sympathy for him?

Examination Questions

The following are typical examination questions.

1   In the opening scene, Brabantio is awakened from sleep to be told that Desdemona has eloped with Othello. Which other characters are awakened from sleep during the course of the play? What do these events have in common? What does Shakespeare accomplish by including so many scenes in which people are awakened?

2   Compare and contrast the reasons Desdemona fell in love with Othello with his reasons for loving her.

3   Concerning the courtship between Othello and Desdemona, noted Shakespearean scholar Harold Bloom comments that Othello was "essentially passive." What evidence can you find in the play that might support the idea that Desdemona was more active in the role of "wooer" than Othello during the courtship?

4   When Othello is informed by the senate that he must leave for Cyprus on his wedding night, he responds, "With all my heart" (Act I Scene 3 line 278). Explain whether you think the actor playing Othello should say this line regretfully, enthusiastically, or in some other way. Give the reasons for your choice, and explain how that reading of the line would support your view of Othello's character.

5   Find as many theatrical terms as you can in the play, and then discuss to whom these terms are being applied and what effect or impression is created by their use.

6   In Act II Scene 3 lines 14–28, why does Iago make so many suggestive remarks to Cassio about Desdemona?

7   To the theatergoers of Shakespeare's time, Venice was known not only for its highly refined culture but also for its outstanding intellectual and artistic accomplishments.

On the other hand, Venice was also noted for its moral decadence; it was inhabited by thousands of prostitutes. In contrast, Cyprus was a remote military garrison vulnerable to Turkish invasion. However, it was also associated with Venus, the goddess of love. Compare and contrast Venice with Cyprus in terms of what each represents and how each location enhances the themes or ideas of the play.

8 In a tragedy, the hero is usually destroyed by a fatal flaw or weakness within himself. Is this the case with Othello or is his downfall strictly the result of Iago's schemes? Support your answer with examples and quotations from the play.

9 To what extent is Iago successful in the play? To what extent does he fail?

10 When Othello and Desdemona are reunited on Cyprus, he tells her, "Honey, you shall be well desir'd in Cyprus" (Act II Scene 1 line 204). In what way does Iago's "poisoning" of Othello's mind result in the perversion of this statement?

11 There are many references to theft in the play. List the various things that are considered to have been stolen. Determine which are concrete in nature and which are abstract. Compare and contrast those things that actually are stolen to those that are merely believed to have been stolen.

12 As Othello's ensign, Iago would have taken an oath to die rather than allow the general's colors [that is, his battle flag] to be captured. Explain how this situation can be interpreted metaphorically. Why is this situation ironic? In what ways does Emilia function as Desdemona's "ensign"?

13 Some critics believe that Othello and Desdemona never consummate their marriage. What might the critics' reasons be for having this opinion? Do you agree or disagree? What evidence can you find to support your opinion? If you think Othello and Desdemona did in fact consummate their marriage, when did this event occur? Support your answer with evidence from the play.

14 Which scenes do you think have the most dramatic tension in the play, and how does Shakespeare create that tension?

15 Although many scenes in *Othello* occur at night, during Shakespeare's time the play would have been performed in broad daylight. Why does Shakespeare have so many scenes occur at night? How does he create and sustain the impression that it is night in these scenes?

16 Think of the different situations in the play in which the spoken word fails to accomplish what the speaker desires, and then compare and contrast one of those situations with one in which the spoken word has great power. Discuss what ideas Shakespeare might have been trying to convey about the power of the spoken word.

17 Othello says that, should he stop loving Desdemona, "Chaos is come again" (Act III Scene 3 line 92). Explain how his allusion to the mythological Chaos enhances the meaning of this line.

18 In Act III Scene 3 lines 97–154, Iago uses the words "think" and "thought" (or "thoughts") seven times, and Othello uses them eleven times. Why does Shakespeare place such emphasis on thinking and thoughts in this particular scene?

19 The word "honest" had several definitions in Shakespeare's time. It could mean "truthful," but it also could mean "respectable," "proper or becoming," or "chaste." Find an example from the play for each of these definitions of the word. Then find a single example in which the word might be used in more than one sense, and explain how the double meaning could enhance understanding of the character or the situation for the audience.

20 What parallels can you draw between the Clown's conversation with the musicians and Iago's dealings with Othello?

21 In addition to Cassio's loss of "reputation," there are many other losses depicted in the play. Tell who experiences some kind of loss and what that person loses.

22 Discuss the symbolism in Cassio's request that Bianca copy the pattern of Desdemona's handkerchief for him.

23 In Act IV Scene 3, just before she sings "Willow," Desdemona comments, "This Lodovico is a proper man" (line 35). What do you think would be her reasons for mentioning him at that time? What might Shakespeare be trying to accomplish by having Desdemona make this comment?

24 Before Othello kills Desdemona, he urges her to confess her sins, yet later in the scene when she begs for time to say just one prayer, he refuses to grant her request. Explain what you think his reasons are for refusing her request.

25 When Othello mistakenly tells Desdemona that Cassio has been killed, she cries, "Alas, he is betrayed and I undone!" Explain what Othello assumes that Desdemona means, and then tell what she actually is saying.

26 In the final scene, when Othello says, "O cursed, cursed slave!" (Act V Scene 2 line 276), he could be referring either to himself or to Iago. Which one do you think he means? What significance is there in the fact that this statement could refer to either one?

27 In the final scene, after Iago stabs Emilia she begs those present, "O, lay me by my mistress' side" (line 437). The stage directions, however, don't actually indicate whether or not her request is granted. If you were the director, would you instruct the actors to place her body on the bed next to Desdemona's or would you have only the bodies of Othello and Desdemona on the bed at the end of the play? What symbolic meanings would the audience be likely to conclude from the two different tableaus?

28 In the final scene of director Oliver Parker's 1995 film version of *Othello*, Cassio (Nathaniel Parker) secretly passes Othello (Laurence Fishburne) the dagger with which he kills himself. The text of the play does not indi-

cate whether Othello already has the dagger hidden on his person or whether he comes to have it in some other manner. What do you think of Parker's decision for the action in this scene? What does he intend this action to reveal about Cassio and/or Othello? Be sure to account for Cassio's statement that follows Othello's death: "This did I fear, but thought he had no weapon" (line 360).

29 Carol Thomas Neely comments that in *Othello*, "Each sex, trapped in its own values and attitudes, misjudges the other." What are the values and attitudes of the women in the play toward love, sex, men, and reputation? What are the men's values regarding these issues? Discuss why the conflict between the women's and the men's values leads to tragedy in this play.

30 The climax is the high point of a story, play, or poem; at the climax, a decision is reached, an action is undertaken, an affirmation or denial is made, or a realization occurs. What would you consider to be the climax of *Othello*? Explain the reasons for your opinion.

31 Why do you suppose that Shakespeare does not have Iago explain or confess in front of the audience during the final scene of the play?

32 Why do you suppose that Shakespeare does not have Iago die in the final scene of the play?

At last! Shakespeare in Language everyone can understand...

SHAKESPEARE MADE EASY Series

Scene 7

Macbeth's castle. Enter a sewer *directing divers servants. Then enter* **Macbeth**.

Macbeth If it were done, when 'tis done, then 'twere well
It were done quickly: if th' assassination
Could trammel up the consequence, and catch,
With his surcease, success; that but this blow
5   Might be the be-all and the end-all here,
But here, upon this bank and shoal of time,
We'd jump the life to come. But in these cases
We still have judgement here: that we but teach
Blood instructions, which being taught return
10 To plague th'inventor: this even-handed justice
Commends th'ingredience of our poisoned chalice
To our own lips. He's here in double trust:
First, as I am his kinsman and his subject,
Strong both against the deed: then, as his host,
15 Who should against his murderer shut the door,
Not bear the knife myself. Besides, this Duncan
Hath borne his faculties so meek, hath been
So clear in his great office, that his virtues
Will plead like angels, trumpet-tongued, against
20 The deep damnation of his taking-off;
And pity, like a naked new-born babe,
Striding the blast, or Heaven's cherubin, horsed
Upon the sightless couriers of the air,
Shall blow the horrid deed in every eye,
25 That tears shall drown the wind. I have no spur
To prick the sides of my intent, but only
Vaulting ambition, which o'erleaps itself,
And falls on th'other –

Scene 7

A room in **Macbeth's** *castle. A* **Butler** *and several* **Waiters** *cross, carrying dishes of food. Then* **Macbeth** *enters. He is thinking about the proposed murder of King Duncan.*

Macbeth If we could get away with the deed after it's done, then the quicker it were done, the better. If the murder had no consequences, and his death ensured success...If, when I strike the blow, that would be the end of it – here, right here, on this side of eternity – we'd willingly chance the life to come. But usually, we get what's coming to us here on earth. We teach the art of bloodshed, then become the victims of our own lessons. This evenhanded justice makes us swallow our own poison. [*Pause*] Duncan is here on double trust: first, because I'm his kinsman and his subject (both good arguments against the deed); then, because I'm his host, who should protect him from his murderer–not bear the knife. Besides, this Duncan has used his power so gently, he's been so incorruptible his great office, that his virtues will plead like angels, their tongues trumpeting the damnable horror of his murder. And pity, like a naked newborn babe or Heaven's avenging angels riding the winds, will cry the deed to everyone so that tears will blind the eye. I've nothing to spur me on but high-leaping ambition, which can often bring about one's downfall.

Shakespeare is Made Easy for these titles:

As You Like It (978-0-7641-4272-7) $6.99, *Can$8.50*
Hamlet (978-0-8120-3638-1) $6.95, *NCR*
Henry IV, Part One (978-0-8120-3585-8) $7.99, *NCR*
Julius Caesar (978-0-8120-3573-5) $6.99, *NCR*
King Lear (978-0-8120-3637-4) $6.99, *NCR*
Macbeth (978-0-8120-3571-1) $6.99, *NCR*
The Merchant of Venice (978-0-8120-3570-4) $6.99, *NCR*
A Midsummer Night's Dream (978-0-8120-3584-1) $6.99, *NCR*
Much Ado About Nothing (978-0-7641-4178-2) $6.99, *Can$8.50*
Othello (978-0-7641-2058-9) $6.95, *Can$8.50*
Romeo & Juliet (978-0-8120-3572-8) $6.99, *NCR*
The Taming of the Shrew (978-0-7641-4190-4) $6.99, *Can$8.50*
The Tempest (978-0-8120-3603-9) $6.95, *NCR*
Twelfth Night (978-0-8120-3604-6) $6.99, *NCR*

To order visit
www.barronseduc.com
or your local book store

A simplified modern translation appears side-by-side with the original Elizabethan text...plus there's helpful background material, study questions, and other aids to better grades.

Yes, up-to-date language now makes it easier to score well on tests *and* enjoy the ageless beauty of the master's works

Barron's Educational Series, Inc.
250 Wireless Blvd.
Hauppauge, N.Y. 11788
Order toll-free: 1-800-645-3476

Prices subject to change without notice.

In Canada:
Georgetown Book Warehouse
34 Armstrong Ave.
Georgetown, Ontario L7G 4R9
Canadian orders: 1-800-247-7160

Each book: paperback
NCR = No Canadian Rights

(#16) R 5/10

SHAKESPEARE MADE EASY

Modernized by Gayle Holste

AT LAST—

Othello

IN LANGUAGE EVERYONE CAN UNDERSTAND

Shakespeare's tragedy of the Moor whose love for Desdemona is destroyed by jealousy unfolds in easy-to-follow English as we speak it today. Othello's passion and Iago's treachery become clear in this straightforward modern version.

The complete original text is laid out side-by-side with a complete modern translation. You'll find this book ideal for instant reference and understanding, whether you are reading Shakespeare for pleasure or studying for an exam.

Also available in this series:

Hamlet • *Henry IV, Part One* • *Julius Caesar*
King Lear • *Macbeth* • *The Merchant of Venice*
A Midsummer Night's Dream • *Much Ado About Nothing*
Romeo and Juliet • *The Taming of the Shrew*
The Tempest • *Twelfth Night*

ISBN-13
ISBN-10

EAN

978-0-7641-2058-9
22 950 $6.95
OTHELLO SHAKESPEARE
02/27/12 Chaucer's

9 780764 120589

$6.95   Canada $8.50
www.barronseduc.com

BARRON'S